The Voice in the Margin

THE VOICE

IN THE MARGIN

Native American

Literature and

the Canon

———

Arnold Krupat

University of California Press

Berkeley / Los Angeles / Oxford

Part of Chapter 4 appeared in different form in Narrative Chance: Postmodern
Discourse on Native American Indian Literatures, ed. Gerald Vizenor and
published by the University of New Mexico Press whose permission to reprint is hereby
gratefully acknowledged.

University of California Press
Berkeley and Los Angeles, California
University of California Press, Ltd.
Oxford, England

Library of Congress Cataloging-in-Publication Data

Krupat, Arnold.
The voice in the margin : Native American literature and the canon
Arnold Krupat.
p.   cm.
Bibliography: p.
Includes index.
ISBN 0-520-06669-3 (alk. paper)
ISBN 0-520-06827-0 (pbk)
1. American literature—Indian authors—History and criticism—
Theory, etc. 2. Indian literature—History and criticism—Theory.
etc. 3. Indians in literature. 4. Canon (Literature) I. Title.
PS153.I52K78   1989   810.9'897—dc20   89-4966
CIP

Printed in the United States of America
1 2 3 4 5 6 7 8 9
The paper used in this publication meets the minimum
requirements of American National Standard for Information
Sciences—Permanence of Paper for Printed Library Materials
ANSI Z39.48.1984

For Donald Bahr and Jimmie Durham

Contents

Men and women do not live by culture alone; the vast majority of them throughout history have been deprived of the chance of living by it at all, and those few who are fortunate enough to live by it now are able to do so because of the labour of those who do not. Any cultural or critical theory which does not begin from this single most important fact, and hold it steadily in mind in its activities, is . . . unlikely to be worth very much.

TERRY EAGLETON

The Voice in the Margin

Introduction

This book is intended as a contribution to American cultural history—of the past, the present, and, at least imaginably, the future—with special reference to the Native American component of that history. I assume rather than argue that, in point of historical fact, American culture has had, has now, and will continue to have some relation to Native American culture—although that relation has most frequently been one of avoidance. As a result, most commentators on American culture generally have managed to proceed as though there were no relation between the two, white and red, Euramerican and Native American, as if absence rather than avoidance defined the New World: as if America was indeed "virgin land," empty, uninhabited, silent, dumb until the Europeans brought the plow and the pen to cultivate its wilderness. From the first days of settlement, Americans sought to establish their own sense of American "civilization" in opposition to some centrally significant Other, most particularly to the Indian "savage." Until a scant thirty-five years ago, the cultural history of America was written pretty exclusively from the point of view of those who had triumphed in the contest between "civilization" and "savagism," in Roy Harvey Pearce's terms, with the result that the voice of the Other was simply silenced, not to be heard. But there is always a return of the repressed in one form or another: and now it is no longer possible to pretend the Other is simply silent or

absent because the formerly conquered write—as they fight—
back. Today, the commentator on American culture who ignores or resists this fact does so at the risk of guaranteeing his
or her own irrelevance to any attempt both to understand the
world or to change it.

Of course there is no such thing as American culture or its
history as a totality, not as an object of ordinary experience
or a subject of academic study. Instead, there are the bits and
pieces of text and hearsay we sojourners and students in
this land unsystematically encounter or intellectually categorize. My special concern is that aspect of culture somewhat
vaguely called literary, what for the University exists as
American literature—periodized (Early American Literature,
Nineteenth-Century American Literature, Civil War to First
World War, Twentieth-Century American Literature, etc.)
and thematized (The American Adam, The Machine and
The Garden, American Romanticism, Love and Death in the
American Novel, etc.) to the point of virtual reification.
Such periodization and thematization, as Nina Baym has
shown it to do for literature by women,[1] also works to
exclude Native literary expression as part of American literature. You cannot make sense of Indian song and story as a
prelude to sectional war among the whites or as related to
their innocent dreams and their subsequent disillusionment
by experience. Of course the University, like the culture at
large, does permit a certain marginalized existence to Native
American literature, but, as is the case with all subaltern
discourse, one's objects of study at the margins are orga-

---

1. See "Melodramas of Beset Manhood: How Theories of American Fiction
Exclude Women Authors."

nized somewhat differently: *if* presented at all, there is Native American oral/traditional literature, or contemporary Native American fiction and poetry, the first treated so far as possible as a body of work untainted by Europe, the other as just-as-good-as the European, in appearance rather like the European, for all that it is marked by certain traces—which the specialist can make manifest in the classroom—of its Other origins. Unlike the situation that prevails, so far as I can tell, in folklore departments, or in some departments of anthropology or religion, center and margin rarely if ever come into fruitful contact so far as the formalized, institutional instruction of literature is concerned.

What chiefly marks the Americanist critic off from the Native Americanist critic today is the relation of each to that thing called theory. Although there are, to be sure, some notable exceptions, Indianists (at least so far as their professional affiliations are to Departments of English rather than folklore or anthropology) have kept their distance from theory rather more than Americanists. It seems worth a moment's speculation as to the reasons for and the consequences of this.

Sigmund Freud late in his life wrote that resistance to psychoanalysis was an inevitability inasmuch as psychoanalysis based itself theoretically upon what Freud called a "third blow" to human narcissism.[2] After the Copernican wound, affirming that we humans occupied not the center of the universe but just another planet revolving around the sun, and after the Darwinian wound, demonstrating that we humans were not descended from the angels of heaven but ascended from the apes of the jungle, the psychoanalytic wound came to say that we were not even masters in our own house: if we were indeed

2. See, "On the Resistance to Psychoanalysis."

sole possessors of reason, we were not exclusively ruled by it. I imagine Paul de Man wished to appropriate something of Freud's unanswerability (albeit with that characteristically canny irony, a sophisticated and somewhat more benign version of what Nixon and Reagan developed into the fine art of "plausible deniability")[3] in his already-classic account of "The Resistance to Theory." The resistance de Man specified was hardly a resistance to literary theory as such, but, rather—the tag references are unfortunate and I ask their indulgence only as a shorthand—to theory in the poststructuralist, Derridaean, deconstructive, or, as I will say shortly, New Rhetorical mode. But in Native American studies there has been and continues to be a resistance to theory *tout court*.

Those who resist theory in Native American studies tend to see it as aligned with the first term of apparently dichotomous sets such as analysis/experience, abstract/concrete, library work/fieldwork, reason/intuition, even culture/nature—sets that (usually quite unknowingly—but resistance to theory, as I see it, is precisely a will to unknowing) would resurrect in practice a structuralist commitment to binary opposition that has been fairly well discredited (in theory). The sets I have referred to are, in turn, equated with a thoroughly historical opposition between the east and the west. The east, which currently includes California most of the time and Chicago some of the time, is culture, books, analysis, and, of course, theory. The west, which usually is limited to Arizona, New Mexico, Montana, and the Dakotas, is raw nature, personal contact, the authority of concrete experience, and so, to be sure, no theory. Once we recall that Indians, in American

3. See also Derrida's defense of de Man's youthful anti–Semitic journalism, "Like the Sound of the Sea Deep within a Shell: Paul de Man's War," as an exercise in the establishment of a case for plausible deniability.

symbology, from the first moment of contact, were always equated to nature and, from at least the Indian Removal Act of 1830, have been considered of the "west," the distance between students of Native American literature and literary theorists becomes understandable.[4]

The consequence of this situation is that one feels put in the position of having to choose between the two terms set in putative opposition, as if it were not really possible to write on Indian subjects without presenting one's *bona fides* in terms of having danced at powwows with so and so or having been taken as blood brother by so and so, as if one's analyses required the authority of personal experience to be valid, as if he who had much experience of Native culture must automatically produce valid analyses of it. Or it is as if one were called upon—I can offer this for its metaphorical force at the least— to read *either* the *Wicazo Sa Review* out of the Indian Studies Center of Eastern Washington University, *Akwesasne Notes,*

4. That Indians stand for savage nature in opposition to civilized culture has been abundantly documented, first and foremost, of course, by Roy Harvey Pearce, as I shall have further occasion to note. This fact has played an important role in attempts to include Indian literature in the canon of American literature (I shall also have more to say on this subject). That Indians "removed" west of the Mississippi with the encouragement of President Andrew Jackson and the acquiescence of the Congress have ever after been taken as "of" the west indicates the degree to which symbolic, one might say ideological, constructs may persist in the face of what would seem to be empirical evidence to the contrary. Just as Euramericans from the earliest contact forward saw Native economies as essentially and irrevocably based upon hunting rather than planting, in spite of detailed evidence that many if not most of the tribes were practiced agriculturists, so, too, do Euramericans persist today in seeing Indians as primarily inhabitants of the western plains or southwestern desert, for all that Native people exist and thrive in the north- and southeast, or the northwest. It is the warbonneted horseman of the plains in buckskin or the near-naked pueblo dancer who continue to constitute the American public's sense of the Indian. Visual iconography, from Catlin's paintings to Edward Curtis's photographs to John Ford's films to PBS's documentaries, has reinforced this westernness of the Indian.

and the *American Indian Culture and Research Journal,* or *Diacritics, Critical Inquiry, Social Text,* and *Cultural Critique.* It seems to me important however to resist such false choices. Anyone interested in the study of Indian literature today needs to read all of these journals, or as many as possible. And to read them more nearly under the sign of sameness than of difference, as engaged in parallel projects, equivalently (if differently) useful for the understanding of Native American and Euramerican culture. To resist this is to continue to perpetuate an us/ them universe. And, as I hope this book will show, that is something I find objectionable in the extreme.

There has been a great deal of talk lately about the need to listen to different voices, to allow the Other to speak, to experiment in the direction of producing dialogic and polyphonic texts. I take up these matters in relation to quite specific critical problems in the pages that follow. In keeping with the purposes appropriate to an Introduction, however, I want to offer some general comments here.

With writing open to otherness or Otherness, it is as with apartheid: you can find almost no one explicitly opposed to the former as you can find almost no one explicitly in favor of the latter. Such pandemic agreement usually indicates wide definitional latitude for the terms under discussion along with a fairly considerable distance from and/or indifference to any real consequences that might ensue from one's position. Just here, I want to consider briefly what it might actually mean to do ethnography, history, or literary criticism with an openness to otherness; in particular, whether this would be to *include* (somehow) the other's point of view or, rather, to *adopt* (somehow) the other's point of view.

If it is the former, cultural studies are in relatively good shape. Among the anthropologists, one would be hard put today to discover an ethnographer indifferent to the Native's view of things, committed only to a full and relentless translation of the Native voice into Western terms. As a branch of historical studies, the discipline of ethnohistory, not yet having celebrated its fiftieth birthday, can already take pride in its accomplishments. Less and less will the historian of Indian–white relations consider Native American actions only in terms of Euramerican categories of understanding. Literary studies lag a bit behind anthropology and history in these regards; there still remain those who assume that Indians have nothing to say worthy of critical scrutiny, that Indians are the academic responsibility of anthropologists or government bureaucrats, not of literary critics. And there are those who read Native American literature as if it consisted of texts written by an incidentally red William Carlos Williams, William Faulkner, or Virginia Woolf. A considerable body of work is currently accumulating, nonetheless, that is concerned to trace the difference as well as the sameness of Indian literature in relation to the Western tradition, with reference to particular linguistic and ethnographic detail.

All this is easy enough to remark. But what if the call to polyphony quite literally intends not so much the inclusion of the Indian point of view but its adoption as one's own? One thing this might mean—although the abundant debates among ethnographic theorists today do not usually put it this way—is a return to the emic mode in anthropology, to the old Boasian concern to present things from the Native point of view.[5] Thus

5. *Emic* and *etic* are the terms offered by Kenneth Pike to distinguish between local and general systems on the model of the phonemic and phonetic distinction in linguistics (see, *Language in Relation to a Unified Theory of the Structure of Human Behavior*). Clifford Geertz's modification of Pike's distinction

a present-day emic ethnography might be, as Richard K. Nelson says of his own work with the Koyukon,

a native natural history . . . outside the established realm of Western science, though it has been organized and filtered through a Western mind. (xiv)

Such a text would attempt to come as close as possible to conveying another culture from that culture's own view, sacrificing any claim to general explanatory ("scientific") force in the interest of a particularized authenticity. But many of those attracted to the other's point of view envision something even more radical than what Nelson provides in his *Make Prayers to the Raven: A Koyukon View of the Northern Forest,* abandoning scientific claims to explanation and even, as I understand it, claims to authenticity in the interest of an affectively evocative criticism in what I can only term the religious mode.

Of course, to adopt the point of view of the other quite literally might lead to the abandonment of critical activity altogether as simply to no point. As Stephen Tyler, perhaps foremost among those calling for the adoption of other-than-Western-scientific ways of encountering the world, writes of the Koya, "thought and thinking—" and by extension, I assume, what we would call the products of thought and thinking, or culture—

----

into the "experience-near" and "experience-far" is not so much a (needed) refinement of the cognitively rigid or insufficiently subtle nature of this distinction as it is a wholesale shift to a different epistemological paradigm, the valorization yet again of interpretation over any attempt at explanation. In the same way, Marcus and Fischer's readiness (via Geertz) to take "Emic and etic categories . . . as relative terms" (181) is not an updating or—as so much in their book would pretend—an escape from paradigm as it is a preference for an alternative (or should I say a *closet*) paradigm.

are not major topics of discourse. The first Koya symposium is yet to be held and what people say, do, and desire is far more important than what they think about thought. (1984, 35)[6]

Ethnographic writing in the Koya mode, *if* it were actually to be carried on, would have in common with religious discourse, as Edward Said has noted, that it "serves as an agent of closure, shutting off human investigation, criticism, and effort" to achieve understanding (1983, 290).

Alternatively, Tyler, as is well known, has called for an equivalently religious postmodern anthropology, which would no longer produce documents of the occult but, instead, occult documents. One would here abandon the Western aim of *representing* (and so of *knowing* or *understanding*) culture and instead seek to *evoke* cultural world views, a kind of anthropological poetics rather than an anthropological science—but, to be sure, a particular *kind* of poetics, one that sees the poem as a quasi-mystical embodiment or incarnation of—whatever. As P. Steven Sangren has noted, even for those who approve this turn, it has thus far been easier to talk about such ethnographic texts than actually to produce them.

Something of this sort might also be said for the hope of writing history, at least the history of Native Americans,

6. Tyler continues, "In the commonsense world inhabited by Koyas, saying and doing—words and deeds—are far more important than thinking, and this is reflected in their linguistic habits" (1984, 35). There would seem to be the acknowledgment, here, that the Koyas' "commonsense world" is indeed no more than their own world, and that Koya common sense, therefore, could only be set *beside* Western common sense as just another cultural construction of common sense (this acknowledging Clifford Geertz's demonstration that what we refer to as "commonsense" is itself not common but a "cultural system" (see Geertz's "Common Sense as a Cultural System") and not used as a critique *of* Western common sense. But the tone of Tyler's argument just here seems to reach for the anthropological critique.

from an Indian point of view. Calvin Martin has recently
called for a shift from the Western "anthropological" view of
history to the Indian "biological" view, and quoted approv-
ingly Robin Ridington's statement that

the true history of these people [Indians] will have to be written in a
mythic language . . . it will have to combine stories of people coming
together with other people, and those that tell of people coming together with animals. (216–217)

Writes Martin, "As long as the Japasas of this land [Japasa was
a Beaver Indian who told Ridington his stories] insist on
linking their life-force to that of Nature around and within
them, we historians are obliged to write about them in just
those terms" (215). The logic of this escapes me entirely—
although Martin's own pages argue and attempt to persuade
by means that Westerners would recognize as logical—for
nothing *logically* "obliges" the critic to write in any particular
way. The strongest *ethical* case can be made for taking the
subject's own view of things seriously, as worthy of detailed
attention and acknowledgment, but this does not necessarily
entail as a consequence the adoption of "just those terms."

The equivalent to this sense of obligation in literary studies concerned with Native Americans is the sort of criticism
which, in the rather mystical—and, indeed, mystifying—
old-fashioned way of Mary Austin or Natalie Curtis Burlin,
reads Indian literature to hear the wind whistling through the
pages, to feel the change of the seasons chapter to chapter, to
note the shape of the surrounding hills in every line, as if that
was actually what Native performers themselves intended,
or what their words executed. The power of Indian literary
expression, in this egregiously mistaken comprehension of

the Indian point of view, has little to do with the artistry of
gifted individuals shaping a subtle and complex tradition,
but, rather, with the ancientness of racial wisdom, or some
such. The newer fashion in mystification is foremost pro-
pounded by N. Scott Momaday, as in his recent assertion,
also in Martin's book, that there are "intrinsic variables in
man's perception of his universe, variables that are determined to *some real extent on the basis of his genetic constitution*"
(Martin, 156; my emphasis). Momaday illustrates his understanding of the genetic determinants of perception by explaining that his probable answer to a child's question, "Where
does the sun live?" would have to be true to "my experience,
my deepest, oldest experience, *the memory in my blood*" (Martin, 157; my emphasis). Now, there is no gene for perception, no such thing as memory in the blood—this latter
construction by now almost a catchphrase for Momaday.
Momaday has become almost an iconic figure for those interested in Native American literature, but, as I shall have occasion to note later, this particular aspect of his work (along
with his continuing refusal, as in the first quotation above, to
generalize gender reference to include women as significant
humans), only places unnecessary obstacles in the way of a
fuller understanding and appreciation of Native American
literature.

I say "unnecessary obstacles" because Momaday's following account of Jemez and Navajo senses of where the sun lives
(it lives in the earth, not in the sky) in no way requires Indians
to have some special "genetic constitution," for such a sense,
nor to acquire that sense from any "memory in [the] blood."[7]

7. Quoting Momaday's use of the phrase "racial memory," H. David
Brumble acknowledges that the "phrasing is unfortunate" (1988, 173) but suggests that "for Momaday . . . 'race' and 'blood' are evocative synonyms for

It is quite possible without the mystifications of Momaday and Martin, to be overwhelmingly impressed by Native American culture and to grant fully that native American cultural production is based upon a profound wisdom that is most certainly different from a Western, rationalistic, scientistic, secular perspective. Nor can anyone who would comment on Native American culture ignore the perspective from which it is produced. But that does not mean that one is "obliged" to adopt that perspective or to insist on the absolute difference of it from the perspectives of the West. I would instance here the statement by Larry Evers and Felipe Molina in their recent study of Yaqui deer songs to the effect that,

> we work for two goals: for the continuation of deer songs as a vital part of life in Yaqui communities and for their appreciation in all communities beyond. Most of the time these goals coincide. (8)

I will return to Evers and Molina, if only briefly, in the final chapter of this book. Here, let me note only that their "two goals," coincidental at least "Most of the time," can only be achieved by those with the patience, perhaps I might even say the Keatsian "negative capability," to work with both an Indian *and* a Western perspective.

For the Western culture-worker, this requires resisting the temptation—to put the matter bluntly—of trying to be an Indian (more modestly, to proceed strictly as an Indian) in one's

---

'culture' " (1988, 174). This conclusion, I think, is based only on Brumble's charitably decent inability to believe that someone as talented and intelligent as Momaday could actually mean the absurdly racist things he says. I don't know what Momaday actually means: the evidence of his writing, however, is overwhelmingly if unfortunately racist in its statement. Schubnell (q.v.) and others, it should be noted, do not so much as blink at regular statements of this kind.

work. For some the former option is far more dramatic than merely trying to understand Indians sympathetically, or practicing secular criticism in anthropology, history, or literary studies. Given the abundantly documented failures of social science to fulfill some of its formerly exaggerated promises of understanding (and, more grimly, of control), that temptation is all the greater. Science, in the terms of Jean-François Lyotard, is just another one of those *grands récits,* the large narratives or stories that have failed. Such a view—the formulation here is again Sangren's—mistakes science as a value for science as an authority, assuming that if the authority of science as a privileged way to sure truth or knowledge has been shown to be mistaken, so, too, must science as a value be shown to be mistaken. Along with a number of other commentators, I would suggest that this conclusion is not only unnecessary, illogical, and premature, but that it leaves its proponents with no recourse but to turn to a religious criticism that is ultimately dependent on the continuing blind faith of its proponents and its audience. This turn, I would claim with Edward Said, seems largely "the result of exhaustion . . . [and] disappointment" (1983, 291); with Said, I would encourage resistance to it.

For all these strong words, I would not want to be understood as denying that one might learn from the Indians themselves how to produce a more accurate criticism of Indian literature. I think here particularly of Dennis Tedlock's observation that Zuni storytellers comment on their stories and those stories' past performances in the act of the storytelling itself as a form of critical activity;[8] recently, as I will show,

8. See "The Spoken Word and the Work of Interpretation in American Indian Religion" in *The Spoken Word and the Work of Interpretation.*

Leslie Silko has affirmed some similar interests and practices among Laguna storytellers. I can generalize that to work critically, not religiously, in an Indian way with Indian literature may mean above all to offer commentary on the effectiveness of variants. Other criticism than this, from the reading I have done, I do not see Native Americans attempting, turning their attention, like the Koya, to other matters. I hope students of Indian literatures will make this part of their work, and I hope some sense of this Indian way of working has, if only implicitly, been *included* in what is to follow, although it has not been *adopted* as a governing perspective.

For all that, I should nonetheless acknowledge that this study is somewhat deficient in that I have only in very small degree managed to include noncanonical or indigenous critical approaches to literature along with noncanonical authors and literary texts. With the help of work by Houston Baker, Hazel Carby, Henry Louis Gates, Jose Limon, Jose David Saldivar, Ramon Saldivar, and Gerald Vizenor, among others, I hope soon to do better along these lines. Others interested in Native American literature are no doubt doing better even as I write.

Let me turn here to some explicit indication of my own sense of polyphony, my quite modest techniques for including otherness and difference. To borrow John Ellis's distinction,[9] I have taken the call to dialogism and polyphony (from

9. See "What Does Deconstruction Contribute to Theory of Criticism?" Ellis, if I have understood him, tends to think that most critical good advice tends along the same lines, as if good advice (like "common sense?") was uniform and universal. Deconstructive good advice (if it is that) does share more with other forms of critical good advice than most deconstructionists have allowed; but some of its advice—regardless of whether this amounts to a theory or not—runs counter to other good advice. Critical good advice, I should say, is like

Bakhtin foremost among others) as offering "good advice" (although advice of a very particular sort) rather than a "theory" (with its almost inevitable commitment to opposing other theories). This is to say that my own sense of the call to polyphony understands it as urging the refusal of imperial domination, and so of the West's claim legitimately to speak for all the Rest. Neither a formal theory nor a program, this call is, rather, an exhortation to proceed humbly and with care; it asks that we Westerners stop shouting, as it were, and that we speak with our ears open. Such a call does not bring with it—inasmuch as formal choices do not of themselves convey moral and political values—the requirement that we write in certain ways, or for that matter that we refrain from writing in certain ways, (e.g., that we avoid all indirect discourse, or refrain from hitherto-conventional methods of documentation—notes, bibliography, and the like). Some radical polyphonists have not sufficiently understood this. For it is not the case that an ethnography that— say—includes "raw" data, extracts from field journals, abundant literal quotation from informants, or references to the fieldworker's anxieties, hopes, and fears will *necessarily* convey textually the layers and nuances (these are, to be sure, metaphors), the *differences* of another culture any better than a more traditional-appearing ethnography. All that is sure— and this is the reason why, I think, influential authors like George Marcus and Michael Fischer have overstated the promise of such experiments—is that the author of the "ex-

---

the folk wisdom of proverbs: there is "He who hesitates is lost" but also "Look before you leap." To take some kinds of advice more seriously than others is to approach having a theory. I hope these remarks may provide some context for my use of Bakhtin and dialogical "theory" later on.

perimental" or unconventional text is thinking about these things.[10] That, indeed, is a start: but that is all it is.

In this book, then, I have tried to proceed with care, to proceed with a certain tentativeness. I have asked the publisher, as will be already apparent, to allow the book to be designed with the notes as footnotes, at the bottom of the page, rather than as endnotes at the back of the book (the more common practice, these days, in my experience). And I can assure the reader that most of what is in the notes is substantive: that is where a number of other voices speak, where I worry and qualify my own statements in relation to those of other writers who, often enough, disagree. But is this no more than what one always used to do, nothing new, but an old fashion? Indeed, it is—but that was then and this is now; and my practice is offered not as blind necessity determined by the past but as a choice in a rather more open present. For many readers of this book will know well that a good deal of the most notable higher criticism today frequently does not offer much in the way of specific citation of other commentators on its subject matter. Locally, for example, Richard Poirier's excellent journal *Raritan* gives no source references even for its authors' direct quotations. But I have

---

10. All of Marcus and Fischer's *Anthropology as Cultural Critique* is permeated by eclectic and largely untheorized enthusiasm for "experimental" ethnography as this may contrast with or oppose what Marcus and Dick Cushman earlier had specified as "ethnographic realism" (see "Ethnographies as Texts"). Marcus and Fischer's enthusiasm for "defamiliarization" as a virtual panacea for all problems of representation is likely to strike the literary reader *familiar* with the Russian formalism from which the concept comes—at least it strikes *me*—as rather simplistic. For all of this, I find the endeavor of *Anthropology as Cultural Critique* admirable and timely—even as I find it thoroughly inadequate to its intentions. There is also P. Steven Sangren's point to acknowledge, that one temptation to overvalue "experimental" ethnographies is simply that students like these texts better than they do more conventional ones (423).

mostly in mind the magisterial manner of Barthes, Foucault, or Derrida whose texts rarely deign to cite any but other great masters. And indeed it has seemed to be the case that cultural critics writing in English may, intentionally or not, signal their own increasing authority by a corresponding decrease in citation: compare Said's *Beginnings,* to *The World, the Text, and the Critic,* or Frank Lentricchia's *After the New Criticism* to *Literature and Social Change,* or Eagleton's *Criticism and Ideology* to *Literary Theory: An Introduction.* The authority of those I have instanced—Said, Lentricchia, Eagleton—is legitimate; I have the highest admiration for these authors—as I have for Frederic Jameson, who, as it happens, an exception to my generalization, does not seem to decrease the number and kind of citations as he moves from, say, *Marxism and Form,* to *The Political Unconscious.* My point, in any case, is that I have wanted the reader to hear as many others as I have heard myself, most of them just plain old others, not Others, and to hear them equally well whatever their status as stars or satellites in this particular universe.

It will be remarked that I have referred to writers whom I have cited as *speaking;* this may be taken as the mark of the purest naiveté in a post-Derridaean age, or it may—I hope it will—be taken, to the contrary, as a willed line of informed approach. I am cognizant of the problematics of textuality in both voice and text; I know that the writer is never present and that nonpresence cannot literally speak. The metaphor of the author as speaker can be asserted, nonetheless, as a hypothesis that might yet retain its force. The world did not begin in 1966 or thereabouts, after all, nor did the long night of logocentrism pass away with nothing at all achieved. No speech or writing can give us *parole pleine*—nor, fortunately, for workaday communication, does it need to. Our intake of meanings are an analog–more/less matter, not a digital–on/ off, all/nothing matter. Bakhtin's determined reference to textual differences as voiced values produced by speakers may also be adduced as contextualizing, if not necessarily authorizing, my practice. And I note happily the inclination of Houston Baker, Jr., to study "the *sound* and *sounding* of Afro-American modernism" (xvi); of Henry Louis Gates to consider the "double-voiced text" (passim); and of a whole host of feminist critics to privilege the voice of a female subject who is unwilling to remain anonymous, absent, silent. As I shall have occasion to note below, it is no accident that those of us who work with hitherto marginalized materials show a certain reluctance to give up the voice in favor of the text as recently defined.

Most of those who have helped me with this book are named in the notes; from these very many I would foremost single out Roy Harvey Pearce. His cross-continental talk by mail and by phone has been an ongoing spur to think better thoughts about important issues. I am grateful for his example, his advice, and his friendship, all of which I value enormously. Pearce, together with Fredric Jameson and Edward Said—whom I do not know and to whom I have not had the opportunity to speak *ultra libros,* as it were—are the tutelary spirits of this book. West Moss, my student research assistant, deserves special thanks here, as do the librarians of Sarah Lawrence College. Andrew Wiget and an anonymous reader of the manuscript offered much good advice, for which I am grateful. David Brumble, with whom I have had the privilege and the pleasure to discuss some of these matters for a good number of years, also read the entire manuscript with tough-minded care. Satya Mohanty's fine editorial eye helped make the second chapter of this book into what it is. Whatever it is, it is better for his attention than anything I could have achieved myself. And I am again indebted to Stan Holwitz of the University of California Press for patience and kindness of the highest order.

New York, 1988

1. The Concept of
the Canon

The concept of a literary canon is generally understood in either of two ways, each very much opposed to the other. Let me state them in their most extreme form: on the one hand, the canon is conceived of as a body of texts having the authority of perennial classics. These texts, "the great books" (as at least one American college has institutionalized them in a course of instruction), are, as they always have been and always will be, nothing less than the very best that has been thought and said. To understand their content—to have isolated for further meditation their themes or ideas—is to gain or make some nearer approach to timeless wisdom; to apprehend their form is to experience the beautiful or at the least to perceive a significant order. Sympathetic contact with these texts cannot help but make one a better person, or—the phrase is a curious one on inspection, to be sure—more human.

On the other hand, however, the canon is taken simply as the name for that body of texts which best performs in the sphere of culture the work of legitimating the prevailing social order: canonical texts are, as they always have been, the most useful for such a purpose (although the modality of their usefulness may, of course, alter with time). To understand their content is largely to accept the world view of the socially dominant class; to apprehend their form is to fail to perceive that acceptance as such. Sympathetic contact with these texts tends mostly—although not always or exclusively—to contribute to that ideological conditioning, the production of that consciousness, necessary to conform one willingly to one's—usually subordinate—class position in society.

The latter conception of the canon derives from what Paul Ricoeur and others have called the hermeneutics of suspicion. Rather than presenting the best that has been thought and said, or the "great tradition," for this perspective on the matter, the canon is simply what Raymond Williams has called "the *selective tradition*" (1980, 39), where "tradition" may be understood as "an aspect of *contemporary* social and cultural organization in the interest of the domination of a specific class . . . ," as "a version of the past which is intended to connect with and ratify the present" (1977, 116). For the hermeneutically suspicious, the texts of the canon have no inherent authority or value; rather, they are socially authorized and institutionally legitimated. Nor do they make their own way into our hearts by appealing unmistakably to an intrinsically human longing for truth, wisdom, beauty, order, and such; instead, they are regularly and insistently urged upon us so that they may promote and sustain by cultural means perspectives and values that are not necessarily consistent with the fullest conceptions of human possibility. This view need not abandon entirely the question of greatness, nor must it deny that ideologically objectionable works may be constructions of great power; rather, it simply points out that, in actual practice, a considerable number of the items that continue to be named among the master texts seem less and less able to sustain their position by any appeal to greatness alone.

In one form or another, hermeneutical suspicion arises, naturally enough, among those who have been impressed by varieties of Marxian, psychoanalytic, and anthropological thought, leading them—here it seems not only awkward but

false for me not to say *us*—leading us to consider ourselves
oppositional intellectuals (neither traditional nor yet organic
in the Gramscian sense). In this country, most of those interested in these matters, no matter what their view, are affili-
ated with the academy—the University, more precisely—and
the disciplinary allegiance of the oppositional intellectuals
tends to be to the *Geisteswissenschaften,* or *sciences humaines:*
most of us would not, today, object, I think, to being described as social scientific workers, although our institutional
and professional allegiance most usually places us in departments of English, language, and literature. As members of
the professoriate, even those suspicious of the canon's claims
to eternal truth and beauty are nonetheless culturally conservative, for one cannot, after all, not teach some of the traditional
canon. And, in any case, there is much in the traditional
canonical texts—in many of them—which, after the appropriate work of historical referencing and demystification has
been performed, still appears even to the hermeneutically suspicious as beautiful and/or somehow true.

If this instrumental or pragmatic view of the canon (to call
it that) I have so sketchily presented derives from suspicion
and generates opposition, the traditional view of the canon—
transcendental and abstractly theoretical—might be said to
derive from a hermeneutics of faith that generates validation
of the society whose noblest cultural productions the great
canonical texts are taken to be. It is only fair to note here,
however, that the canonical validators would—again, so far
as these broad generalizations may hold—object to descriptions of their position that make reference to such things as
cultural opposition and validation as being too politicized to
explain that position. Such descriptions, they would insist—
and in the present instance they would be entirely correct—

could only come from someone with a view very different from theirs. They are interested in literature, not politics; in Man, not individual men (it is only recently that some small opening to women has been worked into the system); in what is enduring and unchangeable in our putatively common human destiny, not in the vicissitudes of epochal accident or of cultural variation.

Oppositional intellectuals, for all that they may appreciate and linger over the internal workings of canonical or even noncanonical texts, must always, as I have noted, engage in a certain historical referencing as they read, relating the literary text to a world that is indeed *hors texte,* "real," and prior to the text.[1] Traditional, validating intellectuals, however, are not, in their reading, particularly concerned with what is socially and materially beyond the text itself (except as "background"), the "real," in the Mallarmean sense, existing mostly to provide materials for a book—which, as they can often demonstrate in a sophisticated manner, performs a complex imaginative transformation of context or reality: this is the artwork that makes art. (And there is, of course, nothing to demystify in the work of art.) For them, literary study has little to do with science (except perhaps as defined by Northrop Frye). Rather, it is either concerned with that compound of ethics and esthetics perhaps best summed up in a phrase such as "the moral imagination," or it is concerned with something now called simply "reading," a purely technical and so wholly disinterested operation. The validators in the mold of Arnold, Trilling, or, indeed, Clifford Geertz tend to consider their professional allegiance to be to the *humanities;* and these are, to be sure, kept alive most

1. This is why, as I shall claim in the following chapter, forms of historicist criticism are more useful to the perspectives and purposes I wish to support than forms of formalist criticism.

diligently, once again, in university departments of English (although Geertz is professionally an anthropologist).[2] Curiously enough, the most recent formalists—let me call them for these purposes, with reference to the New Critics, the New Rhetoricians—for all that they are also conservative vis-à-vis the canon, tend to be antihumanist: their allegiance is not to a universalized, ahistorical concept of Man, but to an equivalently ahistorical, systematized concept of Language. Canonical texts, then, are those that show us either Man struggling to be fully Himself (hopelessly but nobly) or else Language trying to say fully what it means (hopelessly but—in the master texts—interestingly).

There are difficulties with both these views of the canon, as there are attractions in both as well. The transcendental-essentialist view, for example, like all full-blown idealisms, can only be accepted as an act of faith; it requires that one engage in what Edward Said has called "religious" criticism in contradistinction to the secular criticism he so eloquently affirms. Appeals to inherent greatness, to unseen yet dimly felt orders of great power, and the like are not conducive to this-worldly understanding—unless one chooses to say with Saint Augustine *credo ut intellegam*. The traditional view of canonical

2. My placement of Geertz in this company is a consequence of my acceptance of the view of his work held by many that his solution to the problems of the hermeneutic circle (e.g., in "Thick Description . . ." or "Ideology as a Cultural System") comes at the price of a certain trivialization. Geertz's "interpretive" conclusions achieve assurance as they abandon not only claims to explanation but to cognitive force as well. As I have already indicated, critiques of Geertz in the Marcus and Fischer line offer no help in these regards, inasmuch as they adopt a postmodern (not "interpretive" but "textual") epistemology that cannot ground itself sufficiently to permit the achievement of "anthropology as cultural critique," one of their putative aims. Geertz's ongoing rethinking of these problems, I should say in fairness, seems to me much more penetrating than that of (some of) his critics.

authority can be maintained only by rigidly separating literary value from value of other kinds—and by positing literary judgment as a first-order judgment, something that can be formed prior to or independently of our judgments about other kinds of value. Once the introduction of empirical (not to say statistical) evidence is permitted and the condition of cognitive responsibility is accepted,[3] the transcendental–theoretical conception of the canon tends to lose a good deal of its force.

Yet a purely instrumental or pragmatic view of the canon, for all its attractions, has its problems, too. For, at least in its extreme version, it tends to see the canon as formed *exclusively* by power relations: the canonical texts are the surviving victors on the battlefield calling for due praise. If they are an obnoxious group, we can never join them and so we must get out there and beat them. But this is to adopt a Thrasymachean perspective, the world view of primitive capitalism, a crude form of social Darwinism, or indeed an equally crude version of Marxist class struggle. It is to adopt Foucault's bleak vision (somewhat modified in the last work) of discourse as power and power as everywhere, so that even to fight and win is only to become oppressor in one's turn—to force people to read *our* books now, not *theirs* (and, of course, they will fight back, conflict unending). And this sort of Hobbesian war of all against all forever is very far from what most instrumental pragmatists desire.

3. I derive my conception of cognitive responsibility from Hayden White who derives it from Stephen Pepper's *World Hypotheses*. Cognitively responsible positions are those "committed to rational defenses of their world hypotheses" as opposed to those "not so committed" (H. White, n. 23). To the mystic and fascist positions of cognitive irresponsibility mentioned by White we might currently add varieties of postmodernism. Jurgen Habermas's attempts to define conditions of "cognitive adequacy," which I admit to knowing only secondhand, seem also pertinent here.

To avoid it, three positions in relation to the canon have, thus far, seemed open to the instrumentalist. The first is simply to declare a universal peace, as it were, one in which everyone is conceded equal greatness—or, rather, one in which any claim at all to greatness or superiority is automatically suspect. This means, in effect, that one simply dispenses entirely with the concept of the canon—of *any* canon of authorized texts—so that what one teaches and writes about is simply books that happen to be interesting, or useful for one sort of demonstration or another. Not evaluative but only functional criteria are admitted as determining text selection. Cognitive responsibility here consists in a willingness to provide arguments for justifying the functional criteria as generally reasonable ones.

According to this view, one could not claim that *Uncle Tom's Cabin* is either better or worse or even as good as *The Scarlet Letter;* one chooses it for presentation as it fits a particular context of concern in the interest of fully acknowledged extraliterary values; those with other concerns and other values will choose other books—perhaps *The Scarlet Letter,* perhaps the novels of Lydia Maria Child and William Gilmore Simms and the poems of Fanny Fern. Or, if one is still interested in such a category as "nineteenth-century American literature," one may as well found one's view of it upon reading Kit Carson's autobiography and the journals of frontier women as upon novels and poems of any kind. Whether these latter texts are literary texts, indeed, whether it matters whether they are or not, is something I shall take up in a moment.[4] In any case, the series of texts in question has no

---

4. It might be said here that both oppositional instrumentalists (Said, Eagleton) as well as validating essentialists (Derrida, de Man) equivalently tend to bracket the question of literariness, operating simply as cultural critics in the first

authoritative status beyond its functional instantiation in fact; other texts might do as well; at other times, no doubt, other texts will do as well. The body of texts actually taught in any course of instruction or referred to in any work of criticism, far from constituting a canon, now becomes merely a peda-gogical (some might say polemical) series; others may teach and comment upon these texts, if they wish—or they may equally well ignore them.

This solution certainly clears the air of a lot of cant about greatness and inevitability and unquestionable authority, but it also works in the interest of a social vision of pure atomized fragmentation. Everyone does her own thing and we can only hope that our thing will hold up at least well enough to be visible; even should our thing attract the attention of many, there are no grounds for proposing it generally to all, for it remains "ours" only. Barbara Foley's phrase, "the fe-tishization of the refusal of mastery" (129), comes to mind for this strong form of cultural relativism as one way to describe literary life after the canon. Or perhaps an analogy might be made to the poststructuralist infinity of signification: just as there is no decidable meaning to a text, so, too, here, would there be no central or major texts, no ground on which a canon might stand, only the free intertextual play of books taught or read. Of course, in the postmodern world, if one dispenses with belief in the continuity and commonality of a tradition of excellence (moral, political, esthetic) embodied in some form of canon, one then acquiesces in what Fredric Jameson has described, in "Periodizing the '60's," as a "dispos-

---

instance or rhetorical analysts in the second. I will argue for the importance of a specifically literary category of discourse—but I will generally operate, nonethe-less, myself, as a cultural critic interested not only in the texts appropriately classed as literary.

able" culture of the *"metabook,"* a culture made up of those texts that (perhaps against the functional intentions of those who compose and propose them) fill the residual (but dying) book function in our society. Rather "than the ambition to express a proposition, a position or a system with greater 'truth' value"—Jameson is speaking of philosophy—or, for literature, to read or to write a great or central book, one engages in expression of a "radically occasional" nature (in Sayres, 193). This, too, is something most of the hermeneutically suspicious do not desire.

A second way to avoid endless ideological struggle for the canon of great or central books is not to jettison the canon entirely but to propose a canon whose authority is merely statistical. Wayne Charles Miller, for example, has suggested revising the canon of American literature on principles—so it seems to me—of virtually statistical representation.[5] This position on the canon I shall call the ethical–ontological reform. It claims that we should, *in fairness,* read a proportionate number of authors who *are* actually available. Since it is indisputable that America is not almost exclusively made up of white, male, eastern WASPS, courses in American literature should not almost exclusively be made up of texts by white, male, eastern WASPS. With this observation I agree wholeheartedly. But even if one were to accept the principle of proportional revision, the ethical–ontological reform has no way of deciding which authors should finally be taught, or even which authors should represent their particular ethnic and/or racial groups. If it is easy to agree that Black Elk might well be taught instead of William Cullen Bryant (but maybe it isn't so easy to agree after

---

5. See Wayne Charles Miller, "Toward a New Literary History of the United States." I should note that Miller nowhere explicitly proposes a statistical canon.

all, and maybe the most famous Native American autobiographer should yield to some other Native American autobiographer) or that Whittier (if he still shows up) could be dropped to
make room for Frederick Douglass (but why not Linda Brent
or Harriet Wilson?) or Maxine Hong Kingston, it is less easy to
know whether Kingston should be supplemented by Frank
Chin, or whether (for the semester has only so many weeks)
Ferris Takahashi should be taught instead of Piri Thomas.
(And we have still left out immigrant Jewish writers, Chica-
nos, Italian Americans, Scandinavians, and a great many others as yet unmelted into general Americanness.) This inability
or refusal to imagine a principle that might merge valorized
difference into some collective identity (a dialectical principle,
to be sure, so that common identifications do not obliterate
historical differentiations) finally works against the hope of a
common culture; its canon reflects and can reflect nothing but
the changing demographics of each historical moment. We
never approximate an *American literature* but remain instead at
the level of Miller's multiethnic literatures of the United States.

It is perhaps in recognition of this truth that the third way
comes about for hermeneutically suspicious pragmatists to
avoid a view of the canon as inevitably oppressive and end-
lessly contested. Rather than an abandonment of any canon
whatever or the acceptance of a demographically authorized
one, the position I turn to now reconstructs the canon on the
basis of a strictly experiential authority. Recognizing that the
traditional canonical texts have been pretty exclusively the
phallogocentric texts, in Jacques Derrida's term, those representing the experiences and values of a very small group of elite
Western males, this position decides that the books worth
promoting are not just any books, not even those that offer a
kind of proportional representation of what is actually there,

but, instead, those which are directly relevant to their audience's experience. This reform of the canon leads increasingly to the sense that any attempt to consider American or English literature as a whole is just too hopelessly broad, and it is bound to urge a shift more and more to courses in and books about ethnic literature, working-class literature, third world women's literature, regional literature, and so on, and more nearly in isolation from one another rather than in relation to one another.

Here, one gives up the proposal to a wide range of American students and readers even of a multiethnic canon. Instead, one offers to readers of the Plains region, Willa Cather's novels and the epics of John Neihardt; to readers of the southwest, perhaps Paul Horgan and Witter Bynner; New Yorkers may choose from Emma Goldman, Mike Gold, and Abraham Cahan, Langston Hughes and early James Baldwin, Oscar Hijuelos and Piri Thomas, among others. In New England, at least to predominantly male readers, Hawthorne, Thoreau, Melville, even Longfellow and Whittier and Bryant will continue to be taught. Thus Paul Lauter's experience in trying to present Faulkner's *The Bear* to a group of working-class students in New York would rarely be repeated (they thought the story silly; they laughed),[6] for everyone will find his personal concerns more or less closely reflected in what he or she is asked to read.

The latter two of these reactions against the essentialist view of the canon and against the instrumentalism of endless conflict do retain a measure of the authority that traditional views accorded to canonical texts, for the books they propose to us *are,* after all, deemed to be more important or somehow

6. See Paul Lauter, "History and the Canon."

more necessary than others—demographically, or at least in regard to their audiences' own experience. But what they give up is enormous. For they surrender the possibility of attaining just that sort of perspective on our individual experience and our historical moment that a broad acquaintance with literature can provide. Instead of the attempt to define a canon that might become what Elizabeth Fox-Genovese has called a "collective autobiography" and "to introduce some notion of collective standards," they "settle for education as personal autobiography or identity," and thus "accept the worst forms of political domination" (133). In their desire to acknowledge difference and accord it its due, they give up the very possibility of a common culture, one that may at least imply a common society. An American literary canon, I should say, is worth fighting for as the complex record of possible national identities; Crèvecoeur's question, What is an American? is unanswerable, of course. But it needs again and again to be posed.

In these regards, then, the most appealing aspect of the traditional view of the canon is its determination to believe in a common culture, a body of work that defines some part of what we all (whoever "we" are) can believe in and share. To quote Elizabeth Fox-Genovese once more, " . . . however narrow and exclusive the canon we have *inherited,* the existence of *some* canon offers our best guarantee of some common culture" (132; my emphasis), one which, as I would gloss her remarks, in its *heterodoxy* expresses some part of our selves as collective selves, so that we see ourselves neither as simply accommodating or opposing but, rather, informed by others *dialogically.* The idea of the collective self as it is presented in the collective autobiography we call the canon, and the social vision implied by such a collective self, is something I will return to. These are of especial importance in any attempt to keep the concept of an American literature meaningful.

ii.

I began this discussion of the canon with the concept of the canon itself; but at several points it may have seemed that I should, instead, have begun with the concept of *literature:* that is, to have spoken first not of the literary *canon* but of the canon of *literature* and thus to define what is at stake in the various understandings of that term before speaking of the makeup of the literary canon. Even if one abandons not only the traditional literary canon but any canon, choosing, in- stead, only a pedagogical series constituted by no authority other than the intention of the one who instantiates it, one constituted by a purely demographic authority, or only by the authority of its audience's experience, still the question per- sists whether these texts, whatever the principle governing their instantiation, are *literary* texts. Fox-Genovese, for exam- ple, whose work I have cited with approval, does not concern herself with distinguishing between those texts of the canon that may reasonably be designated literary texts and those that may not—as others who would revise the canon, myself among them, on occasion do not. If we would keep the dis- tinction between literary and other texts, whether it is one of kind or of degree, we must not only offer grounds for it but justify it as well: to ask, that is, whether the distinction be- tween literature and other types of written discourse is possi- ble to maintain and also whether it is worth maintaining.

The order I have adopted—canon first, then literature— seems preferable not so much for logical as for strictly em- pirical reasons inasmuch as one can more or less point to the literary canon, at least "as we have inherited it," whereas it is more difficult, probably impossible, to point to "litera-

ture" itself. The canon of Western literature, as this is traditionally conceived in England and America, has consisted of
the texts of Homer, Sophocles, and Dante, Chaucer and
Spenser and Shakespeare, Milton, Donne, Dryden, Words-
worth, Austen, Flaubert, George Eliot, Dickinson, Yeats,
James, Joyce, Proust, Lawrence, Mann, Woolf, and T.S. Eliot, probably Stevens and John Berryman, along with the
texts of many unnamed others—which texts, whatever their
authors' names, would not significantly alter our sense of
the kind and quality of the traditional literary canon. For
traditionalists, to be sure, "literature"—"great" literature—is
simply what these men and some few women wrote. But
just as there is a challenge to the canonicity of these ostensibly "great" authors, so, too, is there a challenge to the view
that their writing defines literature.

For "literature" obviously does not include everything that
even these authors wrote, probably not their letters, for example. Or would it be that *some* of these authors wrote "literary"
letters while others did not? We might possibly admit Milton's
Areopagitica to literature, although that would likely not be the
case with Eliot's *Idea of a Christian Society,* nor with Berryman's
critical biography of Stephen Crane. Henry James's plays
would have to be admitted as compositions of a literary kind—
although these last might be considered *bad* literature. Do
James's novels alone then help us define literature (but what of
the prefaces for the New York edition?)—or is it hopelessly
circular reasoning to say so? Meanwhile, we know today that
all "texts," even menus, ads, and TV programs, can be given
literary *readings,* can be read, that is, *as* literature or in ways
consistent with the sorts of readings that have traditionally
been reserved *for* literature. Are we approaching the time therefore when the canon of literature should open itself to the best-
written ads, or is it, instead, the case that literary readings do

not literature make? And if not, what happens to such apparently nearer-to-literary texts (nearer than ads or menus, anyway) as Rousseau's or Augustine's *Confessions*? It may be that we should indeed speak of the canon without qualification as to canonical type; still, if only for practical reasons (I refer to the traditional ways of mapping subject matter areas in American universities and colleges and the classification systems in our libraries and bookstores), perhaps we would do well, first, to consider what may be meant by literature. (There are also good theoretical reasons for doing so.)

In this matter there are also two opposed views that I will again state in extreme fashion; they parallel the essentialist and the instrumentalist views of the canon. On the one hand, it is held that there is certainly such a thing as literature, a type of discourse qualitatively distinct from other types, with discernible, distinctive traits and unique functions, a thing that changes, to be sure, but only within certain fixed limits (beyond those limits literature would not be literature), so that its lineaments may be traced over time with some assurance. "The existing monuments," as T. S. Eliot put it, "form an ideal order among themselves," an order "modified by the introduction of the new . . . work of art among them," but modified, it appears, only "ever so slightly" (50): for literature, *plus ça change plus ça reste le même.* No wonder, then, that, as a Canadian doctoral candidate in literature complained to me, according to her department head, fur-trade journals are simply *not* literature nor may they be studied as such for the degree. And as Christopher Clausen has recently insisted, "It Is Not Elitist to Place Major Literature at the Center of the

---

7. See Christopher Clausen, "It Is Not Elitist to Place Major Literature at the Center of the English Curriculum."

English Curriculum";[7] so to place it, of course, one needs a certain steady faith that he knows the exact nature of Literature, Majority, and Centrality.

On the other hand, literature is taken as just another socially determined category of discourse: like "greatness," what is or is not "literature" is whatever those empowered to define it say it is. Literature has no essence nor any distinctiveness of its own; it is not inherently recognizable, nor can we know it except insofar as it is institutionally defined. Just as capital gains are what the IRS says they are, so are novels or poems—so is literature—only what the publishers, reviewers, and professors say they are, only what the librarians class under one group of numerals rather than another, or the bookstores place in one section or another. Consider, for example, the opinion of those very differently flamboyant personalities, Leslie Fiedler and Roland Barthes. Fiedler writes, "Literature is effectively what we teach in departments of English; or, conversely, what we teach in departments of English is literature" (73). Or, in Barthes's words, "The 'teaching of literature,' is for me almost tautological. Literature is what is taught, that's all" (1971, 170).

For there is, after all, no single trait that can be isolated in the texts traditionally treated as literature which could unequivocally distingush them from their nonliterary relatives: neither their fictionality (lies and sensational journalism, not to mention Ronald Reagan's accounts of Libyan terrorist activities, are fictional but not usually considered literature); nor their form (greeting card verse has rhyme and meter as do the lyrics of some popular music, but the first of these is never claimed for literature, whereas the second, when claimed, meets vociferous opposition); and assuredly not the figuralism of their language or any excess of signification over semantic communication. William Labov's studies of black

American speech on the one hand, and Paul de Man's studies of philosophical writing on the other, uncover a considerable element of figuralism in ordinary or scientific discourse, but neither of these has as yet—the situation is perhaps in the process of change—been claimed specifically as literature.[8] And as Barbara Herrnstein Smith remarks, there simply are "no *functions* performed by art works that may be specified as unique to them" (14). This is to say that apart from "literature's" existence as an abstract and idealized object of veneration or theorization, what we have to deal with is simply those texts that *for one reason or another* have been treated *as* "literature," literature as a strictly social category of discourse. As Terry Eagleton has claimed, a time might even come when Shakespeare himself would not be seen as a producer of literature; nor is there any fixed and intrinsic manner of determining just what sort of thing *Gulliver's Travels, Our Lady of the Flowers, Glas,* or, indeed, Canadian fur-trade journals might best be considered.

This is a strong position, I believe. But just as one may adopt a generally pragmatic and instrumental view of the canon without denying the usefulness of such a category as the canon, so, too, one may adopt a hermeneutically suspicious view of literature without denying the usefulness of the category itself. Though I agree that there *is*—ontologically, essentially—no such *thing* as literature, the term nonetheless embodies a very specific history and, as well, an aspiration that should not too quickly be abandoned.

We might begin by noting that historically literature was

8. There is a class distinction here, of course, for while philosophical writing by Hume or Rousseau, or anthropological writing by Lévi-Strauss, may frequently show up in literature classes, it is almost unheard of that the transcriptions of sociolinguistic projects should appear.

simply the term for whatever language Western cultures deemed important enough to preserve by means of the technology of writing. Literature, from Latin *littera,* letter, as is well known, served broadly to indicate anything that had been written down and—to achieve a measure of social circulation—copied over. (For oral societies without alphabetic "letters," literature is whatever language is deemed worthy of sufficient repetition to assure that it will be remembered and passed along. From a quantitative point of view, oral cultures will inevitably have less literature than chirographic and print cultures.) Now, although everything written down might have at least an etymological claim to be taken as "littera-ture," poetry, the term that precedes our modern term literature, was always distinguished as a specific kind of writing different from lettered discourse in general because of its curious capacity to appeal either to the emotions, the senses, the imagination, or the fancy—the faculty posited varies with each commentator's psychological understanding and social vision—all of which were contrasted in some greater or lesser degree with the rational or analytical faculties to which other written discourse makes its primary appeal. Poetry, by its rhyme and meter, or —this is the case in literary prose—by its figures and structure, *delights* us; it is pleasurable beyond what can be accounted for rationally. Whether it stands therefore in opposition to rationality is the great question.

In general it may be said that all littera-ture, including the poetic part, was required to be pedagogical to the extent at least that it traditionally was expected to play a role in instructing our reason in how to be the kind of citizens valued by our particular societies. (If littera-ture did not do this it would be against the self-interest of society to preserve it in the first place.) But a type of littera-ture—poetry—which

delights us and appeals to our emotions, imagination, and so
forth, may well be something, as Plato felt, that works
against rationality and so against social formations presumed
to rest upon rational foundations. The problem is to reclaim
poetry for the state, or, less grimly, to show its social value.
Aristotle's cathartic notion of what happens to the emotions
aroused by tragic poetry had exactly this aim; perhaps I. A.
Richards's psychoanalytic revision of Aristotle did, too. As
Sir Philip Sidney summarized Renaissance thinking on the
matter, poetry might be defended by emphasizing its epistemological status, its fictive nature, which permits a more
abundant freedom to mix types of discourse: the philosopher
must teach abstractly, by precept, the historian concretely,
by example. But the poet can do both, and without being
tied, in the latter case, to what actually occurred.[9] The
delight poetry produced was a kind of bonus, one that con-
tributed to the effectiveness of its teaching—which was, to
be sure, the chief reason for preserving and valuing it. Put
another way, the surplus of signification, the excess that
pleased, had cognitive value.

In general, defenders of poetry from Aristotle to Sidney,
Percy Shelley, Walt Whitman, Matthew Arnold, I. A. Richards, T. S. Eliot, Leon Trotsky, and Herbert Marcuse—let
me take them as examples of some of the best-known spokes-
men for (what at this point we must call) literature—have
affirmed the social utility of poetry, the importance of its
pedagogical function, and the compatibility of its extrara-
tional appeal with right reason, regardless of their political

9. This tradition of epistemological defense of literature is continued in Roy
Harvey Pearce's reference to literature as making "conditional contrary-to-fact
statement[s]" (1969, 17) and thus producing "the freedom of fictiveness" (1987,
xi).

differences (and so their stance in relation to an existing society), regardless of their understanding of the component makeup of its delightfulness.

It is only recently—dating perhaps from around the mid- or late nineteenth century—that anyone has attempted to divorce literature from social utility. The argument is that poetry is good in itself, presenting beauty that needs no equation to truth; it is purposeless purpose, and so on. In the art-for-art's-sake line of reasoning (to call it that), poetry's delightfulness is deemed sufficient to justify it without any need to claim a teaching function—or any function whatever. In America, it is not so much the opinion of Verlaine, J. K. Huysmans, Walter Pater, or Oscar Wilde, *mutatis mutandis,* that has weighed in the attempt to isolate literature from the social, but that of Flaubert as passed through Stephen Dedalus's esthetic and expressed by the New Critics, whose poetic theory—for all their abundant concern for social questions—insisted on the literary relevance only of the tensions and ironies internally generated by or in a poem. This separation of the esthetic and the socially useful was reinforced by Roman Jakobson's specification of the poetic function of language as self-reflexiveness, and, most recently, by New Rhetorical deconstruction's insistence on linguistically generated moments of textual aporia as the ultimate horizon of literary language. Recent valorization of "the pleasures of the text,"[10] a turn to *jouissance* and a literary erotics which brackets if it does not overtly scorn questions of poetic functionality, may be seen as only the culmination of a determination to uphold the delighting function of literature in spite of, not as complementary to, its teaching func-

10. See Roland Barthes, *The Pleasure of the Text.*

tion. In America this view animates a range of criticism from Van Wyck Brook's distinction between "art" and "expression," to Lionel Trilling's separation of "genuine" literature from fictionalized propaganda, and Richard Poirier's valorization of a stylistic "world elsewhere." Historically, however, this remains a minority view born of a dissatisfaction with the actualities of social life and a despair of political change in the interest of a transformation of social life.

The foregoing comments are intended to suggest that there are some historically urgent criteria for claiming literature as a distinct category of discourse. Granted, as Saussure said of language, literature is not a positive entity; it has no essence, no body. But it is distinguishable differentially, if only in degree, from other uses of language. The question, What is literature? then, may be answered by positing a range of texts in which the conjoint attempt to teach *and* delight appears, in the old, Russian formalist sense, as the "dominant." In this way we may distinguish literature (although always as the result of an act of interpretation and evaluation that is open to question) from other uses of written language that have aimed at, though certainly not achieved, instruction (philosophy, theology) or pure delight.

But is the effort to sustain the difference between literature and other forms of discourse to any point? If, as I would readily acknowledge, one can delight in philosophical discourse that is primarily oriented toward instruction; if one is always inevitably instructed by discourses of delight of whatever type,[11] why

11. It is harder to provide suggestive instances of texts oriented toward some form of pure delight in a wholly formal and hence abstract order. Perhaps one might adduce Robbe-Grillet's *Jealousy* or some work (which I know but slightly) of Philippe Sollers. An earlier period might present such texts as Raymond Queneau's *Exercises de Style,* untranslated still, I believe, and perhaps untranslat-

then labor to maintain a special category called literature, a category, as I have claimed, that would be constituted precisely by the dominance of its conjunction of the pleasurable and the pedagogical? What answer I can give depends upon an analogy to the canon: just as it is worthwhile to retain the notion of a body of texts centrally significant to a common culture, an approximation to a collective autobiography, the story of our integrated selves as participants in a common society, so too is it worthwhile to retain the notion of literature as comprised of those texts that provide instances of and occasions for the integrated self. Literature is where the affective and rational coexist and complement each other in language, where fancy and imagination press for freedom beyond the bounds of a material constraint to which proper due is given. Literature is that mode of discourse which foremost seeks to enact and perform its insights, insisting that we understand with affect, feel with comprehension. In this sense, T. S. Eliot was wrong: there is no literature of dissociated sensibilities; in this sense, Roy Harvey Pearce was right: literature is always an instance of the search for wholeness.[12]

---

able. Or there is the following text (it is set typographically as a poem and listed in a table of contents as a "Vertigral Document") by Kurt Schwitters, called "abloesung":

> Grimm glimm gnimm bimbimm
> Grimm glimm gnimm bimbimm
> Grimm glimm gnimm bimbimm
> Grimm glimm gnimm bimbimm
> Grimm glimm gnimm bimbimm
> Grimm glimm gnimm bimbimm
> Grimm glimm gnimm bimbimm
> Grimm blimm gnimm bimbimm (38)

This is the first stanza only.

12. See, for example, "Historicism Once More." Also see Wesley Morris's discussion of Pearce in *Toward a New Historicism*. I will discuss Pearce's work further in the following chapter.

Let us then optimistically assume we have staked out a claim for some properly literary territory; let us say we know differentially what literature is. This only tells us which texts are candidates for the canon of literature. How to choose from all of them those that are—what? Great? best? most useful, relevant, cogent? From a purely formal point of view, considering what I will call the *techné* of delight, there probably *are* intrinsic criteria for literary excellence. The only problem is that decisions as to which intrinsic criteria to privilege turn out themselves to be dependent upon prior extrinsic or ideological determinations. And, to be sure, even if we agree upon which texts meet our particular standard of literary "excellence," our further choice from among them must rest upon the *kinds* of imaginative and affective appeals they make, a function of our *phronetic* desire (*phrónēsis,* or "knowing how to act . . . knowing what a situation calls for in the way of action" [Bruns, 16]), or the kind of social pedagogy we wish to further. It is the image of individual wholeness and collective cohesiveness ("content") we approve as presented by means of those techniques ("form") we enjoy that determines our choices for the literary canon. However much we may, with Christopher Clausen, dream of value-free literary judgments, these exist—alas?—only in dreams. (And as Roy Harvey Pearce is fond of noting, in history, not dreams, begin responsibilities.) To acknowledge that in literary studies all is ideology is not suddenly to endorse the Thrasymachean–Hobbesian–Foucauldian view of the endless war of all against all I was at pains to criticize above; rather, it is to say quite simply that literature is not the first thing (nor is it the last and only thing) anybody ever cares about. It is to take my epigraph for this book to heart.

Consider first the question of form, and so the *techné* of

delight. At least from the modernist period up until the current postmodern reaction, subtlety and complexity of verbal texture were the intrinsic criteria for literary excellence: connotation rather than denotation, implication rather than direct statement, irony rather than the metaphoric and metonymic tropes of romanticists and realists. Degrees of subtlety and complexity probably can be determined by intrinsic tests; what *kinds* of subtlety and complexity—and, whether subtlety and complexity of technique *necessarily* mark the "best" texts—cannot be determined intrinsically. That the triumph of modernist taste represents the triumph of a masculinist bias—once more, that these intrinsic criteria rest upon extrinsic grounds—has been noted by feminist critics; what has been noticed less is that this bias represents a privileging of writing over the voice, something readily apparent to students of orality and literacy, if not to deconstructionists.

Thus, current attempts to take women's diaries seriously as types of literature or as cultural documents of more than marginal significance, for example, need to be aware that the values of these texts are not only gender- but technologically-inflected. That is to say that their techniques are not only those assumed to be appropriate to women rather than men, but as well those deemed appropriate to cultures marked by oral rather than chirographic or print modes of information storage and retrieval. In oral cultures, to be sure, these techniques are used not only by women but (even predominantly) by men.

In England—I offer a very broad generalization here—Romantic and Victorian writers, male and female, were thoroughly committed to the values of presence, immediacy, and full communicative intentionality—*parole pleine*—associated with oral forms, as was Whitman in America (but certainly not Thoreau, Hawthorne, and the other "major" eastern WASPS). The sexist part of the modernist shift has to do with the fact that in leaving these values to women, and to men who write like women (curiously, D. H. Lawrence, for one!), it left them stigmatized as outmoded and subordinate. Textuality was new, advanced, and male; orality was old, backward, and female. Not only female, of course, for the backwardness of the oral encompassed the "primitive" as well: the unlettered red savage or black slave. This aspect of modernism is carried forward quite unselfconsciously by Jacques Derrida and Paul de Man: Yale School is Male School, as Barbara Johnson put it. For, although Derrida has been a strong critic of phallogocentrism, he has not extended his critique to the subject of textual complexity. To the contrary, he has reveled in every sort of textual complication as if that were not itself implicated in the Western phallogos. And, to point up the obvious, although he has been tireless in deconstructing phallogocentric/metaphysical texts, he has been completely uninterested in seeking out texts that might be Different.

In America, the new standard of technical excellence, by subordinating not only writing by women but all writing deriving from types of oral presentation, also subordinated the west to the east; Mark Twain's reputation as a major American author, for example, was not securely established until the 1950s, when the first serious critical challenges to the New Critical/modernist program began to make their way. What all this means for Native American literature should be obvious. Its earliest proponents were in fact mostly women and westerners (e.g., Natalie Curtis Burlin, Mary Austin, and Yvor Winters) or those interested in spoken models for verse (e.g., William Carlos Williams), and their strongest case for it often invoked its primitive charm. (Lawrence's sense of the powers of indigenousness is a particular, complex version of similar notions.) At a time when institutional canon-making power was solidly eastern and male and the standard for excellence was based on capabilities apparently possible only to certain kinds of writing, clearly claims for the importance of Native American literature had to go against the grain.

Without endorsing subtlety and complexity as inevitably the stuff of literary excellence so far as the *techné* of delight is concerned, I should still like to take a moment to point out what may not be so well known to many students of written American literature: oral literatures, while they do not privilege ironic tropes, structures, or attitudes, are capable of a wide range of complex and subtle effects in their own right. I will let two brief examples stand here for the very many that might be cited. Consider the much-quoted remark of Maria Chona, Papago woman and autobiographer, in commenting on the fact that Papago songs are very brief: "The song is very short because we understand so much" (23). Chona is usually taken to be referring to the extraordinary degree of condensation in Papago songs and pointing out the very complex interaction between a given singer's words, the culturally defined functional context for those words, and the audience's active awareness of all this at every moment. A different instance of extreme condensation is presented by Keith Basso in relation to the Apache practice of "speaking with names," a technique used in "socially taut" situations, and one in which the enunciation of toponyms invokes "ancient wisdom" as this is contained in stories commonly known to all. As Basso summarizes it,

the expressive force of an Apache utterance seems to be roughly proportionate to the number of separate but complementary functions it accom-
plishes simultaneously, or . . . to the number of distinguishable subject
matters it successfully communicates "about." (1988, 121)

Condensation thus turns out—and this seems to be the case
for some Apache storytelling or "literature," as well—to be
hand in glove with overdetermination, all of it most subtle
and complex indeed.[13] We are very far, here, from the fanta-
sies of primitive simplicity Americans have long attributed to
Native American oral expressiveness. But let us go on.

As with the matter of formal criteria for excellence, in matters of content, decisions as to which books provide the instruction we approve can only be made in reference to a
reader's prior values. For example, in *The World, the Text, and
the Critic,* Edward Said writes that

criticism must think of itself as life-enhancing and constitutively opposed to every form of tyranny, domination, and abuse: its social goals
are noncoercive knowledge produced in the interests of human freedom. (1983, 29)

To produce such criticism, Said may choose to study virtually
any literary or nonliterary text; were he to propose a canon of
the "best" *literature,*[14] however, it would have to be in line

13. See Keith Basso, "Stalking with Stories."
14. Something he might not care to do. It is interesting to note that Fredric
Jameson, Frank Lentricchia, Edward Said, and Terry Eagleton, among the foremost male, anglophone, progressive critics, have not directly taken up discussion
of the canon. To do so has seemed more urgent for feminist critics and those, like
myself, who are interested in marginalized and subordinated traditions. Jameson's work on "third-world literature," animated by his particular interests in
China and Cuba, is a development worth watching in this regard. Wayne
Booth's recent turn to feminist criticism can be covered by no generalization I
can think of.

with his stated values. One further example. Terry Eagleton
conceives the tasks of the revolutionary culture worker to be
consistent with socialist aims. And, he writes, "Ultimately,"

the only reason for being a socialist is that one objects to the fact that the
great majority of men and women have lived lives of suffering and
degradation, and believes that this may conceivably be altered in the
future. (1981, 112)

Eagleton has argued powerfully for no-such-thing-as-litera-
ture, and so it appears unlikely that he would ever propose a
literary canon of "greats." Eagleton's position is that one's
choice of texts to work with, whatever their discursive type,
must and can only be determined by one's intention in working with them—culture criticism, then, in the interest of
mitigating human suffering and degradation. What should be
clear is that any claim to present a canon of literary excellence is inevitably a function of one's prior values and always
implies a social vision; the canon proposed by William Bennett or suggested by Allan Bloom and Christopher Clausen
is as fully determined by extrinsic factors as any canon Said
or Eagleton or I might construct. The difference, let me put
it baldly, is in the willingness of the former to produce
knowledge coercively in the interest of perpetuating an order
whose material effect—doubtless undesired, doubtless inevitable, and resolutely denied—is further suffering and degradation for the many. This is what is at stake in the argument
over literature and the literary canon.

iii.

As we move to proposing principles for a canon of American literature, the example of the twentieth-century's fore-

most canon-maker, T. S. Eliot, is again worth consideration.
John Guillory has recently shown how Eliot came to realize
what I have been arguing, that one's choice of a canon could
not, finally, be defended on literary grounds alone (however
much one may value the category of literature). Rather, Eliot
saw that the choice had to be a reflection of "a more funda-
mental evaluative norm, *extrinsic to literature* (Guillory, 348).
Thus, according to Guillory, "Eliot tells us in *After Strange
Gods* [1933], that he is rewriting 'Tradition and the Individual
Talent' [1919] by substituting [the term] 'orthodoxy' for 'tradition,' and this is unquestionably an ideological correction"
(348). "Orthodoxy," "true opinion," and "right tradition" are
made up of the beliefs inculcated by "a Christian education,"
one that would not so much attempt to produce believers as it
would "primarily train people to be able to think in Christian
categories." Those poets whose teaching was consistent with
orthodoxy had claims to being the "best" poets, the best, at
least in the sense that reading them might help promote the
Christian Society that Eliot envisioned. Eliot did not say
much about the kinds of delight consistent with such teaching, although delight along with teaching there would have
to be for Eliot to attempt to overcome his—mistakenly
theorized—notion of the "dissociation of sensibility" that presumably set in some time after John Donne.

   In selecting his orthodox canon, Eliot had the problem all
of us have when we acknowledge that the literature we most
approve pedagogically is not always or all of it the literature
we most admire esthetically, and vice versa. Eliot's own solution to this problem, as Guillory's discussion makes clear,
was to make a distinction between major and minor poets and
to suggest that the minor poets could turn out to be more
useful—and thus in this regard actually "better"—than the

majors. But Eliot's pleasure in *techné,* in certain kinds of formal prowess, was such that he could not demote to the category of minor author any technical genius whose teaching
alone he deemed counterinstructive, nor promote to majority
the technically lesser author merely because he took the
"right" line.

In time, then, Eliot gave up the claim for an essential, ahistorical (his phrase for this was "timeless"), and universal greatness as intrinsic to the works that make up the "monuments"
of the tradition. Rather, it was the extrinsic principle of *orthodoxy* that came to authorize his choices of the canonical texts
(the "best" if not always the "major" texts)—as it was that
principle which animated Eliot's own religious criticism. The
term Eliot offered for the principle opposed to *orthodoxy* was
heresy; thus, to support the orthodox and oppose the heretical
would be the aims of a religious criticism deployed in the
interest of a religious canon authorizing a Christian Society. A
secular criticism in the interest of a secular canon and a pluralis-
tic democratic society need not, however, oppose orthodoxy
in the name of heresy. To the contrary, it is necessary to reject
heresy along with orthodoxy as equivalently the conceptualiza-
tions of religious thought. Rather than heresy as the principle
(extrinsic, ideological, apart from esthetic valuation), informing my own selections for a canon of American literature, I
would suggest what Guillory, in the final sentences of his article names *heterodoxy,* a term that, for him, is best suited to
"consider what it means that 'difference' has become our central critical category . . . a teaching that will enact discursively
the struggle of difference" (359). That is all Guillory says on the
matter. I have already indicated why I think it is a mistake to
construct and endorse any category that would reify an endless
struggle of discursive difference. This is—to put the matter

another way—only to valorize a radically ironic perspective, a commitment to tension or difference as an end in itself (I shall have more to say about this temptation, a strong presence in American criticism since the modernist period).[15] Politically, as I have heard Cornel West say, it is a commitment not to revolution, which envisions an end however long-postponed, but to resistance, which is a permanent condition of existence. Or, to take Allon White's formulation of this matter,

A politics of pure difference which refuses to theorise the unity-in-difference of humanity ends by replicating the individualism of the self-sufficient bourgeois ego—a dangerous fiction if ever there was one. (233)

I will thus appropriate the term *heterodoxy* and use it to name exactly such a principle as "unity-in-difference," as this principle may inform an American literary canon—a canon of national literature—and an American social order. I shall also try to extend it to the international order of literature and society in taking heterodoxy as informing that *cosmopolitanism* my own discussion will take as its ultimate horizon.

But just here, let me turn again to Edward Said, who has movingly argued against religious criticism and in favor of an explicitly secular criticism. Although Said himself, as I have already noted, is not a canon-maker, still, his theoretical and practical insistence on "how ostrichlike and retrograde assertions about Eurocentric humanities really are" (1983, 29), has strong implications for opening the canon to difference not as a "central critical category" but as the condition of any informed critical stance. Add to this Raymond Williams's comment

15. On the subject of irony, see my "Anthropology in the Ironic Mode: The Work of Franz Boas."

that however dominant a social system may be, the very meaning of its domination involves a limitation or selection of the activities it covers, so that by definition it cannot exhaust all social experience, which therefore always potentially contains space for alternative acts and alternative intentions which are not yet articulated as a social institution or even project. (in Said, 29)

Further adduce almost any typical remark of Bakhtin's on the dialogical nature of language, literature, and society (e.g., "There is neither a first nor a last word and there are no limits to the dialogic context" [quoted in A. White, 220]). Recall "without apology" the canon reformation of the 1960s, and there is in all of this more than enough warrant for a heterodox secular canon of literature, not only in opposition to a Christian society, or, indeed to any monologic orthodoxy, but as well to an insistence upon rather than a permission of difference.

For the canon of American literature, secular heterodoxy on an empirical level means something very specific: it means that any proposed canon of American literature that does not include more than merely occasional examples of the literatures produced by red and black people as well as white people—men and women, of indigenous and African, as well as European origins—is suspect on the very face of it. The history of that national formation called the United States of America is such as to insist upon the primacy of Euramerican, Native American, and Afro-American literary expression in any attempt to define an American literature. In saying this, I hope it is clear, to repeat, that I am not calling for some kind of proportional representation for these groups, nor restricting the canon to texts associated with these groups, aprioristically denying that canonical American books might well be produced by people of Asiatic, or mixed origins, or of any background whatever. In these regards, it is worth noting that Spanish is now the second language of the United States (as it is the second most widely spoken language in the world), a fact sufficiently important to have provoked intense efforts on the part of S. I. Hayakawa and others to pass a regressive and repressive constitutional amendment making English the official language of the United States. As I write, on the eve of Election Day, 1988, proposals are on the ballot in Arizona, Colorado, and Florida to this effect. Given the increase in American Spanish speakers, there is no doubt in my mind that Latino literature will soon exert major pressure on the canon, a development I look forward to with enthusiasm. Nonetheless, to the present, the cultural expression of red, white, and black people seems to me to have a historically urgent claim to primary attention.

I mean, here, to assert that Afro-American and Native American literary production, when we pay attention to it, offers texts equivalently excellent to the traditional Euramerican great books. It is not only that these texts should be read in the interest of fairness or simply because they are available; nor is it because they provide charming examples of "primitive" survivals: they should be read because of their abundant capacity to teach and delight. But for that capacity to be experienced and thus for the excellence of these texts to be acknowledged, it will be necessary, as I have suggested above, to recognize that what they teach frequently runs counter to the teaching of the Western tradition, and that the ways in which they delight is different from the ways in which the Western tradition has given pleasure.

Still, it may be that we have entered into a period in which the prospects for Native American *phrónēsis* and *techné* are rather promising. In terms of its teaching, let me note only the fact that traditional and contemporary Native literatures tend pretty much without exception to derive from an ecosystemic, nonanthropocentric perspective on the world that we may at last be coming to see—as the ozone layer thins, as the polar ice melts, as the nonbiodegradable garbage mounts to the skies—as being centrally rather than marginally important to human survival. This is not to say that Indian literatures are explicitly "about" a particular view of "Nature," far from it; yet this is indeed the perspective with which they all, in my experience, are consistent.

In terms of technique, even the most recent and most complexly composed Native American works are still likely to have roots in or relations to oral traditions that differ considerably in their procedures from those of the dominant, text-based culture: if these works are indeed equivalently excellent, still it must be recognized that they are differently excellent. To the extent that we are perhaps already in what Father Walter Ong calls the "secondary orality of our electronic age" (305) to the extent that print culture is already receding from the importance it had for a full five hundred years, we may currently be producing just the conditions of possibility for such a recognition. That postmodernist fiction, poetry, and painting have found a substantial audience; that the disjointed, even spasmodic styles of "Miami Vice," "Crime Story," and MTV music video have proved popular, indicates that a wide public has lost interest in attempts to represent the world realistically in causally connected, continuous linear narrative. Ronald Reagan's popularity, matched with the unpopularity of his actual political positions, is only further evidence of a paradigm shift whose description is already possible to produce, although its evaluation remains somewhat more difficult. In any event, the material situation as I can understand it, for all that I am wary of it, nonetheless seems to me encouraging for the appreciation of Native American literature.

In the chapters that follow, I first explore the relations between critical perspectives and the canon, most particularly as these relate to the inclusion or exclusion—indeed, the very visibility—of Native American work. This exploration is followed by an essentially historical study that traces attempts to place Indian literatures within the canon of American literature. I embark next upon a lengthy return to the genre of Native American literature with which I have been most concerned, Native American autobiography. I try to do some careful reading here, practical criticism, as it used proudly to be called, of texts that are only marginally literary. My aims are multiple: to call these texts to the attention of readers and make them interesting and illustrative in a variety of ways; to deduce from them some theoretical principles that may, to this point, have occupied a certain "space" but have not been even modestly "grounded." My final chapter attempts to consider the place of Native American literature as part of a heterodox American national, international, and ultimately cosmopolitan world canon of literature. I hope here, as throughout, to provide some theoretical basis for the enormous amount of practical work that needs to be done. A brief conclusion rounds out this book.

2. Criticism and
the Canon

As for "historicism," it has never really disappeared from the scene, though like "naturalism" it has indeed passed through many stages. In most quarters historicism has long since put aside the old values and habits which had drawn the scorn of Nietzsche and brought about the much publicized "crisis of historicism" of the earlier part of this century; and it seems too soon to place it (along with consciousness and the self) among the unliving or make it a candidate for disinterment. (Donald R. Kelley, 168)

Let us begin with R. K. Meiners's question,

[W]hat might have happened if a model of historical criticism such as that represented by Erich Auerbach had been sufficiently present in American institutions to furnish a real antagonism to New Criticism rather than the largely eclectic and untheoretical historicism that prevailed more through default than energy[?]. (130)

What indeed. But the question needs to be rephrased as not so much a matter of prior presence/absence as a matter of contemporaneous contest. Granting that an older academic historicism offered little resistance to the onslaught of New Critical formalism,[1] we may yet wonder why the more sophisticated

[This chapter first appeared as an essay–review in *Diacritics*, where it was dedicated to Roy Harvey Pearce. The present version is slightly revised and expanded. I am grateful to the editors of *Diacritics* for permission to reprint.]
1. Formalism and historicism are, of course, terms to which a great deal of discussion has been devoted. In what follows I try to do no more than to make

historicist work being produced at exactly the same time as that of the New Critics achieved so little visibility or effectivity. If, that is, we date the emergence, establishment, and dominance of those varieties of critical theory and practice subsumable under the broad rubric of the New Criticism from the 1920s to the 1950s, we are looking precisely at a period in which strong historical study of a sort very different from whatever "eclectic and untheoretical historicism" may have been present *was* being produced. Most of the references can be found in Wesley Morris's *Toward a New Historicism,* from which I would select for mention, first, the monumental three volumes by V. L. Parrington, *Main Currents in American Thought* (1927); also in the 1920s Van Wyck Brooks is in print with *The Pilgrimage of Henry James* (1925) and studies of *Emerson and Others* (1927). By 1933, we have Granville Hicks's *The Great Tradition;* in that same year, the Johns Hopkins philosopher, Arthur O. Lovejoy, delivered the William James Lectures at Harvard that would appear in 1936 as *The Great Chain of Being.* Also in 1936, William Charvat published *The Origins of American Critical Thought.* Frank Lentricchia's recent attention to Kenneth Burke may remind us that Burke's *Attitudes toward History,* in two volumes, appeared in 1937. Perry Miller issued the second volume of his *The New England Mind, From Colony to Province* in 1939, and F. O. Matthiessen's *American Renaissance* dates from 1941. Throughout the 1940s Leo Spitzer and Lovejoy carry on a debate in public on the value of Lovejoy's "history of ideas" for literary studies. Finally, to make this survey no longer, Henry Nash Smith's *Virgin Land: The Ameri-*

---

my own rough working definitions of these terms clear. As will be apparent, I have thought it reasonable to bracket the Kantian dimensions of formalism—as I have also not specifically engaged the question of whether historicisms must inevitably align themselves with Marxisms.

can West as Symbol and Myth came out in 1950, to be followed in
1953 by the first major publication of the critic whose work I
shall examine in detail, Roy Harvey Pearce's *The Savages of
America: A Study of the Indian and the American Mind*—these
latter two texts influenced by Lovejoy's method. Whatever the
problems one might discover in these texts, or in others I have
not named, they could not accurately be described as "eclectic
and untheoretical," although all of them take seriously "the
conviction," as a recent comment on the sociology of literature
states it, "that literature and society necessarily explain each
other" (Ferguson, et. al., 421). Only to the extent that such a
"conviction" can be accepted as a virtual commonplace can we
claim to have marginalized the formalist legacy of the New
Criticism, to have moved historicist criticism from margin to
center.

Returning to Meiners's formulation, perhaps we may say
that if the New Criticism did not have a powerful historical
antagonist in place, it certainly had competition from a theoretically sophisticated historical criticism contemporaneous
with it. One reason this criticism did not establish its methods
as the norm, I believe, is that it was being produced chiefly by
Americanists, two of the most powerful of whom (belatedly,
so far as any contest for critical influence was concerned)
worked with what were considered (even by the standards of
Americanists and historicists) eccentric materials. Smith attended to such things as the popular dime novels; Pearce, as I
shall note further, centered his study on texts concerned with
the Indian. I am positing here, as others have done, a relation
between critical theory and the canon, and suggesting that
from the 1920s to the 1950s a persistent Eurocentrism in
American institutions aided the New Criticism in its progress
to a position of dominance. If this is so, then the only way

some hypothetical American Auerbach could have helped a historicist criticism to become the dominant practice would have been, first, of course, to have published here a good many years before the actual Auerbach published his major book,[2] and, most of all, like the actual Auerbach, to have worked predominantly with the standard canon of European literature, touching only a very few, if any, American books.

For it is important to recall that New Critical formalism established itself against the moralism of its predecessor, the "New Humanism" (I think this must be what Meiners has in mind as unsophisticated historicism) of Irving Babbitt and Paul Elmer More, among others, by questioning its method but not its relation to American literature. Just as Paul Elmer More might admit to feeling that "American literature is indeed a wilderness of mediocrity" (in Tanner: 174), so might the New Critics find few authors in three hundred years of American writing who engaged their interest. More precisely, the American authors they did work with were not those who seemed most to require consideration of their *implication in* American society and culture—I borrow, here, a favorite phrase from Pearce. As Russell Reising has noted, this was part of a program that, to the extent it granted any "socially mimetic element in American literature," systematically "devalue[d] it" in order to "privilege the aesthetic, symbolic, or linguistic elements" of it (17).

Of course it is precisely the strategy of formalisms, whether

2. Auerbach's *Mimesis,* after all, is a book that not only follows but, as we know, from the copyright page, *survives* World War II—published in Berne in 1946, "Written in Istanbul between May 1942 and April 1945" (n.p.), according to Auerbach, first American edition published in 1953, just a few years before New Criticism was to be challenged not so much by any historicism but by Frye's "New Mythography"; the phrase is Roy Harvey Pearce's in "Historicism Once More" (20).

they are theorized by Rene Wellek or Paul de Man,[3] to subordinate if not wholly ignore a range of potential contexts for the
text as not centrally relevant to their study. For formalists,
literary inquiry differs from that of sociology or psychology
or, indeed, of history, in limiting itself to the internal system
of a text—its ironies and tensions for New Critics, its tropes
or figures for deconstructionists. For this reason, formalist
criticism must generally accept the canon as it finds it, for
there is no formalist method for raising questions of evaluation; texts are "good" as they work interestingly or—what is
the same thing—as they provide interesting work to a particular method. For older European authors, we know who is of
first rank, time and the opinion of those competent to judge
having made the selection—or at least we know those worthy
of attacking. In regard to newer writing, authors are proposed
for consideration as their work seems amenable to formalist
method, which is again to say as it seems not to insist on any
relation to history, at least to no history other than literary
history.[4]

3. It may be worth recalling that René Wellek, flying the banner of the New
Criticism against historicist work even to the present moment in the sixth and
seventh volumes—1980 and 1987—of his *History of Modern Criticism,* earlier, in
the 1940s, in his *Theory of Literature* (1949, with Austin Warren) and in the 1950s,
in the first volume of his *History* (1955), intervened against the historicist influence of both Lovejoy *and* Auerbach. For a telling corrective, see Pearce's notes to
"Historicism Once More" (see nn. at pp. 15–16 and p. 24). Wellek's criticisms of
Pearce have always been severe.

4. Of course, we know very well now that New Critical formalism was not
in the least apolitical but committed to a determined, if sometimes vague, feudal-
ist program, one that Smith—a southerner like the Fugitives, but a southwest-
erner, altogether a different thing—criticized explicitly, disapproving its per-
petuation of " 'the myth of the plantation, and American Arcadia,' even as it
neglected the South's actual economic problems" (Bridgman, 261). And Pearce's
position, as will be apparent, is also firmly one of demystification, "liberal," in
general, rather than "conservative." These issues.continue to count as witnessed

This is why for the New Critics, and, as we shall see, for the deconstructionists, Henry James's comments in his early book on *Hawthorne* (1879) on America's presumed lack of social texture amenable to esthetic working, become a necessary first premise for the study of American literature. Let me quote the passage at some length. James, writing about the difficulties in the way of Hawthorne's becoming a fully achieved realist novelist, notes "the items of high civilization, as it exists in other countries, which are absent from the texture of American life." There is

No State, in the European sense of the word, and indeed barely a specific national name. No sovereign, no court, no personal loyalty, no aristocracy, no church, no clergy, no army, no diplomatic service, no country gentlemen, no palaces, no castles, nor manors, nor old country-houses, nor parsonages, nor thatched cottages, nor ivied ruins; no cathedrals, nor abbeys, nor little Norman churches; no great Universities nor public schools—no Oxford, nor Eton, nor Harrow; no literature, no novels, no museums, no pictures, no political society, no sporting class—no Epsom nor Ascot! (1963, 34)

It is the thinness on which American cultural production is presumably based that becomes, for formalists, a kind of supplementary justification for the "intrinsic" treatment of American literature; the formalist canon is made up of those

by the "Note" commenting on John Fisher's eulogy of Smith by Louis Kampf, Paul Lauter, and Richard Ohmann claiming that Fisher misrepresents "Henry Smith's politics and thus, deeply, his life." Kampf, Lauter, and Ohmann believe "Henry Nash Smith would have preferred to have been remembered as a supporter of change and of bringing the MLA into the world we actually inhabit" (374). Reising is also to the point when he writes that "To argue that the New Critics either attempted or succeeded in depoliticizing literary thinking is to miss the profoundly political recoil from history and politics implicit in their work" (17).

few figures who recognized what the New Critics knew all along and James had shrewdly expressed, that there is not much point relating an American text to its context. Hawthorne and Dickinson, acute in their ostensible hermiticism/ hermeticism, are interesting to work with inasmuch as their interest cannot possibly be a function of their relation to American life (what is there, after all?); beyond these, there is not much to be done with the older American literature. Of the new, there is Eliot who, in all the quotation of the *Waste Land* could find need for no American author; and Pound, who, despite his "pact" with Walt Whitman, was never deeply engaged by any American. Frank Norris and Dreiser and Dos Passos are untouched or denigrated. And the European canon is simply given, the result of time's selective wisdom; how could it be otherwise, for to question the canon would be to engage material and ideological issues that are outside the purview of the *literary* critic. The estheticization of the literary/historical—the denial, in Reising's phrase, "of the possibility (or the desirability) of studying American literature as a vehicle of social knowledge" (17)—is itself profoundly ideological, as are, to recall a point made earlier, all calls to keep literature free of any values but those of "greatness."

Now, the Americanist–historicist critics, it must be admitted, also seem to have accepted the Jamesian assessment of American life in comparison to that of Europe in ways fairly similar to the New Critics, thereby abandoning ground that might well have been held against the onslaught of intrinsic criticism. The difference is that for them, as historicists, this thinness is a problem rather than a permission: Parrington, Brooks, Matthiessen, and others were constantly worrying the question of how American culture, for all its deficiencies, might not only disable but also empower somehow the likes not only of Hawthorne and James but of Poe and Twain, and of Melville and Whitman—whose status as canonical figures is exactly what is at stake. What is missing from their critique, of course, is any attention to the possible development of American life not only in relation to what was missing in reference to England but to what was encountered, newly, here, most particularly in relation to Native American peoples. This is to say that the historicists were also oriented eastward.

In these regards, perhaps it is worth a moment to recall the regional conflict between east and west so strongly patterned in American life since the time of Andrew Jackson. Both the New Critics and their historicist contemporaries, as proponents of high culture, were inevitably proponents of the east (and, if they pushed further, just as inevitably of Europe). They were thus opposing—as late as the 1920s and 1930s—the west-oriented "frontier" thesis of Frederick Jackson Turner, the notion that American culture came out of the "forest," the catch-all term for the "wilderness" of noncivilization or savagism. (Turner did not, I think, mean high culture, James's "items of high civilization," but culture as the anthropologist would define it, the various institutions and manners taken as "natural" by the populace at large.) An extreme reading of Turner would thus deny that eastern high culture was really American at all—Barry Goldwater was not innovating when he suggested some twenty-five years ago that New York be cut free of America and set adrift upon the ocean—and those who admired eastern high culture could disagree with Turner only in longing that one day it might indeed be American, once the west caught up, as it were, became "civilized" itself (westerners, thus, becoming the east's Indian "sav-

ages"). This was not, of course, the west's view of the matter,
nor is it today. And I have already indicated the degree to
which east/west disputes remain unresolved—in academic as
well as general culture. Here it may not be irrelevant to note
that Henry Smith and Roy Pearce, the first to engage in sophisticated study of the images of popular culture and the
popular images of Indians, are themselves not easterners,
Pearce hailing from California and Smith from the Southwest. Only with Pearce's historicist work does it become
possible to consider what I have taken as axiomatic, the influence of Native American culture on American culture.

The historical developments I have noted are such as to
make the legacy of even a subordinated historicist criticism in
American Studies still a thoroughly hierarchical matter. To
this day, in every case, those who work on American subjects
privileging the canonical WASP, eastern, male writers (and,
to be sure, Emily Dickinson) struggling with cultural thinness have had primary claims to attention. Consider, for example, that at least one reason for Yvor Winters's tangency to
both the historicist and formalist criticism of his day, lies
partly in his determination to champion both Frederick Goddard Tuckerman *and* Native American literature (not to say
Winters's position as a Californian before that state's university system had the high repute it does today).[5] Those who
attend to feminist materials (just now, for the moment) come
next. Afro-American literary expression takes third place on

---

5. In a curious sense these interests came together when N. Scott Momaday
chose to take his doctorate under Winters at Stanford and produced as his doctoral dissertation a complete edition of Tuckerman's poems, while also beginning
the text—first projected as a long narrative poem—that became the novel, *House
Made of Dawn* (1968), a book that, in winning a Pulitzer Prize, had the effect of
making contemporary Native American writing visible to a wider public. I
discuss Momaday's autobiographical work in a later chapter.

this particular scale. Next, in large measure due to the recent work of Eve Kosofsky-Sedgwick, among others, come studies of "homosocial" discourse, the writing of gay men and lesbians. Popular literature of the sort that Henry Nash Smith pioneered in studying probably occupies fifth place on this odd but powerfully operative scale, whereas work attentive to Native American literature comes, to date, only a distant sixth. For all of this, it remains the case that clear rankings and accurate classifications of canonical importance become increasingly difficult to establish as one sinks lower on this scale: Is Smith's work more nearly focused on the regional or the popular, after all? Is Annette Kolodny's recent work with women's journals of the nineteenth century more feminist or regional—or popular? And, given the fair degree of rigidity that still prevails in academic English departments, the classificatory unclarity of the *hors* canonical texts works against their visibility: What if the Department hasn't been able to afford its feminist, its regionalist, its Afro-Americanist, its specialist in Native American studies?

I note that Smith's book still has no major *theoretical* influence outside American studies, if there. Smith, however, was asked to publish his "reassessment" of *Virgin Land* for the volume *Ideology and Classic American Literature,* edited by Sacvan Bercovitch and Myra Jehlen,[6] but Pearce was not asked to publish his "reassessment" of *Savages* (in *The Journal of Ethnic Studies*) whose theoretical component has to this

6. Where Smith himself acknowledged that *Virgin Land* would have been richer had it attended to the Indian materials Pearce examined (see Bercovitch and Jehlen, 28), Kampf, Lauter, and Ohmann correctly remark this recognition as indicative of the view of Smith's politics they wish to present. Smith reviewed Pearce's *Savages*—quite favorably—for the Ohio State University house organ, *The Graduate Record.*

day been overlooked in false tribute, as it were, to its substantive riches. (Pearce's own assessment of *Virgin Land* appears in the title essay of his new book, *Gesta Humanorum,* to
which I refer below.) Nor was he asked to contribute to
Bercovitch's *Reconstructing American Literary History*—neither
of which collections, let it be noted, has a single essay dealing with Native American materials. One further potentially
illustrative reference: Jane Tompkins chooses to demonstrate
the *importance* of feminist criticism by studying *Uncle Tom's
Cabin,* a novel by a woman dealing with Afro-Americans
(see "Sentimental Power: *Uncle Tom's Cabin* and the Politics
of Literary History" in Bercovitch/Jehlen: but the essay has
appeared in a great many places). When Tompkins wishes,
however, to produce an essay in non-sequiturial criticism,
whose theoretical point (presented as "against theory" neo-
pragmatism) is that research and interpretive and evaluative
effort are to no special purpose because we are always
thrown back on whatever it may be that we already believe—can it be an accident that such an essay just happens
to have as its focus a subject involving Native American
materials? See her " 'Indians': Textualism, Morality, and the
Problem of History," in which "Indians" exist only between
inverted commas for Tomkins although textualism, morality, and even the problem of history need no such marking.[7]

To recapitulate: from the 1920s to the 1950s, both our increasingly dominant formalist criticism and our active but

---

7. Thus, if we take Paul Rabinow's advice to include "an anthropology of
anthropology" (253) as part of the interpretive process, anthropologizing literary
and cultural studies reveals that the way to a major career is not by work in
Native American literature. That a hierarchy of *content* so persists in the present
moment may be surprising, but persist it does.

pedagogically less visible historicist criticism seem to have shared curiously similar views of American culture but not quite similar views of American literature as a whole. Although the New Critics pretty much always knew which American writers were worth study, whether of the past century or of the present, the historicists were not quite sure, and historicist criticism, as it actually developed, increasingly approached the possibility of a challenge to the canon it was itself helping to establish. Finally, I have claimed, with Smith and Pearce, historicist criticism did begin to take seriously work that required consideration of the social production of meaning, work whose importance could not be ascribed foremost to its internal system of relations. For a variety of reasons—economic, political, and social, quite as much as "literary"—it turned out that the canon was preserved intact and only the rationale for its preservation changed; thus the New Criticism won the day, and we have not yet had an effective historical criticism (as we have not had an effective socialist party) in America.

Indeed, although Wesley Morris may have pointed us *Toward a New Historicism* fifteen years ago, it is only today that we find something called—in the best old fashion—the New Historicism coming center stage, sending into the wings *its* predecessor, another formalism, the one known generally as poststructuralism or deconstruction. Here we may note yet another curious overlapping of essentially opposed positions, for, just as older historicists and older (New Critical) formalists seem to have agreed on the sociocultural thinness of American life, so, too, do the New Historicists and new formalist deconstructionists seem to agree on the determinative power of impersonal forces in the making of texts. As Roy Harvey Pearce states it in the Foreword to his book, *Gesta*

Humanorum: Studies in the Historicist Mode, it seems to be the fact for the New Historicism that its "practicioners too often have an awkward and embarrassing difficulty with the concept of Self—and, along with it, with the concept of specifically human intentionality" (ix).

Pearce's own historicism in its recent humanist form certainly does privilege the Self; but his practice of historicist criticism has not always done so, or not to the current degree. So here is Pearce, once more it would seem, going against the grain: some thirty-five years ago it was his historical method and his choice of American thought about Indians as subject that marginalized his work; now, as a new historicism comes to the fore, his militant humanism may serve to obscure his contribution to a historicist criticism of American literature. I want to embark, here, on a closer examination of Pearce's work which can, I think, serve to provide something of a test case for understanding what our dominant formalist criticism has suppressed—and what a newly emerging mode of historicist criticism may itself suppress. My particular interest in all this is to promote an increasing visibility for Native American literature, both traditional and contemporary, and to encourage its inclusion in the canon of American literature.

Pearce's *The Savages of America: A Study of the Indian and the Idea of Civilization,* appeared at a time when, to cite Myra Jehlen, "ideological analysis and literary criticism appeared inherently contradictory to most critics of American literature" (2), largely as a result of the New Criticism's achieved dominance, as noted above. Against the grain, then, Pearce's book offered ideological analysis and literary criticism, or, given the extraordinary range of his study—from seventeenth-century travel writing to Indian plays of the nineteenth century—

offered discursive analysis, a broad cultural study of the kind we now associate with writers such as Gramsci and Raymond Williams, Bakhtin, and, of course, Michel Foucault.[8]

Pearce's work was an attempt to elevate Lovejoy's "history of ideas" approach to intellectual history from the stage of "analysis" to that of "synthesis": as Pearce describes the analytic stage (typical of most of Lovejoy's own work) in *Gesta Humanorum,* this meant "the thinking through of the logical possibilities latent in any statement of belief or in any idea" (1987, 9) as found in a text, or, as he put it in 1956—in a form, I think, much closer to his own use of Lovejovean "analysis" in *Savagism:* "the searching of literature, along with philosophical, historical, economic, and analogous forms of writing, for the explicit or implicit expression of ideas of significance for the history of our culture" (1967, 2). On the level of synthesis, however, not only were what Lovejoy called "unit ideas" considered; rather, "Combinations of unit ideas . . . were placed in their socio-cultural contexts and were shown as they shaped men's minds and opinions leading them to acts" (1987, 10). The "history of ideas" as it might be practiced in the "synthetic mode" thus led to the question, "How do ideas, as we have come to know them through this kind of historical analysis, function and have meaning in the contexts in which they have appeared and have had their immediate cultural impress?" (Pearce, 1956: 3). In *Savagism,* then, Pearce in effect was show-

---

8. I have remarked Foucault's hostility to historicism, and, in particular, to the history of ideas in my Introduction to the new California edition of *Savagism and Civilization: A Study of the Indian and the American Mind:* this is the title of *Savages'* revised appearance in 1965, and I will refer to the book as *Savagism.* Parts of my discussion here also appear, in slightly different form, in that Introduction. See also Frank Manuel's recent "Lovejoy Revisited," for a fuller comparison of Lovejoy (not Pearce) and Foucault.

ing how Lovejoy's work might indeed lead to a "social history of ideas," or as we might now put it, to a cultural critique.[9]

It would be Pearce's task to show the way in which "the history of American civilization would . . . be conceived of as three-dimensional, progressing from past to present, from east to west, from lower to higher" (1967, 49), and how, for almost two hundred and fifty years, that conception would establish itself in relation to specific socially produced definitions of Indian "savagery." American "civilization," that is, invented itself as the obverse or opposite of Native American "savagism," what *we* would be, defined in relation to what *they* presumably were—or sensibly were not and could not be. In a later essay, Pearce would incorporate material from *Savagism* in a study of Melville's "The Metaphysics of Indian-Hating: Leatherstocking Unmasked," in which, as he says, "Melville shows how Indian-hating and its metaphysic have been taken to be necessary in God's scheme of things American" (1969, 117), a kind of *summa* of savagist logic where "destruction . . . [is] conceived as necessary to a cultural mission" (1969, 130). Those who remember Vietnam, or, more recently, the televised testimony of Oliver North, may shudder at the persistence of the metaphysics of Indian-hating.

In terms not only of his concern for the ideological contours of discourse in history, then, but also of his choice of subject matter, Pearce's study must have seemed strange. For, although the years between the two wars had seen a flurry of interest in the Indian, anthologies of Native poetry appearing for the first time and such diverse luminaries as Mary Austin, D. H. Lawrence, William Carlos Williams, and Yvor Winters

---

9. Donald Kelley provides references for the criticism of Lovejoy as not attentive enough to social factors in his "Horizons of Intellectual History."

attending to things Indian, I can think only of Albert Keiser's
1933 study, *The Indian in American Literature,* as preceding
Pearce's in its attention to European–American thought about
the Native American. The canon—the effective and visible
selection of texts—had, after all, stood firm.

Pearce's book, as I have said, is substantively rich, but it is
theoretically clear and coherent as well. The Foreword to the
first publication of *Savagism* proposed to work with "Idea,
Symbol, and Image" as terms "meant to categorize, however
roughly, stages in the history of an idea as it becomes part of a
system of thought and action." "By Idea," Pearce wrote, "I
mean a predication, explicit or implicit, which offers a solution of a major human problem. By Symbol I mean a vehicle
for an Idea. . . . By Image I mean a vehicle for a Symbol."
The idea was the notion of the savage and savagism: "the
Symbol is the Indian; and the Images are those found in social, historical, and imaginative writing of the period" (1609–
1851). Thus, as Pearce had announced at the beginning of his
Foreword, *Savages* was "a book about a belief," but one that
was also "planned according to [a] structure of thought *and
action*" (my emphasis); and in a 1966 Postscript to the original
Foreword he reaffirmed that "the book is a study of one of
those unattractive 'isms' which taught our forebears how to
make up their minds and *also how to act*" (1967, x; my emphasis). Pearce's practice of historicist criticism (he does not call it
that yet) in *Savagism,* reconciles an orientation toward "ideas"
and toward "actions," developing a concern, as I would gloss
these, both for the social production of meanings as located in
texts and for the material consequences or effectivity of those
meanings as expressed in social action. One may reasonably
see this practice as fundamentally enabling for such major
Americanist studies—all of which take the place of the Indian

in the development of American society and culture as significant—as Richard Slotkin's *Regeneration through Violence* (1973), Michael Paul Rogin's *Fathers and Children: Andrew Jackson and the Subjugation of the American Indian* (1975), and Richard Drinnon's *Facing West: The Metaphysics of Indian-hating and Empire-building* (1980), among others.

But there is a very considerable difference between this version of historicist criticism and the version we find in *Gesta Humanorum* where, as I shall try to indicate, history becomes less a matter of shifting social belief and action, for Pearce, and more the unchanging record of the "tensions . . . between self and culture" (1987, x). The texts chosen for examination will be those most useful for the dramatization of that tension.

The change in Pearce's critical emphasis from the social/ collective to the individual (and the parallel change in the texts studied) may be noted in three introductions to Hawthorne's work (*The House of the Seven Gables* [1954], *Twice-Told Tales* [1955], *The Scarlet Letter* [1957]) he prepared for the J. M. Dent, Everyman Library. Here there is an intense emphasis on inwardness and the affective experience of the individual self (e.g., a concern for the "true and authentic self," a phrase repeated several times in the few pages of *The Scarlet Letter* piece). Full theoretical expression of this shift of emphasis comes in a densely brilliant (but neglected) essay of 1958 called "Historicism Once More." Curiously enough, this piece first appeared under New Critical auspices, at least to the extent that it was accepted by John Crowe Ransom for the *Kenyon Review*. In "Historicism Once More," history is no longer understood as the interaction of socially produced "beliefs" and of the social "actions" that result from those beliefs;

rather, for the first time I think in Pearce's work, history becomes thematized as that constant which serves as a check upon the individual self's longing for freedom and plenitude, as essentially the reified forces of "self-limitation and self-definition" (1967, 32). Sociocultural contexts and the individual's responsibility for her actions continue to be of importance, but increasingly any social and material detail thins out before a growing fascination with the thick possibilities of selfhood.

Pearce remarks the fact that we have certainly had historical critics concerned with backgrounds and sources, in order to ask, "what does it mean to be . . . a 'critical historicist' instead of an 'historical critic'?" (1967, 6). One thing it means is that we will try to see how the pastness, as Pearce calls it, of the literary work is involved in any apprehension of it we may achieve in the present. The concern is "not only to see literature in history . . . [but] to see history in literature."[10] But the question remains, What is one to understand by history? Since literature (because of its fictive nature presenting what Pearce in several places refers to as conditional contrary-to-fact statements) is the form of writing best suited to record the human struggle for wholeness, the broad range of discursive materials examined in *Savages* is now largely abandoned for a concentration exclusively on literary writing, and that, indeed of the canonical authors. For, as Pearce unequivocally states it, "man, the self, is at the center of all literature and . . . literary works are necessarily created in terms of a fixed, unchanging and unchangeable sense of what it is to be aware of oneself as a

10. Stephen Greenblatt, whose name is virtually synonymous with the New Historicism, echoes Pearce in his concern for "both the social presence to the world of the literary text and the social presence of the world in the literary text" (6).

man, whatever one's situation in historical time" (1969, 26).[11]
To be sure, one's "situation" is never to be ignored, but the
historical situation for Pearce is rarely materially and quantitatively but only "qualitatively *in,* existentially *in,* a literary
work" (1969, 15), thus becoming fixed as a constant thematic:[12] history is always and ever no more than the record of
those forces that inevitably and necessarily condition the individual self's longing for freedom and plentitude. (This latter is
no nostalgia for Pearce inasmuch as its achievement is for him
as for Derrida an impossibility. I suspect a comparison between
Pearce and Derrida on this subject would, among other things,
reveal the aridity of the latter's response to human struggle—
although since I first wrote this, Derrida seems to have been
moved at least to textual gestures against apartheid.) Degrees
of freedom—history as quantitatively allowing now something more now something less of human potentiality to be
actualized—are not considered, nor is the category of social or
collective freedom set in relation to the existential freedom of
the apparently autonomous individual.

"In literature," Pearce writes, "humanitas triumphs over
history, even as it triumphs by means of history" (1969, 31).
At this point it would still be theoretically possible to bal-

11. The new book attempts to modify this type of formulation, urging that
we read the masculine pronouns as applicable as well to women; whether this is a
sufficient response to the issue is open to question.

12. The theme, as now stated is that "the human project . . . [is] gloriously
tragico-comical" (1987, 19): thus, in Hayden White's scheme, Pearce's "mode of
employment" would be "satirical"; his "mode of argument" would be "contex-
tualist"; and his mode of "ideological implication" would be "liberal"—all of
which, as White elaborates them, are, I think, fairly accurate as macro-descriptions
of Pearce's work (passim). *Gesta Humanorum* also has a chapter sharply critical of
those who would substitute a fixed plot (Marxists and deconstructionists in the
prophetic mode—e.g., the coming of free play and the death of man) for Pearce's
sense of—an equivalently fixed—theme.

ance the concern for self with an attention to the social and material; the turn to the self is not, that is, in itself necessarily destructive of history as the record of temporal difference. As Fredric Jameson writes, "any critical insights of whatever variety (stylistic, psychoanalytic, archetypal, typological, generic, semiotic) can always be historicized" (1981, 375), and so, of course, there is no dismissing the existential/ phenomenological concerns Pearce expresses as inherently suspect. After all, Jameson himself would only echo Pearce in writing that "History is . . . the experience of Necessity. . . . History is what hurts, it is what refuses desire and sets inexorable limits to individual as well as collective praxis"—and this, of course, in a book whose call to arms is "Always historicize" (1981, passim). The question, as I understand it, concerns what kind of self we envision, and what sort of tensions exist between the self and the experience of History/Necessity. The question is also whether we will let the upper-case initials of History and Necessity be the final word on the subject or whether we will descend to the lower-case (as it were) and examine the details of their working.

In *Gesta Humanorum,* the agon of self and history, desire for freedom and confrontation with finitude, provide the central theme, with Pearce developing and refining his understanding of humanitas through the elaboration of the concept of the two humanisms, what he calls the Humanism of the One and the Humanism of the Many. The first is "Humanism overdetermined by Self [where the demands of the id are felt to dominate or exert major power] and Humanism overdetermined by Culture [where the demands of the superego are felt most strongly] (1987, xii). Because the focus is on American

literature, "The studies collected here are mainly concerned
with that predominating Humanism, for well and for ill, in
American society in its history, the Humanism of the One"
(1987, xii). Pearce traces the claims of the cock-crowing ego
(I allude to Thoreau, a writer Pearce does not treat in these
studies, although his two humanisms might indeed prove
useful ways to come at Thoreau) and its shortfalls in the
poetry of the "age of Paine," in Hawthorne, Whitman,
Twain, and in Wallace Stevens (the Stevens essay is particularly fine), and in the "New Poetry" of Snodgrass, Duncan,
Wright, Ignatow, Ashbery, and others. It is in the Stevens
essay that Pearce, as I read him, points to the way his critical
project may be brought full circle. Stevens, to whose sense of
the ambiguity, duality, and "tragico-comical" thematic of life
Pearce responds so deeply, must, in this brave and moving
essay, finally be rejected as the full examplar of American
literature. Pearce unsentimentally recognizes how the Humanism of the One may become "an isolating humanism" (1987,
153), and he pulls back from Stevens because "what cannot be
decreated is the fact, the factuality of the self in its history—
that is, historicity as such" (1987, 153).[13]

Pearce catalogues current critical perspectives "according to
the sort of anthropology (or anthropological commitments) in
which they are grounded" (vii), sketching relations between

13. Pearce's attention to the "Fireside Poets" and other distinctly non-
modernist authors—in his useful terms, poets submitted too thoroughly to the
Humanism of the Many—in *The Continuity of American Poetry* needs to be remarked. Alan Golding notes that "The first critical overview of the American
long poem did not appear till the third chapter of Roy Harvey Pearce's *Continuity
of American Poetry* in 1961" (298). Pearce always has the good sense to discrimi-
nate between more and less successful texts, but he does not therefore steer clear
of such as Whittier or Longfellow—in full knowledge that a Pound had to
swallow hard before swallowing even Whitman.

"forms of Symbolic Anthropology" and the problem of representation, and "Geertzian and Frankfort School anthropology" and ideological work, before announcing that his "studies have as their matrix psychological anthropology—what in the past was called culture–personality theory," where "culture," as I have indicated above, equates pretty much to superego demands on the ego and "personality" is constituted by how the ego handles those demands in opposition to the demands of an ever-present, all-desiring id. Now, it seems to me that it will not do to dismiss this concern for humanitas—for the "consciousness of self and self-consciousness" on which Pearce centers his most recent work—as merely a bourgeois illusion. I would instantiate here Allon White's commentary relating to Bakhtin (to whom I will turn soon) as humanist to the effect that the "notorious" antihumanism of poststructuralism has defined humanism in a "perfunctory and impoverished" manner so that it might dismiss it, to its own self-aggrandizement, in a pragmatic "rhetoric of revaluation" (230). White cites Kate Soper's important distinction between humanism as primary locus for the question of human agency (my primary concern here) and humanism as teleology, the belief in "the idea that there is a particular social grouping 'destined' to realize humanity's essential being or historic purpose" (in White, 230–231).

As Terry Eagleton (in "The Subject of Literature") has noted bitterly, to treat literature as the locus of an aimless, contentless, Kantian subjectivity, and the self as merely the playground for swirling affect has been and can be the cruelest of mystifications. But there are other ways to conceive the project of producing the Subject, and these may well be important to consider just now, both for literary theory in general and for the study of Native American literature in particular. Bakhtin, as Allon White remarks, is "certainly a humanist . . . believing in a strong sense of human agency operating on the basis of structures and conventions already in place and not freely chosen" (231)—although he is not, as Pearce is not, a teleological humanist.

Here, some anthropology may be useful. For one thing, as Clifford Geertz writes—in what may be seen as a *qualified* reaffirmation of the classic statement of Marcel Mauss ("A category of the human mind: the notion of person; the notion of self" [1938])—the "concept of the person . . . exists in recognizable form among all social groups," although "the actual conceptions involved vary from one group to the next, and often quite sharply (in Shweder and LeVine, 126). Thus it is that

The Western conception of the person as a bounded, unique, more or less integrated motivational and cognitive universe, a dynamic center of awareness, emotion, judgment, and action organized into a distinctive whole and set contrastively both against other such wholes and against its social and natural background, is, however incorrigible it may seem to us, a rather peculiar idea within the contexts of the world's cultures. (in Shweder and LeVine, 126)

Nevertheless, as Richard Shweder points out in a discussion of Geertz's essay,

the concept of the self [Geertz] refers to as a *Western* conception . . . is precisely the concept that most developmental psychologists would say has to be there in childhood in all societies, not just in the West. . . . In other words something that fits [Geertz's] description of the Western adult conception of the self may also be a universal infant and early childhood conception of the self. (in Sweder and LeVine, 13)

one which "gets expressed among adults in the West and over-ridden or reversed among adults in Bali" or other cultures.

These anthropologists do not tell us whether that expressed self is uniformly Western or predominantly middle class, nor do they begin to specify ways to ascertain—I am thinking again of Eagleton's essay—the content of that "bounded, unique, more or less integrated motivational and cognitive universe" as described by Geertz. If one thinks of the quotations from the Children's Employment Commission Report in the first volume of Marx's *Capital,* one may wonder of the children not yet in their teens working twelve-hour days regularly with frequent four-day shifts of fourteen hours each (and some days eighteen-hour and round-the-clock shifts) whether they were free to express their "best selves." Less dramatically but as tellingly, one may try to imagine the everyday situations of those who appear in the two family histories in "Life at the Edge" in *Consumer Reports* and wonder how bounded, unique, and more or less integrated these selves are likely to be. (I deliberately mention here a nonspecialized, mainstream publication outside any "left" orbit.) And one may think also of the postmodern "self" marked by "schizophrenic euphoria," in Fredric Jameson's powerful account (1984, passim), and wonder the same. As Steven Lukes has pointed out in commenting on Mauss's essay, at just about the time that Mauss's "sacred" *moi* was being founded by Fichte as "a being possessing metaphysical and moral value . . . a sacred being" (23), so, too, was that self being constituted negatively. In the apt quotation Lukes chooses from Foucault, the "individual is not to be thought of as a sort of elementary nucleus, a primitive atom"; rather, it is

one of the prime effects of power that certain bodies, certain gestures, certain discourses, certain desires, come to be identified and constituted as individuals. . . . The individual which power has constituted is at the same time its vehicle. (in Lukes, 295)

Add (as Lukes does) Musil's representative modernist observation on the difficulties of self-consciousness in mass society
(Musil: "In earlier times one could be an individual with a
better conscience than one can today" (in Lukes, 295); add
Mary Midgley's account of the self as always gender inflected
(Midgley: the "whole idea of a free, independent, enquiring,
choosing individual, an idea central to European thought, has
always been essentially the idea of a male. . . . In spite of its
force and nobiliity, it contains a deep strain of falsity . . .
because the supposed independence of the male was itself
false. It was parasitical, taking for granted the love and service
of non-autonomous females [and indeed often of the less en-
lightened males as well]" (51); add, to be sure, the mushroom
cloud over Hiroshima; the millions killed in the Holocaust;
and it is not hard to see why the concept of the "sacred" or
"transcendental" self would have to be dispersed, rethought
in order for new work to be done.[14]

But perhaps the reaction against the older privileging of self
and self-consciousness *itself* went too far, so that today, both
the self-pronounced humanist, Roy Harvey Pearce, and the
self-pronounced antihumanist Terry Eagleton must each point
out "an awkward and embarrassing difficulty with the concept
of Self—and along with it, with the concept of specifically

14. But it is worthwhile also to take into account Fredric Jameson's correla-
tion of antihumanism and technological development. Jameson remarks on the
"Third Technological Revolution in the West (electronics, nuclear energy)—in
other words a whole new step in the conquest of nature by human praxis . . . "
in relation to the

> kind of thought officially designated as "anti-humanist" and concerned to
> think what transcends or escapes human consciousness and intention. Simi-
> larly the Second Technological Revolution of the late 19th century—an unpar-
> alleled quantum leap in human power over nature—was the moment of ex-
> pression of a whole range of nihilisms associated with "modernity" or with
> high modernism in culture. (1981, 191)

human intentionality" (1987, ix), and so a need "to confront the problem of the subject" all over again (Eagleton, in Milner, 133). Eagleton continues:

What one is asking for is less a rethinking of the subject than, to use an old term, a rethinking of the agent, a rethinking of the subject as agent in a context where unworkable ideas of agency, the agent as transcendental source, have been properly discredited. (in Milner, 133)

And this sort of rethinking, it seems to me, is not foreclosed by Pearce's focus on the self, which is always for him *implicated in* history.[15] In the studies that make up *Gesta Humanorum,* as Pearce writes,

I tried to find those quite specific critically determinative sociocultural, historical situations out of which the writings I have studied have come, so to see how those situations (which I would declare are in effect ideological) have in good part made the achievements of those writings both possible and impossible. (1987, xiii)

Now, if ideology, albeit in parenthesis, stands in for the *meaning* of "sociocultural, historical situations," stands, therefore, as a symbol for what Pearce in other places named *history,* or *society,* leading always to a *sense* of the past rather than an account of it, then we are not likely to examine the content of ideology that will, once again, be thematized as yet another constant, the factor of time's constraints upon desire. But Pearce's own theory in no way requires this.

15. As it is not foreclosed by Bakhtin's focus on the nature of speech to the apparent neglect of the individual speaker. As Allon White observes, Bakhtin is thus "a specific kind of humanist, a sort of class-conscious and sociologically informed Auerbach[!]" (233). To go from Pearce to Bakhtin, as I do, two chapters hence, is not therefore so long a journey as one might have thought.

One can see history dialectically, as an agon not of freedom and finitude taken at so general a level as to have the battle's conclusion (not to say its meaning as tragico-comical) always foreordained. One can see history as the attempt on the part of individuals and groups to gain specific increments of freedom, as these are as much dependent on objective, which is to say material, conditions as on subjective sensations alone. As Mary Midgley has put it, "The choice now is between promoting everybody, equally to the position of a Hobbesian or Sartrean solitary individual, or re-thinking the notion of individuality radically from scratch" (55), a rethinking that must pay detailed attention to the specific social and institutional structures of complex social formations. Roy Harvey Pearce's work can provide a theoretical base from which to engage such work—which, for American criticism, now must include a specific and historical rethinking of individuality in relation to Native American collective concepts of the self.

The preceding discussion proposed the usefulness of, in effect, joining the earlier and later work of Roy Harvey Pearce to produce a model for a more comprehensive criticism of American literature as a national body of texts and as a specific selection of texts. In the 1950s, Pearce told us that the American concept of "civilization" depended upon various projections of Native American "savagism," our positive national self-definition achieved by insisting upon a certain negative definition of "them." And Pearce showed that a great deal of our American writing, whether strictly "literary" or not, was concerned with the meaning, morality, and implications of this process. This we had had from no one before. Now, in the 1980s, as I read him, Pearce's humanist historicism in its most fully developed form in *Gesta Humanorum* tells us that our new awareness of national definitions (to use a somewhat homely locution for what may otherwise be described as the ideological, hegemonic, or epistemic) may have caused us to ignore the ways in which individuals still struggle to align their own situated and highly particular sense of things with this always-already-given national sense. And a great deal of our writing, mostly of the kind formally considered "literary," now speaks of this struggle, however much it may also speak of and by means of collective representations.

These two sides of Pearce's work appear quite clearly in a talk he gave in 1973 to the American Historical Association (published as "From the History of Ideas to Ethnohistory"). There, he offered a reconsideration of his *Savagism and Civilization,* claiming that *Savagism,* his study of an American ideology, would have been a better book had it "dealt in richer detail with the experiential qualities of those whose beliefs and actions it tries to comprehend" (1974, 90), and this "from the perspectives of Red as well as White" (1974, 91). Pearce urges that we read the work of Edward Sapir, A. I. Hallowell, and the largely neglected ethnoanalyst (to call him that) Georges Devereux, quite as much as that of Lévi-Strauss and Clifford Geertz. It is the perspective of the red in a variety of expressive forms, of course, that has been ignored, marginalized, or, more recently, reduced to a merely statistical potency as one of the "multiethnic" literatures of the United States. But the cultural production of indigenous people, like the cultural production of Afro-American people, for obvious historical reasons has, as I have noted, a special status in relation to the canon of American literature. The case for the Indian, at least, has been made recently by a number of writers whose arguments I will not attempt to summarize; instead, I shall simply let Walt Whitman speak briefly for them all. In a letter dated July 20, 1883, Whitman wrote,

As to our aboriginal or Indian population . . . I know it seems to be agreed that they must gradually dwindle as time rolls on, and in a few generations more leave only a reminiscence, a blank. But I am not at all clear about that. As America, from its many far-back sources and current supplies, develops, adapts, entwines, faithfully identifies its own— are we to see it cheerfully accepting and using all the contributions of foreign lands from the whole outside globe—and then rejecting the only ones distinctively its own—the autochthonic ones? (in Chapman, 21)

This letter, included by Whitman in the "deathbed edition" of his work, as Abraham Chapman notes, does not appear in the MLA-approved, five-volume edition of Whitman's correspondence. Nor has it, to my knowledge, been cited by those who quote James's contemporary insistence on the continuing absence of an American "own."

The perspective of the red in relation to that of the white appears particularly clearly in Indian autobiographies (texts, as I have elsewhere noted, that are compositely rather than individually produced) as the textual equivalent of the frontier. The Native self documented in the text called an Indian "autobiography" is the result of a specific encounter—adversarial, cooperative, or whatever—between the Native American and the European American. There is good reason to use such a model, in appropriately dilute or concentrated form as the individual case may demand, for the study of selected American texts.[16] American fiction, poetry, or autobiography, after

16. For American autobiography, for example, this could mean that the student of Benjamin Franklin's *Memoirs* might do well to read the contemporaneous autobiographies of the Christianized Indian Samson Occom, who wrote in the 1780s, and Hendrick Aupaumut, who wrote in 1791. Crevecoeur's *Letters of an*

all, is produced culturally not only as a system of differences between here and there, in the Jamesian paradigm (where "there" is fullness and "here" only lack), but as a system of differences between here and the "autochthonic" priority of what is "distinctively" America's "own," as in Whitman's model—a model in which both parties to the relation have occasionally found themselves face to face. As a *national* literature, American literature needs to know its *local* components better, and all the more so if it is to play the role it should in the constitution of an *international,* indeed, a *cosmopolitan* literature.

Here, for example, is the Cheyenne warrior Wooden Leg, in his autobiography, describing an important moment in the cultural "development" of his individual "personality":

The soft whisperings of an eagle wing bone flute came into my ears. The sound seemed to come from the roof and from other points in the utterly dark interior of the lodge. After a few of the gentle blasts, I felt the instrument being placed in my hands. My father put it there. It now was mine, to keep. It was to be worn around my neck, suspended at the midbreast by a buckskin thong, during all times of danger. If I were threatened with imminent harm I had but to put it to my lips and cause it to send out its soothing notes. That would ward off every evil design upon me. It was my mystic protector. It was my medicine. (137–138)

American Farmer (1782), in particular Crevecoeur's chapter, "What Is an American?" are regularly anthologized, but a full consideration of the question of American identity might also take into account the letters of Eleazar Wheelock's Indians at Moors Charity School (precursor of Dartmouth College), among them such as David Fowler (1735–1807), a Montauk Indian farmer and schoolmaster who planted when he could and went hungry when his harvest failed; unlike Crevecoeur, who went back to France, Fowler had no Old World to return to. I offer a few more possible comparisons below: but a good deal of American literature might be considered, even today, in relation to ethnohistorical conceptions of the frontier as the space of cultural intersection (not, as in the older ethnocentric view, the point to which "civilization" had advanced).

Not every Cheyenne boy had exactly this experience, although some such experience was apparently typical. And, despite the stiffness of the translator's prose, we can, if we choose, easily think of Wooden Leg and his father in the sweat lodge in relation, say, to their contemporaries, Huck Finn and his Pap in their dark interior. The point, of course, would not be to sentimentalize Indian wholeness and harmony in comparison to white fragmentation (Huck's experience of his parent, I take it, is probably not historically and culturally typical, although this might, of course, be interesting to know—for a certain kind of critic, at any rate) but to compare aspects of the formation of subjects in specific historical and cultural settings. The reader of Wooden Leg's autobiography, too, would have a different sense of the ending of Twain's novel inasmuch as he would know well that the territories for which Huck lights out were hardly "virgin land" but the home of the Cheyenne, among others, and with the coming of the whites soon to be, in Francis Jenning's phrase, "widowed land" (15).

For the criticism of Native American fiction and poetry, production of which has been rich of late, the humanist (ethno)historicism Pearce suggests, a compound of history of ideas, psychohistory, and psychological anthropology, has many possibilities—provided, to be sure, detailed attention is paid to the material context of culture-and-personality, to the objective conditions of possibility defining human agency. This, for any study of Indian literature, must include such things as historical alterations in patterns of production and exchange: the Reservation system; the Allotment experiment; attempts to impose compulsory, monolingual education; and then the whole dreary ledgerbook of statistics on the incidence of tuberculosis, alcoholism, unemployment, and suicide. This is not at all to suggest that contemporary Native Americans do nothing but languish; quite to the contrary, expressively, at least, on the reservation or off, there is great vitality. Let me offer two brief examples.

Here is part of a poem by Wendy Rose, from a fine book called *The Halfbreed Chronicles* (1985):

> *What My Father Said*
>
> when lightning danced
> west of the mesa
> was this: that for us
> among the asphalt
> and black shadowed structures
> of the city
> there is some question
> about living our lives
> and not melting back
> to remembered stone, to adobe, to grass,
> innocent and loud, sweetly singing
> in the summer rain
> and rolling clouds.
>
> Begin, he said, by giving back . . .

The poem ends,

> come and eat
> come and eat
> live in my tongue
> and forget
> your hunger.

This recalls the last lines of Robert Frost's "Directive," for example, and one may wonder how the imperative to "drink and be whole" with which it concludes may compare to that of the speaker's father in Rose's poem to "eat," to "live," and to "forget . . . hunger." Frost's little poem "The Vanishing Red" might be remembered, too, in this context. Its shrewd recognition that "Indian-hating" can take the form of an insistence upon Indian silence, its presentation of Native people as those who have "no right to be heard from," can illuminate the various forms of Native speech in Rose's work—and that of many contemporary Indian poets. I offer these highly subjective intuitions not as adequate analysis but, rather, as merely indicating the possibility of another perspective on one canonical poet—as the brief passage from Wooden Leg may indicate a perspective on a canonical novelist.

Let me offer just one more contemporary example. I want to try to convey something of the quality of Ralph Salisbury's highly condensed and complex story, "The Sonofabitch and the Dog." I should perhaps make the point explicit that in choosing to cite Rose and Salisbury, I am intentionally avoiding examples from Louise Erdrich, N. Scott Momaday, and Leslie Marmon Silko, currently, as it seems to me, the most visible Native American writers. The intention is not in any way to devalue these authors' works, but to suggest instead that there are many others worthy of consideration besides the most visible.

Salisbury's story is the first-person narrative of a teenaged Indian soldier, a commando in an unspecified American war—very likely the Korean conflict in which Salisbury himself served: but the references to helicopters may bring Vietnam to mind. The Indian commando winds up in an unusual alliance with a dog named Commando, as both of them engage in efforts to survive in a white world that often seems far more threatening than the war itself. What I take as the climactic moment of this extraordinary piece occurs when the narrator

was only two days back from my first behind-the-lines mission. I'd killed seven people. . . . All three of my buddies had been blown up by the same land mine. (184)

Then, the dog speaks to him:

Commando said [,] "You're an Indian. You understand the earth. You understand animals. You understand what I'm saying, and you understand that I'm not just bullshitting you."

I was pretty sober in the chill night, and I thought Commando was correct in what he was saying, but I'd never heard a dog talk White language before. I'd been hearing my dead buddies' voices. And I wasn't sure in just what way I was hearing the dog. And it didn't seem right to answer back in an ordinary way.

"How old are you?" Commando asked.

"Seventeen."

"Do you want to be eighteen?" (184)

Commando informs the narrator that his choice is between being "proud and stupid and dead, or humble and freaked-out and alive" (185). Choosing the second alternative, the narrator

[n]ext day . . . went to the only piece of earth that wasn't covered with concrete or grass cut short like a military-haircut—the firing range.

Spreadeagle in the sacred way, I gazed at shaggy white buffalo clouds and prayed while stones under me softened. (185)

He stays out there through target practice, as bullets pass over him. Then "For seven days I fasted. For seven days I prayed." After a visit to the base psychiatrist, he is made chaplain's assistant, although he is no Christian. The story concludes, "I do what I'm told. I remember every detail. And by now I'm eighteen" (187). From a thematic point of view, it seems to me this story provides a striking allegory of the historical experience of most Native American tribes, what I will later call the *tribal allegory*. I will reserve further discussion of this point for the final chapter. Here, I will only repeat that we have in Salisbury's story (as in other contemporary Native American fiction) a perspective on our putatively "common" American experience that we are not likely to have from non-Indian sources. To understand better what Native American artists know and think and feel, personally and historically in their material situation; to understand better how a certain traditional commitment to speaking or singing such knowledge and thought and emotion has adapted itself to writing, may well provoke a rereading, even a reevaluating of other American writers, both older, canonical authors and newer authors on the verge of canonical status. I cannot specify just how such rereading and reevaluating might actually proceed beyond the lines—thematic and technical—already indicated. I would, nonetheless, reaffirm that such rereading and reevaluating must be the consequence of the inclusion of Native American writers (as also of Afro-American writers, and women of all groups).

Yet, given the relationship between critical perspectives and the composition of the canon, the chances for Native literatures to position themselves within, or at least at the margins of the canon of American literature are poor should a formalist paradigm persist.

For there are unmistakable connections between critical paradigms and canon formation. New Critical formalism, as I have said, took the supposed thinness of American culture and society with reference to Europe as a supplementary justification for its practice of an "intrinsic" critique. It did this in the interest of a conservative political program that it sought to further—covertly—by divorcing literary studies from social and political questions. Curiously (or maybe not so curiously), history returns upon itself as we find J. Hillis Miller, among the foremost American deconstructionists, in his 1986 Presidential Address to the Modern Language Association, citing none other than James in the interest of authorizing the particular formalism of his choice.[17] Miller says that what we have of culture here in America "is recent, datable, relatively simple. It has not been accumulating long enough to be thick on the ground" (J. H. Miller, 287), and so it would seem, for all the politeness initially offered in his address toward cultural critique and historicist criticism, it is formalism that must will out. Who could expect otherwise, if we must indeed go on evaluating American culture in regular, direct, and monolithic comparison to that of the Europe from

17. It is interesting to note how fixated on this single passage of James formalist Eurocentric critics tend to be, as if James had nothing more to say about America after 1879. In 1904, however, after a visit to Ellis Island, he wrote (in *The American Scene* [1907]):

> The after-sense of that acute experience, however, I myself found, was by no means to be brushed away; I felt it grow and grow, on the contrary wherever I turned; other impressions might come and go, but this affirmed claim of the alien, however immeasurably alien, to share in one's supreme relation was everywhere the fixed element, the reminder not to be dodged. (1963,85)

Poor James! first an America barren of culture, then an America almost overwhelmed by the "affirmed claim of the alien." Miller's conservatism on the canon is explicit and acknowledged—although I do not think he has accepted the connection between his critical preference and his canonical preference. It may also be worth pointing out that Miller's appropriation and fetishization of "rhetorically sophisticated reading" (289) in the MLA address as the particular expertise of deconstructionists, ignores the fact that rhetorical reading, historically, properly encompasses occasionality quite as much as figurality: the purposes of persuasion as well as the means appropriate to persuasion. Deconstructionists have shown remarkably little interest in the concrete occasions for the deployment of figures.

which, in its dominant forms, at least, it derives. Thus, Miller can imperially announce, "I affirm that the future of literary studies depends on maintaining and developing that rhetorical reading which today is most commonly called 'deconstruction' " (J. H. Miller, 289).

Miller's is not only an elitist position, blind, as I have already noted, to the history that is thick on the ground here as nowhere else, but also a position that is sadly out of date. For, although Miller recalls Gertrude Stein's comment about Oakland, California, that place where there is no there there, he forgets her remark that America is the oldest country in the modern world, having occupied it the longest. For it is only in regard to an older "higher" culture that America can now be considered a major importer from anywhere. Miller's choice of the Orange County (California) Performing Arts Center as his "allegorical emblem" of American culture offers an extremely narrow illustration: it is as if one chose to watch only PBS to gauge what the actual living present and possible future of television might be. In fact, it would rather seem to be the case, for better or worse, that America is the world's major exporter of culture, and that contemporary Europe is much concerned to see whether it has yet managed to produce cultural goods as slick, as efficiently commodified, as readily disposable as what is Made in the U.S.A.

Past historicisms, I have said, while worrying the thick and thin, did not much question the metaphor. But of course it is possible to take a historicist position for which history however "recent, [and] datable" can never be so "relatively simple" as Miller, following James, makes it, for the simple reason that America never could be defined adequately in terms of absence alone. Rather, it is a dialectic of presence/absence—of difference—to which we must turn. No State? No England, to be sure; still, the Iroquois Confederacy about the time of our Revolution was arguably as complex a political entity as the Papal confederacy, complex enough to influence the framers of our Constitution. There even was a king here, whose English name was King Phillip. No church? Decidedly there were deep-rooted "heathen practices" everywhere—and these of such power that Christian "praying Indians" were never so many as the missionaries hoped. A sporting *class* assuredly there was not, but brilliant players of what we call Lacrosse, and some of the finest long-distance runners of their day. Abundant descriptions suggest that the Comanches, among others, might well have taught Ascot riders a thing or two about horsemanship. No ruins? well, there were the great mounds of Mississippi, and the Hohokam (Pima-Papago, *huhugkam,* "the finished ones") prehistoric remains in the Southwest. And of course there were and there still are the Native literatures, the creation stories and the stories of Coyote, and Hare, and Raven, the ritual and personal songs, the indigenous "autobiographical" forms like the coup story—on which, to be sure, some Native American autobiographies, those of Yellow Wolf, Plenty-Coups, and Joseph White Bull, among others, depend. Is there not here American history? is none of this to bear upon our understanding of American literature? Perhaps not, if a formalist criticism prevails—nor if only a narrow new historicism does.

In the heyday of formalism, both D. H. Lawrence (in his *Studies in Classic American Literature* [1925]) and also William Carlos Williams (whose mention of the Indians in *In the American Grain* [1925] is cited but instantly abandoned by Hillis Miller) recognized the need for Americans to come to terms with the indigenous peoples and cultures they had subordinated but not quite destroyed. Native American people and their cultural productions have not disappeared, but, in the wake of New Critical and deconstructive dominance, and a certain historicist narrowness, they are probably not familiar to most students of American literature. It is my hope that some form of materially situated historicism will take upon itself the task of seeing what is actually there—both subjectively and objectively—for a broadly defined American literature. This criticism, surely not far off, will also attend carefully to Native American literary expression, which, as Whitman so clearly saw, is distinctively important *here*.

3. Native American Literature
and the Canon

Although the rich and various literatures of Native American peoples, apart from their inherent interest and excellence, by virtue of their antiquity and indigenousness, have a strong claim to inclusion in the canon of American literature, this claim, as I have noted, has not yet been granted with any fullness.

[Most of the account that follows was first published in *Critical Inquiry*'s special issue on the canon of September 1983 (I thank *CI* for permission to reprint). That same year, Michael Castro published *Interpreting the Indian: Twentieth-Century Poets and the Native American*. Working independently of each other and from somewhat different perspectives (e.g., among other things, Castro notes his own position as a poet and one interested in the "spiritual aspects of . . . 'revolutionary' consciousness" [xiii], whereas my position is that of the cultural critic of materialist bent), it turns out that we covered a good deal of the same ground, even on occasion choosing the same quotations for illustration and display. I urge the reader interested in these matters to consult Castro's book. Why, then, reprint my version here? Largely because, although I admire the scope and detail of Castro's work, I find myself frequently unsatisfied with the explanations offered—unsatisfied because so few explanations are even attempted, unsatisfied because those explanations are too little tied to social factors (e.g., Castro's acceptance of Vine DeLoria's dismissal of the many questions about John Neihardt's editing of Black Elk: "The transcendent truth that Deloria speaks of is attested by the national and international popularity of *Black Elk Speaks*" [95]. Now *Black Elk Speaks* is a lot less *popular* nationally and internationally than—say—*Dallas,* but in any case—lest the comparison seem too cheap a shot—I think it more likely that any popularity the book does have might be explained by a good many things other than its putative "transcendent truth"). So I reaffirm here my own view of these matters—in a spirit of dialogue once more pointing the reader to Castro.]

From the very first period of invasion and settlement until the close of the "frontier," Americans tended to define their peculiar national distinctiveness, as I have several times noted, in relation to a perceived opposition between the Europeans they no longer were and the Indians they did not wish to become. The development of autobiography as a major genre of American writing is instructive in this regard, as in so many others. Eastern autobiographers like Jonathan Edwards in the colonial period, Benjamin Franklin in the Revolutionary period, and Henry Thoreau in the period preceding the Civil War, all wrote and thought about Indians, although finally choosing the European polarity as decisive for self- and literary definition. In contrast, western autobiographers like Daniel Boone, Davy Crockett, Kit Carson, and William F. Cody ("Buffalo Bill"), all ultimately loyal to white "civilization," nonetheless fashioned themselves and their books on models deriving in varying degrees from Indian "savagery."[1] But this particular tension never operated in the definition of an American literature generally for the simple reason that Indians, who did not write, were not regarded as actually possessing a "littera-ture" that might be studied and imitated.

"Littera-ture," of course, meant precisely the culture of letters (as agri-culture meant the culture of the fields), and the man of letters, European or Euramerican, was the man of culture; Native Americans—Indians—were "children of nature" precisely because they were not men of letters. And oral literature, at least until near the nineteenth century, was simply a contradiction in terms. American literature, seeking to define itself as a body of national writing and as a selection of

1. See my "American Autobiography: The Western Tradition."

distinctively literary texts, considered only European models because no other models—no local or Native models, no "autochthonic" own—seemed to be present. Here is just that relation of avoidance justified by an imagined absence that I noted at the outset.

Yet even after Indian literature was "discovered," attempts to open the canon to it based themselves—mistakenly, to be sure, yet powerfully, nonetheless—on an appeal to the "naturalness" of this literature, as though it was not individuals and cultural practices but the very rocks and trees and rivers that had somehow produced the Native poem or story, and somehow spoke directly in them. This peculiar "naturalness" of Native American literature, currently linked, as I remarked in the Introduction, to a "biological" consciousness, continues to be its primary claim to attention. Thus I will not apologize for repeating yet again that for all the dramatic immediacy of Native American discourse; for all its rootedness in a consciousness very different from that of the West, it nonetheless remains the complex product of historical tradition and cultural convention as these are manipulated by individual performers who take technical problems—of pacing and pronunciation and pausing; the use of archaisms and neologisms; possibilities of condensation and expansion, and the like—altogether as seriously as the authors known to the Western tradition. In these regards, Native American literary expression is like literary expression everywhere. Nor does this contradict the point I insisted upon earlier, the cultural and technical difference of Native American literatures from the literatures of the West. To urge the inclusion of Indian literature in the canon of American literature, then, is not only to propose an addition but a reevaluation of what "American literature" means.

For all that sporadic attempts to read, teach, and use Native American literature as a model for written literature extend back well over a century, it is only in the past thirty years or so that the formal principles of many Indian languages have been established on anything like a sound scientific basis. Only in this time have dictionaries and grammars of some of these languages become available so that the scholar might come closer to an accurate understanding of what Indian performers actually said and meant. Ethnographic studies have also developed over these years to provide an enriched sense of the cultures that provide the matrix for specific performances. Still, as Dell Hymes has remarked, it would yet be premature to specify a canon of Native American literature area- or continent-wide. There remain too many old recordings to listen to and retranscribe; too many older texts to retranslate and compare to contemporary variants; too much sorting and typing, comparing and evaluating yet to do for anyone to propose the "masterworks" of the Indian tradition. And so it is too soon to say exactly which Native American texts ought properly enter the canon of American literature. For all this, efforts have been made to urge some Native texts upon the broader national literary awareness. Thus I now turn to some literary history.

The first invader–settlers of America responded to the verbal productions of Native orality as a satanic or bestial gibberish that, unmarked in letters nor bound in books, could never be thought to constitute a littera-ture. John Eliot translated the Bible into an Algonquian language in the seventeenth century, but the Puritans did not inscribe the wicked or animal noise of Native song or story. The scientist–revolutionaries of the eighteenth century were more interested in Indian cultural activity than were their Puritan forebears and made efforts to describe, catalogue, and subdue its various manifestations—just as they did with other natural phenomena like lightning or steam pressure. Although the child of nature, in this period, was as frequently deemed the noble as the murderous savage—a change prompted less by Rousseau than by the colonists' need to establish trade and military alliances with the powerful interior tribes—it was still difficult to conceive that without writing he could have a littera-ture. Washington, Franklin, and Jefferson, according to Roy Harvey Pearce, "encouraged the collection of Indian wordlists as part of an international project in comparative linguistics," and Jefferson quoted a well-known (perhaps apocryphal) speech of Chief Logan as an example of Native oratorical ability (1967, 80). But this was still far from recognizing an Indian capacity for literary production. Nonetheless, what may be the first translation of an Indian "poem" dates from the pre-Revolutionary period. This appears in the *Memoirs* of Henry Timberlake, a young Virginian, who, after serving under Washington, embarked upon a mission to the Cherokee. Timberlake apparently did not know Cherokee and so had to work from the rendition of an interpreter. In his "Translation of the WAR-SONG. *Caw waw noo dee,* &c.," we encounter Indian poetry in the form of heroic couplets. Here are the first few lines:

> Where'er the earth's enlighten'd by the sun,
> Moon shines by night, grass grows, or waters run,
> Be't known that we are going, like men, afar,
> In hostile fields to wage destructive war;
> Like men we go, to meet our country's foes,
> Who, woman-like, shall fly our dreaded blows. (81)

Timberlake made no effort to transcribe the original Cherokee; only scholarly reconstruction might provide an approximation of what this song was like.

In the Romantic nineteenth century, littera-ture came to
mean not simply the written culture generally but a selection
from it of imaginative and expressive utterance—in writing,
to be sure, but also in the speech and song of common men
and the "folk" who might themselves be unable to write.
"Nature" became the "keyword" of culture, and "oral literature," something other than a contradiction in terms. Once
these ideas crossed the ocean to the American east, it was but
a short step to hear Native expression as "naturally" poetic
and as constituting a literature in need of no more than tex-
tualization and formal—"civilized"—supplementation.

English Romanticism had reached the east by the 1830s
(Timberlake had reached England earlier: Robert Southey
used the *Memoirs* for his 1805 epic, *Madoc*), but in those years
the social and cultural dominance of the east was challenged
by the Jackson presidency and the "rise of the west." So far as
Indians were concerned, the 1830s were the years of President
Jackson's Indian Removal policy, which made the forcible
relocation of the eastern tribes to the west of the Mississippi a
national priority. During that decade, easterners interested in
Indians were primarily concerned to preserve Indian lives and
lands before trying to preserve Indian literature. History writing rather than poetry writing appeared the more urgent task.
For, as B. B. Thatcher put it in the preface to his *Indian
Biography,* published in Boston in 1832, "We owe, and our
Fathers owed, too much to the Indians . . . to deny them the
poor restitution of historical justice at least" (n.p.).

In the 1840s and 1850s, it was American "civilization" that

began to proclaim itself "Nature's nation," in Perry Miller's phrase (1956, 209), proclaiming all the louder as aggressive expansion threatened to destroy the forests, the grasslands, and, as always, their aboriginal inhabitants, nature's children, the Indians. In this period, the work of Henry Rowe School-craft came to wide attention. Schoolcraft, an Indian agent interested in *la pensée sauvage*—"savage mentality," as he called it—had been publishing since 1839, but it was what Roy Harvey Pearce calls his "masterwork," a study under-taken, appropriately, at the instigation of the secretary of war—the *Historical and Statistical Information Respecting the History, Condition, and Prospects of the Indian Tribes of the United States* (1851–1857, and reissued under various titles)—that marks the increasingly important contribution of what we would call anthropological scholarship to our understanding of Indian literature. Indeed, according to A. Grove Day, "the beginning of wide interest in native poetry in translation prop-erly dates from the year 1851, when a history of the Indians was published by Henry Rowe Schoolcraft which included samples of Chippewa poetry" (27).

One example from Schoolcraft, quoted by Day, has repeat-edly been anthologized; it has also occasioned some trenchant commentary by John Greenway and, particularly, by Dell Hymes. Schoolcraft's procedure—a transcription of the origi-nal, a literal translation, and a "literary" translation—continues often to be followed today. His Chippewa "Chant to the Fire-Fly" is literally translated:

Flitting-white-fire-insect! waving-white-fire-bug! give me light before I go to bed! give me light before I go to sleep. Come, little dancing white-fire-bug! Come, little flitting white-fire-beast! Light me with your bright white-flame-instrument—your little candle. (Day, 28)

The first few lines of his "literary" translation read:

> Fire-fly, fire-fly! bright little thing,
> Light me to bed, and my song I will sing.
> Give me your light, as you fly over my head,
> That I may merrily go to my bed. (Day, 28)[2]

This translation is as typical of its period's deliquescent Romanticism as Timberlake's couplets are of the high Drydenesque. Obviously, the translation of Indian poetry (like

---

2. See John Greenway, *Literature among the Primitives;* and also Dell Hymes, "Some North Pacific Coast Poems: A Problem in Anthropological Philology" (rpt. with some additions and alterations in his *"In Vain I Tried to Tell You": Essays in Native American Ethnopoetics*). Schoolcraft's translation also appears in John Bierhorst, ed., *Songs of the Chippewa.*

Hymes's attempts to retranslate Schoolcraft's text—and other texts—are particularly instructive because Hymes is committed to the examination of existing Native language originals. The Laguna writer, Leslie Marmon Silko, has disparagingly claimed that "white poets use the term 'translation' very loosely when applied to Asian or Native American material; few, if any of them, are conversant in the Asian or Native American languges they pretend to 'translate.' What they do is sit down and rearrange English transcriptions done by ethnologists, and then call this a 'translation' " (1979, 3). She is, in general, correct regarding some poet–translators' practice; but the matter is not so simple. "White poets," also "translate" from other white poets whose language—Dutch, Russian, Polish— they may not understand very well, but in any case, all translators, no matter how "conversant" they may be with the language of the original, face problems that are not only a matter of knowledge. Brian Swann who published Silko's piece has insisted that his own "rearrangements" are not translations but *versions* (see his *Song of the Sky: Versions of Native American Songs and Poems*)—a usefully modest stance, no doubt, but one that cannot circumvent the problems Silko raises. Hymes does know the language from which he translates—as does Tedlock, Howard Norman, Donald Bahr, and a number of others. But they still do not agree (see my "Post-structuralism and Oral Literature" on this matter) as to what constitutes an adequate or accurate or simply useful translation. And, in any case, the shift from oral to textual media means that there are problems of *presentation* as well as translation. For a very basic account of this matter, see the Introduction to Brian Swann and Arnold Krupat, eds., *Recovering the Word: Essays on Native American Literature.*

poetic translation generally) reveals as much about the translator's culture and literary predilections as it does about the
Indian's. Schoolcraft also published, without literary elaboration, some brief Chippewa Midé—medicine society—songs
such as the two following:

> All around the circle of the sky I hear the Spirit's voice.

> I walk upon half the sky. (Day, 146)

His contemporaries, however, did not seem interested in
these—which, today, probably appear both more attractive
and more "Indian." In any case, although Schoolcraft's translations spurred interest in Native American poetry, they seem
to have had no influence on American poetry in their time.
Not Indian poetry but, rather, poetry with an Indian subject
did enter the American canon in the 1850s, however.

Composed by a Harvard professor of European literature,
the first to teach *Faust* in an American college, Henry Wadsworth Longfellow's *Song of Hiawatha* (1855) sold out its first
printing of four thousand copies on the day of its publication
and completed its first year in print with sales of thirty-eight
thousand. Longfellow derived his Indian materials from
Schoolcraft's earlier work, the *Algic Researches* (1839); he derived his attitudes toward Indians from eastern progres-
siveist thought (Alas, the Noble but Vanishing Savage); and
he derived his meter from the Finnish epic, *Kalevala*. Longfellow's Hiawatha comfortably counsels the people to abandon the old ways and adapt themselves to the coming of
"civilization," and he does so in a meter that only "civilization" can provide. It is necessary, of course, to mention
Longfellow in any consideration of possible Indian influence

on American literature, but *The Song of Hiawatha,* in fact, shows no such influence at all. Longfellow did not make use of Schoolcraft's Chippewa translations (themselves mostly "civilized" in their formal conventions), nor did he have any sense of his own about what Native American literary composition might actually be like or whether it might somehow stand without Finnish support and supplementation. The admission of *Hiawatha* into the American canon had nothing to do with the possibility of expanding the canon; *Hiawatha* merely assimilates the Indian to the persisting Eurocentrism of the east.

Euramericans continued to move westward, appropriating Native American lands by force and by fraud. Once the west had been "won," as the "frontier" approached its "close" in 1890, American thought about Indians situated itself within a broader debate between Americanism and cultural pluralism. The "Indian problem" was related to the "immigrant problem"; the various "solutions" proposed rested upon particular visions of the social order. The "Americanizers" gained the ascendant in 1887 with the passage of the General Allotment Act, known as the Dawes Severalty Act. The Dawes Act was an attack on Indian culture ("for the Indians' own good") by way of an attack on the Indians' collectively held land base—a "mighty pulverizing engine to break up the tribal mass," as Theodore Roosevelt called the act in presciently cyclotronic imagery (Washburn, 1975, 242). The Dawes Act was also— and intended to be—an attack on all "communistic" systems. Opposed (for the most part) to Dawes and the Americanizers were the anthropologists of the newly founded Bureau of Ethnology (1879; after 1894, the Bureau of American Ethnology), whose studies of the rich, Native tribal heritage committed them to its preservation rather than destruction. An important exception, however, was Alice Fletcher. One of the first, in the 1880s, to study the forms of Native American music, Fletcher, nonetheless, was "one of the most vigorous opponents of tribalism and played an influential role in the agitation . . . to force the allotment of land in severalty upon the Indians without tribal consent," as Wilcomb Washburn has commented (1975, 245).

Fletcher was more interested in the music of Indian songs than in their texts; her influence on the study of Native American poetry comes through Frances Densmore and, more particularly, Natalie Curtis Burlin, whose work she inspired. Densmore, trained in piano, organ, and harmony at the Oberlin Conservatory of Music and at Harvard, began in 1901 a lifetime of work with Indian music by transcribing a Sioux woman's song that she heard near her home in Red Wing, Minnesota. Densmore continued to publish on Indian music until her death in 1957. Of the vast body of material she transcribed and translated, it may be the Midé songs of the Chippewa—these attracted her as they had Schoolcraft—which she published for the Bureau of American Ethnology in 1910, that have most often appeared in the anthologies (although not in the earliest ones).

It was Burlin, the third of these early collectors of Native song, who had the greatest impact on the anthologies. In 1907, Burlin published *The Indians' Book,* a wide-ranging collection that presented not only the music of Native American songs (in special notation) but also poems and short narratives from the tribes. Burlin's particular appreciation of Native artistic production is entirely that of the antiquarian looking back upon what President Theodore Roosevelt called, in a prefatory letter to her book, "the simple beauty and strange charm—the charm of a vanished elder world—of Indian po-

etry" (Burlin, n.p.). Like Fletcher, Burlin had no doubt that
the "child races" of Indians must give way to the "adult races"
of Anglo-Saxon peoples. She recommended the charming and
simple songs of the Indians to her white audience for the
wisdom they might—somehow, vaguely—teach, and, as
well, as an act of—sentimental—justice to this soon-to-be-
vanished race. Indeed, Burlin's Indians are so childlike and
simple as to be entirely creatures of nature; their art, she says,
is "spontaneous," the talent to produce it "inborn" in every
member of the race (Burlin, xxviii–xxix). In these beliefs,
Burlin completely ignores the major developments of scientific anthropology in her time, which insisted upon the cultural, not racial, explanation of cultural things. Some of her
translations—they are, curiously, the ones chosen by Louis
Untermeyer for his 1931 anthology of American poetry,
which I note below—are full of exclamation points and ar-
chaic diction, but others, like this Winnebago "Holy Song,"
are somewhat less elaborated and point more nearly forward:

> Let it fly—the arrow,
> Let it fly—the arrow,
> Pierce with a spell the man, oh!
> Let it fly—the arrow.
>
> Let it fly—the arrow,
> Let it fly—the arrow,
> Pierce with a spell the woman!
> Let it fly—the arrow.
>   (256–257)

Burlin's work, for all its mistaken inspiration and its partly
dubious execution, remains the locus of much that is available
nowhere else.

The Dawes Act was a disaster for the Indians; yet it was not officially abandoned until the 1930s. By that time, American anthropology was no longer based in the government bureau, nor in the great urban museum, but, instead, in the university. Franz Boas, who had come to Columbia University just before the turn of the century to train a new generation of anthropologists, was the dominant force in ethnographic science. I will not attempt a full discussion of Boas's contribution to the preservation of Native American culture but, rather, quote Hymes at some length; his description of what happened on the northwest coast of America is largely true for the literatures of most Indian peoples.

Often non-Indians did not wish to preserve the culture of the Indians. Conviction or guilt persuaded them that it was already gone, or best gone. It is a shameful fact that most of what can be known today about the cultures of the Indians of my state, Oregon, is due to the efforts of men who came across the continent. Franz Boas, a German Jew unable to aspire to scholarly advancement in his native country but versed in the German intellectual tradition that valued individual cultures and their works, recorded Shoalwater and Kathlamet Chinook. His student Sapir recorded Wishram and Takelma; another student, L. J. Frachtenberg, recorded Alsea, Siuslaw, Coos, and Kalapuya. Frachtenberg was followed by a later student with a better ear, Melville Jacobs, who provided superior texts from Coos and Kalapuya, all that has been published so far in Sahaptin, and all that is known, save for one scrap, of Clackamas. To repeat, most of what we can know of the first literature of Oregon is due to representatives of German and Jewish intellectual tradition, who crossed the continent to record it. With regard to that first literature, they are the pioneers. The pioneers of Western song and story and their descendants did little or nothing. (1981, 6)

These German and Jewish intellectuals were entirely skeptical of the Americanizers' claims to WASP cultural superiority and asserted their sense of the importance to American culture not only of Continental philosophy and philology but of the aboriginal American culture of the Indians as well. Whereas early attempts at "ethnographic salvage" were made in the name of history, and the Americanizers' attempts at ethnographic destruction were made, generally, in the name of religion, what Boas and his students preserved was in the name of science. The work of Fletcher, Densmore, and Curtis began specifically from an interest in Indian music and coincided with imagism and a movement in poetry to privilege the genre of the brief lyric. But Boas and his students sought knowledge. Although they recorded songs, which would early be anthologized, they also recorded lengthy narratives that were performed but not sung. Hardly inimical to poetry,[3] their commitment to science led them to prefer the most literal prose translations—which usually obscured completely the dynamics of Indian performances and made it very difficult for anyone to discover a genuine poetry among Native peoples. The full value of what Boas and his students recorded would only begin to be revealed in the 1950s and after, when developments in anthropological linguistics would permit their translations to be modified for accuracy and to yield new translations of more apparent poetic value.

It was just after World War I that the first concerted effort to present Native American poetry as a part of American literature occurred. This effort was associated with the Amer-

3. Edward Sapir and Ruth Benedict, among Franz Boas's early students, wrote a good deal of verse. Contemporary anthropologist–poets include Paul Friedrich, Dell Hymes, Nathaniel Tarn, and Dennis Tedlock. Native American poets with training or a degree in anthropology include Paula Gunn Allen, Wendy Rose, and Jack Forbes.

ican radicals' call for cultural pluralism, with the imagist challenge to a canon still dominated by Emerson, Longfellow, and James Russell Lowell, and, in particular, with the work of Mary Austin. If Schoolcraft's Chippewa translations may be said to have opened the way to interest in North American poetry, then it was George Cronyn's anthology of Indian poetry, *The Path on the Rainbow* (1918), that began to broaden that way. Cronyn's volume was hardly, as Austin called it in her introduction, "the first authoritative volume of aboriginal American verse," for Cronyn was often uncritical and/or misinformed (Austin, 1918: xv). (It might be said that no "authoritative" collection appeared before Margot Astrov's in 1946; it might also be said that no "authoritative" collection has yet appeared.) Yet Cronyn had the acumen to take translations from the superb student of Navajo, Washington Matthews, from John Swanton, and from Boas himself. Whatever its quality, finally, Cronyn's volume—which attracted a good deal of attention—at least made it possible to imagine, as Austin predicted in her introduction, that a relationship was "about to develop between Indian verse and the ultimate literary destiny of America" (Austin, 1918: xv–xvi).

In Austin's view, to know the Native American heritage was not, as Curtis believed, for the "adult" American to honor some indigenous childlike past; rather, it was for the contemporary American poet to "put himself in touch with the resident genius of his own land" in the living present (1918, xxxii). There is an "extraordinary likeness," Austin remarked, "between much of this native product and the recent work of the Imagists, *vers librists,* and other literary fashionables." Thus, "the first free movement of poetic originality in America finds us just about where the last Medicine Man left off" (1918, xvi).

A year later, in 1919, Austin wrote in the *Dial* that "vers libre and Imagism are in truth primitive forms, and both of them generically [*sic*] American forms, forms instinctively selected by people living in America and freed from outside influence" (1919, 569). Austin ascribed these "forms" to nature, most particularly to what D. H. Lawrence was soon to call "the spirit of place." In Indian poetry, Austin wrote, "the shape of the lines is influenced by the contours of the country" (1919, 570). So determining was this geographical influence that "before 1900" she "could listen to aboriginal verses on the phonograph in unidentified Amerindian languages, and securely refer them by their dominant rhythms to the plains, the deserts and woodlands," as she explained in 1923, in the introduction to her own collection of versions of Indian poems, *The American Rhythm* (19).[4] Austin wittily admitted that she took the anthropologists of her day more seriously than they took her; but if she did take them seriously, she understood them badly, for her sort of simplistic environmental determinism was unacceptable to them as an explanation of cultural variation.

Nonetheless, Austin's often-repeated conviction "that American poetry must inevitably take, at some period of its history, the mold of Amerind verse, which is the mold of the American experience shaped by the American environment" (1930, 42) took a clear stand on the future of American poetry. This stand was not only in opposition to the Longfellow–Emerson–

---

4. My quotation is from the "enlarged and expanded edition" of the text originally published in 1923.

Lowell eastern past but in opposition, as well, to the futures envisioned by Austin's contemporaries, T. S. Eliot and Ezra Pound,[5] who looked not to the West but to the East and Far East, and to a past very different from that of "the last Medicine Man." Yet Austin shared with Eliot and Pound what F. H. Matthews has called the "revolt against Americanism."

"In the 1920's," in Matthews' cogent summary,

> the revulsion from Americanism and the search for a viable cultural community intensified into a major quest. Intellectuals in a position to assert their identity with some minority now fanned the embers of recently-declining traditions, or raised folk arts to self-conscious status. . . . Writers who lacked a vital region or ethnic minority with which to identify turned instead, like Sherwood Anderson and William Carlos William[s], to quarrying the national past in search of lost virtue. (14)

This "revulsion from Americanism" serves to link Austin, Williams, Eliot, and Pound, although the solutions each proposed to the common problem they shared were incompatible with one another. The modernist internationalism of the "paleface" and the nativism of the "redskin" were united in the young Yvor Winters.[6] As poet–critic, first, and, subsequently, as scholar–teacher, Winters urged the claims of Indian literatures as part of a broader challenge to the established canon.

---

5. For all the sympathies shared by Eliot and Pound, they diverge considerably in relation to issues that might bear on Native American materials. Pound's interest in ideographic languge, in varieties of Japanese practice, in charms and spells and incantations make him available as a sympathetic elder in ways that Eliot simply is not. Jerome Rothenberg takes an epigraph from Pound for his "Pre-Face" to a collection of Cree translations (1976; ix), and Nathaniel Tarn invokes him in a discussion of Gary Snyder's work.

6. The quoted terms are from Philip Rahv (1–6), in an essay first published in 1939, although to my knowledge Rahv was not interested in Indians.

In 1922, that *annus mirabilis* of *Ulysses* and *The Waste Land,* Winters published *The Magpie's Shadow;* the "Indians especially were an influence on *The Magpie's Shadow,*" Winters would later write (1978, 13). The linked poems of *The Magpie's Shadow* are introduced by an epigraph from Rimbaud, and Japanese poetry is also an influence, although it is impossible to tell what Winters may have taken from the Native American and what from the Japanese[7] (the two non-Western traditions have often appeared as parallel influences on those poets looking beyond the European tradition—and William Stafford has published a "Sioux Haiku"). The brief, titled stanzas of the poem's three sections seem familiar enough from imagist practice. Thus, from part 2, "In Spring":

May
Oh, evening in my hair!

Or, from part 3, "In Summer and Autumn":

The Walker
In dream my feet are still.

Blue Mountain
A deer walks that mountain. (1978, 32, 33)

A year earlier, Winters had published in *Poetry* magazine a poem with an Indian subject, "Lament, beside an Acéquia, for the Wife of Awa-Tsireh." He later identified Awa-Tsireh as a painter from the pueblo of San Ildefonso. That was in 1928, in "The Indian in English," a review for *Transition* of

---

7. Winters: "I was familiar also with many translations from the poetry of the Japanese" (1978, 13).

two important Native American poetry anthologies, Cronyn's *Path on the Rainbow* and Nellie Barnes's *American Indian
Love Lyrics and Other Verse*. Winters quoted from the translators he admired and also offered, "finally," what he called an
example of "nonreligious and purely dramatic material" in a
"more modern group of Chinook songs" translated by Boas
(1975, 39). I should also note Winters's 1926 "Open Letter to
the Editors of *This Quarter,*" in which he protested the exploi-
tation of Indian materials. This "notion of interpreting the
Indian," Winters wrote, "is too much for me. They are in no
need of assistance whatsoever, as anyone is aware who has
ever read the really great translations of Frances Densmore,
Washington Matthews, Frank Russell, and Jeremiah Curtin—
translations that can take their place with no embar[r]assment
beside the best Greek or Chinese versions of H. D. or Ezra
Pound and which some day will do so" (1975, 33).

Winters's own poetic development would not follow Native
American models; yet Winters continued to press the canon to
open itself not only to Frederick Tuckerman, Thomas Sturge
Moore, and Elizabeth Daryush but to Native American poetry
as well. Winters directed A. Grove Day's doctoral dissertation,
which became one of the important anthologies of Indian
verse; another of his doctoral students was the Kiowa N. Scott
Momaday, whose work I will discuss.

In Winters's *Transition* article, he approved of Cronyn's collection as, of the two reviewed, "by all odds the better and
larger selection, despite its being saddled with a selection of
'interpretations' " (1975, 35). In his approval of Cronyn, he
placed himself at odds with Untermeyer, another great canon
maker of the time. In 1919, Untermeyer had also reviewed
Cronyn's volume, for the *Dial,* rather sniffily concluding that
this Indian anthology was "as an ethnic document . . . of

indubitable value; as a contribution to creative Americana [?] it may grow to have importance. But as a collection for the mere man of letters it is a rather forbidding pile—a crude and top-heavy monument with a few lovely and even lively decorations" (1919, 241). Austin quickly responded in a piece from which I have already quoted. Characterizing Untermeyer as "one whose mind has so evidently never visited west of Broadway," Austin made the telling point that "if Mr. Untermeyer could get his mind off the Indian Anthology as a thing of type and paper, he might have got something more out of it" (1919, 569).

By the 1930s, however, Untermeyer had apparently come nearer to Austin's estimate of Native American poetry. His *American Poetry: From the Beginning to Whitman* (1931)—according to H. Bruce Franklin the "most widely used anthology of poetry" in the schools (100)—included a section on American Indian poetry along with sections on Negro spirituals and blues, cowboy songs, and city gutturals.[8] Untermeyer quoted from Austin's introduction to *The Path on the Rainbow* and recommended Curtis's *Indians' Book,* Barnes's *American Indian Love Lyrics,* and Austin's *American Rhythm.* This last, he said, included "a penetrating essay in interpretation" (1931, 693). Austin's essay, however, offers no more than the geographical determinism I have already remarked; Untermeyer tended to prefer "adaptations" rather than more literal translations, just the sort of "interpretations" Winters, quite wisely, warned against.

Translation versions of Native American poetry had earlier

8. For an evaluation of the standard school anthologies in relation to the literature of American minorities, see Ernece B. Kelly, ed., *Searching for America,* a Publication of the National Council of Teachers of English Task Force on Racism and Bias in the Teaching of English.

appeared in another anthology widely used in the schools. In 1928, Mark Van Doren, also an admirer of Curtis, had published his *Anthology of World Poetry,* consisting of poetic translations from literatures around the world. A section on "American" poetry comes last; this contains twenty poems from translators ranging from Schoolcraft to Austin and Curtis; there is nothing from Boas and his students.

These influential anthologies, for all their confusions about Indians and Indian literature—not to say their thoroughgoing ignorance of what anthropological scholarship of their time had made it possible to understand about Native Americans and their literature—nonetheless were clear gestures toward that pluralism intended to open the canon. In this regard, they were cultural equivalents of the political change from Herbert Hoover to FDR, from the Dawes Act's policy of cultural destruction and Indian assimilation to the Indian New Deal of Roosevelt's commissioner of Indian affairs, John Collier, who sought to preserve and protect traditional Native cultures.

World War II brought Claude Lévi-Strauss to the New School for Social Research in New York, where, as legend has it, he learned structural linguistics from his colleague Roman Jakobson, another displaced European. Lévi-Strauss's essay "The Structural Study of Myth" appeared in the *Journal of American Folklore* in 1955. Whatever its influence on method in America, this text was an important encouragement to the study of Indian "myth," if not—and the two were distinct for Lévi-Strauss—Indian "poetry." It was just after the war, in 1946, that Astrov's anthology of Native prose and poetry, *The Winged Serpent,* was published—still, in 1965, as Hymes judged, one of the "two major contemporary anthologies in English" (1965, 317) and, according to William Bevis in 1974, "the best general anthology in paperback" (323). Astrov's introduction and notes pay special attention to the scientific, anthropological contexts of Indian literatures, and the translations she chooses, as well as the commentary she provides, reflect the considerable advances ethnography had made in the Boasian period.

The second of the "two major contemporary anthologies" is Day's *The Sky Clears,* published in 1951. Unlike Astrov, Day pointed, as Austin had, specifically to the possibility of Indian influence on modern American poetry—although only, as Hymes has noted, in relation to existing translations. Day was, as I have said, Winters's doctoral student, and he dedicated the anthology, an outgrowth of his dissertation, to "Yvor Winters, Singer of Power."

Boas had died in 1942; but by that time his students occupied major positions of influence in American anthropology. It was one of Boas's later students, Melville Jacobs, who, in 1958, published the first of an important series of narratives from the Northwest. These appeared as numbers of the *International Journal of American Linguistics,* issued by the Indiana University Research Center in Anthropology, Folklore, and Linguistics. It was also in 1958 at Indiana that Thomas Sebeok convened the interdisciplinary conference on style that provided the occasion for Jakobson's well-known concluding paper, "Linguistics and Poetics." (Sebeok's earlier symposium on myth had provided a forum for Lévi-Strauss's "Structural Study of Myth.") Through the work of Hymes, a participant in that conference, the insights and method of Lévi-Strauss and Jakobson would be brought together to advance the study of Native American literatures as they might be encountered and/or restructured in their original languages.

As early as 1953, while working at Indiana University,

Hymes began to conceive the possibility of what he has called a "living relation, through fresh translation and study of the [Native American] originals, to modern poetry" (1965, 318). But in the 1950s—to take a single suggestive instance—it was Sputnik and the challenge to further conquest of nature, rather than nature itself, that most engaged Americans. The federal government renewed its efforts to Americanize the Indian under the policy known as "termination." Washburn has described it as "the forced dissolution of tribal organizations and the break-up of existing tribal assets" (268). This was not a time in which the social order encouraged a cultural opening to Native American influences—although some would turn to it for alternatives.

But by 1960, neither presidential candidate supported the termination policy; and by 1970, Richard Nixon, as president, declared government policy toward the Indians to be self-determination without termination. One of Nixon's first official acts was to return the sacred Blue Lake of the Taos Pueblo people. The rights not only of Native peoples but of all those who had traditionally been excluded from full social and literary representation were asserted in the 1970s, arousing a broad increase of interest in traditional Native American culture and literature.

As early as 1951, Gary Snyder, then a senior at Reed College, had written his B.A. thesis on a Haida myth and, in 1960, Snyder's *Myths and Texts,* work done between 1952 and 1956, appeared; I shall return to this shortly. In 1961, Kenneth Rexroth's important essays "The Poet as Translator" and "American Indian Songs" were published, while, a year later, Jerome Rothenberg inaugurated what would be a major and ongoing poetic program with his performance- and event-oriented *From a Shaman's Notebook: Poems from the Floating World.* This was an early attempt, as Rothenberg wrote in 1969, "to get as far away as I could from *writing*" (in Chapman, 303). By that time, Rothenberg had also published *Technicians of the Sacred: A Range of Poetries from Africa, America, Asia, and Oceania* (1968), Rothenberg's presumptuously global reach has been properly and abundantly criticized;[9] yet this volume performed a service for non-Western poetries generally, and for Native American poetry in particular. Rothenberg was not only perspicacious in his selection from the older translators—he included Densmore, Washington Matthews, and Pliny Earle Goddard, while excluding Austin, for example—but also collected newer translations by William Carlos Williams, W. S. Merwin, and Rochelle Owens. Perhaps most important, Rothenberg went to great lengths to demonstrate the way in which some modern and contemporary poetry follows "primitive" (" 'primitive' means complex") directions (1968, xx).

In the section of his "Pre-Face" to *Technicians of the Sacred* called "Primitive and Modern: Intersections and Analogies," Rothenberg tried to show "some of the ways in which primitive poetry and thought are close to an impulse toward unity in our own time, of which the poets are forerunners" (1968, xxii). Rothenberg lists six "important intersections" in some detail, which I shall abbreviate. These are: (1) "the poem carried by the voice," (2) "a highly developed process of image-thinking," (3) "a 'minimal' art of maximal involvement," (4) "an 'intermedia' situation" in which "the poet's techniques aren't limited to verbal maneuvers but operate also through song, non-verbal sound, visual signs, and the varied activities of the

9. William Bevis's "American Indian Verse Translations" contains the most telling critique. More recently, see William M. Clements, "Faking the Pumpkin: On Jerome Rothenberg's Literary Offenses." *Shaking the Pumpkin* has stood up well, however, recently appearing in a new edition (1987).

ritual event," (5) "the animal-body-rootedness of 'primitive' poetry," and (6) "the poet as shaman" (1968, xxii–xxiii). Some of the "important intersections (analogies)" Rothenberg lists are: jazz and rock poetry, "Blake's multi-images," surrealism, random poetry, concrete poetry, happenings, dada, "lautgedichte (sound poems)," projective verse, "Rimbaud's voyant, Rilke's angel, Lorca's duende," beat poetry and psychedelic "poetry" (1968, xxii, xxiii).

Rothenberg then illustrated contemporary intersections with the "primitive" by quoting a number of contemporary poems in his extended commentaries. He drew from his own work, as well as from Owens, Robert Creeley, Denise Levertov, and Diane Wakoski, among others, and included a translation from Pablo Neruda done by Robert Bly. Rothenberg also quoted a poem from Snyder's *Myths and Texts*. This volume of poems, published, as I have noted, in 1960, takes its title, as Snyder later wrote, "from the happy collections Sapir, Boas, Swanton, and others made of American Indian folktales early in this century" (vii). It is no surprise, then, to find, as the poet and anthropologist Nathaniel Tarn puts it, "Indians everywhere" (xv).

In the 1960s, a considerable number of American poets turned from European models and sources to acquaint themselves with Native American models and sources—as they also turned to the cultural productions of Afro-Americans and women.[10] To turn to Indians was to valorize the natural,

10. Some of the poets who showed interest in Indians in the 1960s were Robert Bly, Robert Creeley, Edward Dorn, Richard Hugo, Galway Kinnell, W. S. Merwin, Rochelle Owens, William Stafford, David Wagoner, and James Wright, among others. Theodore Roethke's 1964 collection, *The Far Field*, contains a "North American Sequence." A section of that sequence called "The Longing" ends (rather awkwardly) with: "Old men should be explorers?/ I'll be an Indian./ Ogalala?/ Iroquois."

the communal and the collective; it was to seek the dramatically immediate, and to reject the New Critical conception of
the poem as object. Many poets in the 1960s wrote, in Louis
Simpson's phrase, "Indian poems"; so many, that it seemed,
in Simpson's 1972 recollection, that

the Indian was being taken up again as a symbol. It was nostalgia, and
something more: in their search for a way of life to identify with, poets
were turning to an idea of the dark, suppressed American. . . . Poems
about Indians were a fantasy of sophisticated twentieth-century people
who were trying to find ways out of the materialism that was everywhere around them (241–242).

In 1975, in response to an interviewer's question, Simpson
elaborated:

We were trying to use the Indian as a means of expressing our feeling
about the repressed side of America that should be released. However, if
I or anyone were to continue to try to write Indian poems, we should
know more about Indians than we did, than I did. (L. Smith, 1975, 105)[11]

This is surely correct; and it may serve to point up the obvious fact that poems with Indian subjects do not necessarily
have much to do with Indians or, even less, with Indian models. Poets like Rothenberg and Snyder have an informed
awareness of Native cultures and their literary productions;

---

11. Simpson continued, "I was writing with sympathy and an historical sense
of feeling, but to write about Indians you should in a sense become an Indian" (in
L. Smith, 105). Leslie Silko has quoted Simpson's remark to criticize "the unmiti-
gated egotism of the white man,, and the belief that he could 'in a sense become
an Indian' " (1979, 3). Unfortunately, for Silko's "attack," Simpson had gone on
to say, "you have to know how they think and feel. *And that I know I could never
do, so I wouldn't even bother trying*" (in L. Smith, 105; my emphasis). Not to quote
Simpson to this effect is simply dishonest on Silko's part.

others like Stafford and Richard Hugo have a deep feeling for
the places so important to traditional Native cultures. Then
there are poets like James Tate, whose "One Dream of Indians" proclaims:

> When I thought of Indians
> before, I thought of slender
> muscular men with feather
>
> heads wailing hallelujah,
> of blood spears on white flesh, their
> two-toned ponies insane. (54)

But, the speaker tells us, ". . . There was one dream / of
Indians I didn't / dream, however. That was you." Here is
that determined reduction to the merely personal that marked
a good deal of writing-school verse in the 1950s, that carried
into the 1960s, and that persists today. The appearance of
Indians in such poems is purely incidental and indicative of no
particular relation whatever to Native Americans and their
literature.

It was in the 1960s as well that a number of powerful Native American writers began to appear in print, among them
Duane Niatum, Simon J. Ortiz, Roberta Hill, and James
Welch. By the end of the decade, in 1969, the Pulitzer Prize
for literature went to the Kiowa professor of English literature N. Scott Momaday for his novel *House Made of Dawn*.
That same year, Momaday published his widely noticed,
cross-cultural experiment in autobiography, *The Way to Rainy
Mountain*. Momaday, as I have noted, was a student of Winters and for his doctoral dissertation prepared an edition of the
poems of Frederick Tuckerman, Winters's candidate for ma-

jor American poet of the nineteenth century. Momaday, like
Welch, writes both poetry and fiction; his verse, however,
seems closer to the formal manner of later Winters than to
anything discoverable in traditional Native literature. Here
are the opening stanzas of Momaday's "Angle of Geese,"
which appeared in a volume of the same name:

> How shall we adorn
> Recognition with our speech?
> Now the dead firstborn
> Will lag in the wake of words.
>
> Custom intervenes;
> We are civil, something more:
> More than language means,
> The mute presence mulls and marks.
>   (in Sanders and Peek, 461)

And here is Welch's "Snow Country Weavers":

> A time to tell you things are well.
> Birds flew south a year ago.
> One returned, a blue-wing teal
> wild with news of his mother's love.
>
> Mention me to friends. Say
> wolves are dying at my door,
> the winter drives them from their meat.
> Say this: say in my mind
>
> I saw your spiders weaving threads
> to bandage up the day. And more,
> those webs were filled with words
> that tumbled meaning into wind.
>   (in Sanders and Peek, 470)

In Welch's poem, regular reference to animals is made, but formally the regular stanzas and irregular rhymes (in particular, the final "mind"/"wind" and the brooding-earnest tone) derive from the Euramerican rather than the Native American literary tradition. This is often the case as well with the work of Hill and Niatum, who, with Welch and Momaday, probably appear most frequently in general anthologies of American poetry. Their technical conservatism seems a recognition of the inevitable presence, in written verse in English, of the European poetic tradition.

I am far from implying, with these observations, a negative judgment upon the work of these writers; obviously, Native American poets are entitled to the same freedom accorded their non-Native counterparts in their choice of subject matter and formal manner. And, in any case, there are decided occasions on which these poets adopt a more open, more voice-oriented style. The relation of other contemporary Indian poets—I think of Ortiz, Ray A. Young Bear, and Joy Harjo—to European poetics is more tentative, more marginal. I will quote in full Ortiz's "This Preparation" as an example:

> these sticks i am holding
> i cut down at the creek.
> i have just come from there.
> i listened to the creek
> speaking to the world,
> i did my praying,
> and then i took my knife
> and cut the sticks.
> there is some sorrow in leaving
> fresh wounds in growing things,
> but my praying has relieved

some of my sorrow, prayers
make things possible, my uncle said.
before i left i listened again
for words the creek was telling,
and i smelled its smell which
are words also. and then
i tied my sticks into a bundle
and came home, each step a prayer
for this morning and a safe return.
my son is sleeping still
in this quietness, my wife
is stirring at her cooking,
and i am making this preparation.
i wish to make my praying
into these sticks like gods have taught.

(in Sanders and Peek, 467)

On one hand, the reverential stance toward "ordinary" life, the sense of human responsibility to nature, the commitment to a relationship of "participant maintenance" (in Robert Redfield's phrase) toward the universe: these are all attitudes familiar to the Native tradition. The poem is presented as spoken–performed, with gestures implied, as an aspect of some larger (ritual) event. On the other hand, "This Preparation" is not radically different from poems by certain non-Native poets; it is by and large assimilable to the Euramerican tradition. It will take further work on traditional Native American literatures—new translations and new studies and greater general familiarity—to indicate to what degree its methods as well as its outlook can figure in written verse in English.

In any case, it should be obvious that just as the mere existence of poems with Indian subjects by non-Native poets does not in itself constitute evidence of a genuine opening to Native American influences, so, too, the mere existence of poems in print by Native American poets does not indicate any effective influence of traditional Native American literature on the canon. It does not seem possible or fruitful to attempt strictly to distinguish Native American from European influences in the work of Indian writers and non-Indians interested in Indian traditions, although the nature of the technical mix may well be worth attention. The errors to avoid, I believe, are to urge (as Leslie Marmon Silko has done) that Anglos simply stick to their own traditions, on the one hand, and, on the other, to insist (as Thomas Sanders and Walter Peek have done) that some "remembered Indianness" or "inherited and unconsciously sublimated urge to employ the polysynthetic structure of Native American languages" must somehow come through the English of poetry written by Native Americans (449).[12]

Some other developments of the late 1960s also bear importantly on our subject. For it was in 1968—the year Dover reissued Burlin's *Indians' Book,* while fighting was reported in Vietnam and the streets of Chicago—that rebellion took place among the professoriate at the MLA convention in New York City: a concerted effort to naturalize the canon and to revise its traditional hierarchies of race and gender. Earlier that same year, students in France had rebelled against their professors and the government that employed them, calling for the burning of the libraries and a return to nature: "Sous les paviers, la plage!" ("Under the pavement, the beach!"). Earlier still, in 1966, French structuralism—*hors de Lévi-Strauss*—had arrived

---

12. These two Native American editors have put together a fine collection, but their own commentary, although sometimes excellent, also includes the kind of essentially, if unintentionally, racist remarks ("remembered Indianness," "inherited . . . urge") I have quoted.

in force upon American shores to deliver the fourth blow, as it were, to Western humanistic narcissism (following the first three blows that Freud specified, those delivered by Galileo, Darwin, and Freud himself), with the symposium called "The Languages of Criticism and the Sciences of Man," held at the Johns Hopkins University. Michael Foucault was not present, but Barthes, Jacques Lacan, and the youthful Jacques Derrida were in attendance. At Johns Hopkins, Barthes announced that "to write" might be an intransitive verb; and Lacan dissolved the individual subject as "a fading thing that runs under the chain of signifiers. For the definition of a signifier is that it represents a subject not for another subject but for another signifier" (194). Derrida, already displaying his characteristic total assurance, told his audience that "one can say in total assurance that there is nothing fortuitous about the fact that the critique of ethnocentrism—the very condition of ethnology—should be systematically and historically contemporaneous with the destruction of the history of metaphysics. Both belong to a single and same era" (in Macksey and Donato, 251–252). This denial of the privileged place of man—and modern anthropology's contribution to the conditions of possibility for such a denial (an early subject, as well, of Foucault's discourse)—projects exactly the sort of revision of the Western consciousness that would bring it nearer to appreciating the world view of Native American peoples and thus contribute to a more ready understanding of traditional Native American literatures and their claims upon the canon.

Throughout the 1970s and to the present moment, the developments I have been tracing have continued. In 1973, an excellent formal textbook, *Literature of the American Indian,* appeared; by 1975 there were at least five available anthologies of American Indian poets, many of whom had originally published in prestigious quarterlies.[13] In 1981, Joseph Bruchac, himself part Abnaki and a poet, collected the work of more than thirty Indian poets in *American Indian Writings,* a special issue of the *Greenfield Review.* Duane Niatum's *Harper's Anthology of Twentieth-Century Native American Poetry* has just come out (1988). The 1970s also saw the publication of John Bierhorst's valuable anthologies of Native American materials; Rothenberg's erratic but powerful volume of translation-versions, *Shaking the Pumpkin;* and Merwin's working of some of Robert Lowie's *Crow Texts.* Merwin's work appeared in *Alcheringa,* a journal of ethnopoetics, edited by Rothenberg and by the anthropologist Dennis Tedlock. *Alcheringa* not only published non-Western texts but occasionally included recordings with some of its issues. In 1979, Snyder's B.A. thesis was published as *He Who Hunted Birds in His Father's Village: The Dimensions of a Haida Myth,* with a preface by Tarn. *Myths and Texts,* which had been in and out of print since its original appearance in 1960, was finally reissued by Snyder's principal publisher, New Directions, in 1978.

Two important books of poetic translations from the 1970s deserve particular mention—one by Tedlock and one by Howard Norman. On the basis of recent work, I think it's reasonable to require that translations of Native American literature, if they are to be considered approximately accurate, meet two specific conditions. First, they must derive from an actual, taped, or re-creative audition of the Native performance. Second, they must be produced in accord with what Hymes has

13. In addition to Niatum's collection, *Carriers of the Dream Wheel,* one might also note Terry Allen, ed., *The Whispering Wind: Poetry by Young American Indians;* Robert K. Dodge and Joseph B. McCullough, eds., *Voices from Wah'Kon-Tah: Contemporary Poetry of Native Americans;* Dick Lourie, ed., *Come to Power: Eleven Contemporary American Indian Poets;* and Kenneth Rosen, ed., *Voices of the Rainbow: Contemporary Poetry by American Indians.*

called "philological recognition of the original, not bilingual control," at least a rough working knowledge of the language in question (1965, 336). [14] To produce his translations from the Zuni, *Finding the Center* (1972), Tedlock himself tape-recorded the narratives he would translate. Highly competent in Zuni, Tedlock sought to indicate the structural principles of Zuni narrative performance by attention to its metalinguistic features, its changes of pace and volume, the gestures of the narrator, and the audience responses; these he attempted to present by means of typographical variations. Although a shift from large to small type does not strictly represent a shift in volume from loud to soft, it does insist that something has changed; spaces on the page are not silences—but we are sufficiently accustomed to the analogy to respond to it.

Tedlock's translations are of Zuni *narrative;* yet they are arranged on the page in a manner that corresponds more closely to Euramerican poetry than to the more usual Euramerican medium for narrative, prose. Tedlock has argued long and well, however, that prose has "no existence outside the written page" (1977, 513). In one way or another, he has been supported in this conclusion by the practices of Barre Toelken and Hymes, who have both advanced the artful science of what Toelken calls the "poetic retranslation" of Indian narrative that formerly had been transcribed in blocks of "prose." [15]

14. Very little that we have in the anthologies of traditional Indian literature meets the two requirements for approximate accuracy I have posited, but I am far from suggesting that we should ignore all but that little. Rather, we need to be acutely aware of the mode of production of Native American texts, taking into account the varying contributions of Native performers, informants, interpreters, and the like, as well as those of non-Native editors. Whatever understanding of traditional Native American literature may currently be achieved, it will have to take into account the role Euramericans have played in its textual production. This is only one price of our history of domestic imperialism.

15. See Barre Toelken and Tacheeni Scott, "Poetic Retranslation and the 'Pretty Languages' of Yellowman."

Similarly, Norman's collection, *The Wishing Bone Cycle: Narrative Poems of the Swampy Cree* (1976), translates Indian stories into what appear, on the page, as poetry. Norman, a non-Native, grew up in proximity to Cree people and learned their language. A poet himself, he gathered these stories and presented them so effectively as to make a strong case for the power of Native American literary production—as well as to point out that traditional examples of that production are still discoverable. (Tedlock's collection performs the same service.)

The Wishing Bone Cycle, according to Norman, is a trickster cycle, but "the inventor and initiator of these particular poems was Jacob Nibenegenesabe, who lived for ninety-four years northeast of Lake Winnipeg, Canada" (3). Nibenegenesabe says, "I go backward, look forward, as the porcupine does," and Norman explains: "The idea is that each time these stories about the past are told they will be learned for the future" (1976, 4). These are, again, stories; they are narrated rather than sung or otherwise accompanied by music or dance; and they are both traditional and original, more or less in the same ways that traditional "authors" in Native cultures were always both originators and augmenters—as, indeed, the etymology of our word "author," from the Latin *augere,* indicates. An example:

> One time I wished myself in love.
> I was the little squirrel
> with dark stripes.
> I climbed shaky limbs for fruit for her.
> I even swam with the moon on the water
> to reach her.
> That was a time little troubled me.

> I worked all day to gather food
> and watched her sleep all night.
> It is not the same way now
> but my heart still sings
> when I hear her
> over the leaves. (1976, 8)

Among other interesting texts in Norman's volume are a group of "short poems," which "may be spoken by anyone in a Cree community. Once told, even poems derived from the most personal experiences become community property" (1976, 93). Here is one from John Rains:

> I am the poorest one.
> I cook bark.
> I have bad luck in hunting.
> A duck caught my arrow
> and used it
> for her nest.
>
> I am the poorest one.
> I sit in mud and weep.
> I have bad luck in hunting.
> A goose caught my arrow
> and broke it
> in two.
>
> I am old, old.
> Don't bring me pity,
> but food
> yes.
>   (1976, 93–94)

I shall return to materials of this kind in the concluding chapter.

4. Monologue and Dialogue in Native American Autobiography

i.

Because of the relation between critical paradigms and the literary canon—some texts being more visible and more interesting to certain procedures than to others—I have proposed the importance of a historicist emphasis for American literature as far more likely than any formalist turn for the purpose of noting the contribution of indigenous, Native American literature to American literature (as well as to see what it might mean to value Native productions in their own right). The sort of historicism I am interested in is one that allows for human agency, not teleologically destined to some foregone conclusion but as it engages in struggle to reconcile a maximum degree of individual freedom with a maximum degree of social justice. This struggle takes place in the material world—in society—and it takes place in the cultural world—in literature. To think of the human agent in this way requires that one theorize a different sort of self than the Western "bourgeois ego." In this project, as in so very many others, Fredric Jameson offers help, if only in passing. Jameson has said,

I always insist on a . . . possibility beyond the old bourgeois ego and the [postmodern] schizophrenic subject of our organization society today: a *collective subject*, decentered but not schizophrenic. (in Stephanson 45)

Jameson goes on to say that this subject "emerges in certain forms of storytelling that can be found in third-world literature . . . ," but neither here nor in a more extended consideration of this matter (I will examine it in the next chapter) does Jameson indicate whether this problematic category, third world literature, might also encompass the literature of Native Americans—in which, I want to claim here, this "collective self" has at least its nearest, as well as one of its most powerful models.

Autobiography is the type of literary discourse to which we have regularly looked for models of the self, and Native American autobiography, in both its individually written (autobiographies by Indians) and its compositely produced (Indian autobiographies) forms, offers what I would call *dialogic* models of the self. In Native American autobiography the self most typically is not constituted by the achievement of a distinctive, special voice that separates it from others, but, rather, by the achievement of a particular placement in relation to the many voices without which it could not exist. As the textual representation of a situated encounter between two persons (or three, if we include the frequent presence of an interpreter or translator) and two cultures, Indian autobiographies are quite literally dialogic. In autobiographies by Indians where only the autobiographical subject writes, there is not the dialogue of specific persons, although cultural cross-talk persists; as an Indian *and* a writer, a Lakota (for example) *and* a Christian (or a self-conscious artist in the Western sense), even the apparently monologous Native autobiographer is likely to show his or her biculturalism.

For any person who identifies himself or herself as an Indian, the writing of autobiography, whether done alone or in conjunction with a non-Indian person, generates a textual self that is in greater or lesser degree inevitably dialogic. But this textual self derives from a prior actual or biographical self, and this, too, in its historical formation, is collectively rather than individualistically constituted. I mean to say only that Native American autobiographies, so far as their subjects have been formed in relation to tribal-traditional cultures (the assumption one makes in calling these texts Native American autobiographies in the first place) provide illustrations of the social constitution of the individual in variants that have not much been present in the West since perhaps the sixteenth century. While cases will differ, traditionally, Native American selves are better accounted for, in Mauss's classic terms, by *personnalité* or role theories rather than by *moi* theories of inwardness and individualism (although the situation is considerably more complex than Mauss allowed). Native American autobiographies, then, are the textual result of specific dialogues (between persons, between cultures, between persons and cultures) which claim to represent an Indian subject who, him- or herself, is the human result of specific dialogical or collective sociocultural practices. They are particularly interesting, it will be my claim, as providing images of a collective self and a collective society.

For all of this, it is the case, as I shall try to show, that some Native American autobiographies work in such a way as to suppress the dialogic or collective constitution of both Native self and autobiographical text. It is the aim of these autobiographies to attain to—in my view, to submit to—one or another monologic model of the self and the text as given by the dominant Euramerican culture at a particular moment in time, to accommodate themselves to a reigning authoritative discourse. But I have already invoked a number of theoretical contexts that it may be useful to speak of further before proceeding.

ii.

To introduce the terms "monologue" and "dialogue" is, of course, to invoke two important developments in literary and social scientific theory. I refer to recent interest in the Russian theorist, Mikhail Bakhtin, and to the effort to define what has been called a dialogical anthropology.

So much has been written on Bakhtin of late that any attempt to summarize his thought is bound to be both incomplete and partial. Incomplete, because what is generally to be understood by reference to "Bakhtin," is very far from settled. To be sure, "Freud" and "Marx" mean different things to different people, as well; but there seems to be in Bakhtin, more than in these other major thinkers (and it is by no means universally agreed that comparison of Bakhtin to major thinkers is justified), an openness or ambiguity of a particularly pronounced kind. This openness, if we choose to call it that, may be functional, a practical illustration of what had been theoretically proposed, a textual gesture on the part of Bakhtin himself in the direction of dialogism. Or perhaps it is not "openness" but, instead, flawed thinking and ambiguity to the point of confusion that makes it so hard to specify the particulars of Bakhtin's thought; not rhetoric but logic is at issue. For these reasons, any attempt at an approximately neutral "summary" automatically becomes partial, a choice not between nuances but real differences; there is indeed, as the title of Allon White's essay conveys, a ". . . Struggle Over Bakhtin."

For Bakhtin, human language is, as he calls it, heteroglossic and polyvocal, the speech of each individual enabled and circumscribed not so much by language as a *system* (hence Bakhtin's difference from Saussurian structural linguistics and its fascination with *langue*), as by the actual speech of other individuals. Speech is social and meaning is open and in flux, inevitably a dialogue among speakers, not the property or in the power of any single speaker. "[A]ll there is to know about the world is not exhausted by a particular discourse about it . . ." (1984, 45), Bakhtin notes in a typical statement; or, "Nothing is absolutely dead: every meaning will have its homecoming festival" (in A. White, 219). In writing, it is what Bakhtin calls the novel which most fully testifies to its own (inevitable) incompleteness, to its ongoing indebtedness to the discourse of others; the novel, for Bakhtin, is the prime literary instance of dialogized speech. Still, some forms of written discourse, and some forms of social practice, do seek to impose a single voice as alone authoritative, thus subordinating or entirely suppressing other voices. What Bakhtin calls the epic is the literary genre preeminently marked by the monologic tendency, while the totalitarianism of the Stalinism under which Bakhtin lived provides the sociopolitical model of monologism. Bakhtin seems to be committed to dialogue on empirical grounds inasmuch as the term "dialogic" claims to name the way speech and social life "really" are. But Bakhtin seems also to be committed to dialogue on moral and esthetic grounds; he approves of and is pleased by that which he finds di-, hetero-, poly-, and so on.

What is at issue here for criticism is the meaning of this preference both in language and in political practice. Semantically, it is not clear whether Bakhtinian dialogic envisions a strong form of pluralism in which all possible significations have at least some legitimate claim in any determination of meaningfulness, or, rather, a kind of infinite, unbounded free play of signifiers in regard to which decidable meanings simply do not exist. In the same way, Bakhtin's dislike of what he calls monologue may or may not leave room for some forms of relatively stable or normative assertion. We do not yet know whether such statements as those I quoted above—and, to repeat, there are innumerable such statements in Bakhtin's writing—intend a radically ironic (a deconstructive, postmodern) refusal of any form of grounded meaning however relativized, or, instead, an insistence that no single language act has the capacity to encompass the entire range of humanly possible meaning—as no single mode of political organization can give full latitude to human potential. In this latter regard, the issue is particularly complicated. This is to say that, while we do know from Bakhtin that something called the "novel" is supposed to provide the best illustration of relativized, dialogic discourse, we do not quite know whether the nearest thing he gives us to a sociopolitical equivalent of the "novel," Rabelaisian "carnival," represents an actual model for social organization or only an escape from too-rigid social organization.

In more or less similar fashion, we find the same questions arising when we consider the implications of the various principles, definitions, and proposals for a dialogical anthropology, some of them developing more or less independently of the Bakhtinian milieu. Here, it is the refusal of the hegemony of Western social science as monologically authorized to represent, interpret, or explain (in the languages of the West, in books by single authors, who have written alone in their offices or studies, etc.) that is of foremost concern. In every case there is a dissatisfaction with that set of oppositions—us and them, center and margin, hot cultures and cold, science and superstition, and so on—which always, in practice, leads to a privileging of the former term over the latter. This dissatisfaction focuses most specifically on what George Marcus and Dick Cushman have termed "ethnographic realism,"[1] the mode of writing which, in their view, has expressed the absorption and explanation of them by us, their marginality centralized in the metropolitan terminologies that we, scientifically, provide, and so forth. Dissatisfaction with "ethnographic realism" has expressed itself variously. Marcus and Michael Fischer, for example, as I noted earlier, have turned to a naive and untheorized faith in "innovation" in the interest, it would seem, of a "defamiliarization" that quite unhistorically is taken as likely to produce "better" ethnographies than those in the "realistic" mode. But most generally, the dissatisfaction I allude to has involved a retreat from at least the most blatantly imperial forms of (the phrase is James Clifford's) "ethnographic authority," or (the phrase here is Dennis Tedlock's) "analogical anthropology."[2]

As Tedlock presents it, analogical anthropology "involves the replacement of one discourse with another" (1983, 324), "their" voice either disappearing entirely or appearing only in what amounts to a full translation by the anthropologist. Dialogical anthropology, however, "would be a talking across, or alternately, which is something we all do in the field if we are not purely natural scientists." Moving from an empirical argument (dialogue represents how it really is) to an essentially ethical or esthetic argument, Tedlock goes on to assert that "There is no reason this dialogue must stop when we leave the field." Thus the essay in which these sentences appear begins with an account of its first presentation as a talk, consistent with Tedlock's belief that "the circumstances of

1. See George Marcus and Dick Cushman, "Ethnographies as Texts."
2. See James Clifford, "On Ethnographic Authority," and Dennis Tedlock, "The Analogical Tradition and the Emergence of a Dialogical Anthropology" (in *The Spoken Word and the Work of Interpretation*).

anthropological discourse . . . should be kept in open discussion rather than being hidden away in footnotes, appendixes, and unpublished manuscripts" (1983, 321). Tedlock's argument here is carried forward not logically but rhetorically by means of the opposition between the adjective "open" and the verb particle "hidden." My point is not to criticize Tedlock; I generally agree with him, and he has put the case as eloquently as—and in rather a less mystified and "millenial" fashion than—anyone. Rather, I want to reaffirm my remark in the Introduction that there is no way logically to demonstrate that the use of appendixes and footnotes, for example, is *necessarily* imperialistic or functions *always and everywhere* in the service of domination. Those of us who wish to speak in favor of dialogue will have to take a dialectical and specifically historical approach to the subject.

The different ways in which "circumstances" and cross-talk may be conveyed are explored in the work of dialogical anthropology where the intention—to say what by now should be apparent—is to find ways to let the Other speak for him- or herself, to open one's text to difference, to defer to the authority of alterity, at least to the fullest extent that this is possible. How to do this is by no means clear. Marcus and Fischer vaguely invite a formal eclecticism—so long as it strikes the "reader" (for whose taste in these matters they are ready to speak with quite monologic authority) as "sophisticated." As P. Steven Sangren has shown, this "sophistication," with its tendency to privilege either "the experience of fieldwork [or] the problematics of ethnographic rhetoric," in actual practice may well border "on self-congratulatory, narcissistic decadence," (423) or, at best, produce something like Kevin Dwyer's somber recognition that a certain kind of ethnographic search for the Other works best when it acknowledges

that what it can most securely discover is the Self.[3] But this is
not to say that a commitment to dialogue in the interest of a
dialectical anthropology (as in the title of Stanley Diamond's
excellent journal) cannot be more fully aware of textual problematics than has hitherto been the case, more modest and/or
self-conscious about its inevitably totalizing categories, and so
hope to produce ethnographic accounts that may well advance
our sense of truth and knowledge, however relativized these
may be.

It turns out, thus, to be the case that dialogical anthropology broadly conceived, in quite the same way as Bakhtinian
dialogic, may desire forms of fuller and more authentic, more
relativistically scientific (the conception here need not be
taken as oxymoronic) representations of others—or, to the
contrary, it may desire a refusal of representation altogether.[4]
It is difficult to imagine what this refusal would mean in
actual practice, although Stephen Tyler's call for poetic evoca-
tion in anthropology as the next step beyond explanation and
even interpretation may give us some idea. Tyler's program
to move anthropology from the production of "documents[s]
of the occult" to "occult document[s]" (in the phrase he takes
from Robert Duncan)[5] envisions a postmodern anthropology
that would abandon all "scientific" claims to epistemological
status as "truth" in favor of moments of insight or "knowing." Tyler himself, however, seems aware that an "evocative" ethnography is easier to imagine/desire than to produce.
In any event, to read dialogical anthropology this way is the

3. See Dwyer's *Moroccan Dialogues: Anthropology in Question,* along with
work by Paul Rabinow and many other self-conscious ethnographers.
4. James Clifford's discussion of this problem in Edward Said's *Orientalism* is
particularly useful. See Clifford's "Review Essay of Edward Said's *Orientalism.*"
5. See Tyler's "From Document of the Occult to Occult Document."

same as to read Bakhtin in poststructuralist fashion; both readings, in their different ways, lead to what I see as an essentially religious criticism.

Now Indian autobiographies are, as I have said, the products of historically specifiable dialogues between two persons from different cultures, and autobiographies by Indians are written by one person alone who has had significant experience of two different cultures (the self-identification as a Native person and the writing themselves testifying to this fact). Although Indian autobiographies are quite literally dialogic productions, nonetheless a number of these texts have tended toward monologism: there is an attempt in them to permit only a single voice to sound. In practice that voice has been not so much the voice of the individual Indian subject or even the individual white editor, that is, not so much a personal voice, as—in the Foucauldian sense—the voice of a dominant order or discipline (at the very least a dominant period style that defines which texts are candidates for being taken seriously). I shall take this up in more detail below.

And, curiously enough, when we consider a range of autobiographies by Indians, we discover that although they are literally monologues, written by one speaker alone, some among them have sought to achieve a high degree of dialogism—to acknowledge and dramatize, as I indicated earlier, the bicultural nature of their textual formation and also the collective formation of their particular sense of self. But—to speak generally for only a moment more—this commitment to dialogue in autobiographies by Indians is no more universally present in them than a commitment to monologue is universally present in Indian autobiographies. Indeed, as I shall try to show, even the determined Indian monologist usually finds it difficult or impossible to hide all traces of other voices.

Dominant in the Pilgrim century, revived in the mideighteenth century during the Great Awakening, and residually operative even in our own time, a major American discourse is the discourse of what I shall call *salvationism.* A dialect of aggressive Protestantism, salvationism is the discursive equivalent of a glass trained on Heaven through which all this world must be seen. The category of concern here—of "knowledge/power" in Foucault's term—is *religion.* In the second quarter of the nineteenth century, this discourse is secularized; in relation to Indians, the will of God becomes translated into the law of nature, an evolutionary law that insists upon the accession of "savagery" to "civilization." The category of concern now is (natural) *history.* In the twentieth century, Indians become not so much candidates for salvation or for historical documentation as subjects for anthropological study. The category of concern is (social) *science.* Just as the subjects of salvationist autobiography were those whose life stories were offered as illustrating God's plan and power; just as the subjects of savagist autobiography were those whose life stories were offered as illustrating the historical progress of civilization; so, too, were the subjects of social scientific autobiography those whose life stories were offered as representative of their cultures. In the past twenty years or so, the Native American autobiographies—autobiographies by Indians rather than Indian autobiographies—that have been most noticed have presented themselves in relation to the category (not of religion, history, or science, but) of the *esthetic,* as art,[6] adopting presen-

6. I use salvationism/religion, savagism/history, scientism/social science, and esthetic/art, here and in the discussion to follow as terms to indicate both a perspective and a practice, a point of view and a style. In their perspectival aspect, they are related to Foucault's sense of the master discourse or episteme governing a particular epoch. Foucault is almost exclusively epistemic in his

tational techniques that derive more or less from types of literary modernism.[7]

I propose to examine in some detail two Indian autobiographies, J. B. Patterson's *Life of Black Hawk* (1833) and L. V. McWhorter's *Yellow Wolf: His Own Story* (1940), and two autobiographies by Indians, William Apes's *A Son of the Forest* (1829), and Leslie Marmon Silko's *Storyteller* (1981) for their relation to dialogism. My sense of the matter is that this relation has social as well as cultural consequences, some of which I will try to indicate.

iii.

Born in 1798 of a mixed blood father and a Pequot mother, William Apes suffered through a particularly brutal childhood. He learned Christian doctrine along with his letters from white foster parents—with whom, for all their kindnesses, he did not dwell long. In his early teens he enlisted as a soldier and participated, on the American side, in the attempted invasion of Canada during the War of 1812, a war in which Tecumseh and Black Hawk fought for the British. After leaving military service, Apes worked at a variety of

---

concerns having little interest in the details of written practice (as opposed to institutional practice on which subject he is enormously useful) or style. He does not, therefore, devote himself much to that careful *reading* which so occupies the disciples of Derrida and de Man—who, it must be said, have had little interest in the perspectival dimensions of the texts they read (or of any practice other than the practice of writing), all of which are seen as variants of one master perspective only, that of Western logocentrism in all its undifferentiated sway.]

7. I am thinking most particularly of the work of N. Scott Momaday who remains the best known and most influential Native American artist today. I look at Momaday's autobiographical writing just below. The great exception to this generalization is the Chippewa novelist Gerald Vizenor who has explicitly identified himself with postmodernism in fiction, criticism, and autobiography.

trades and was eventually attracted to the teachings of evangelical Methodists. He obtained first an "exhorter's" and then, with great difficulty, a preacher's license. It is with this latter achievement that Apes concludes his autobiography, filling thereby, a familiar Western autobiographical pattern, the discovery of identity in vocation. Apes's *Son of the Forest* is a tale of trial and test, the story of the bark that has safely crossed the stormy sea—at least, that is, so far as this life is concerned. Safe haven for Apes is nowhere short of heaven— where, as he says in the final paragraphs of his narrative, he hopes to meet his readers.

So far as we know, Apes wrote his story alone (he seems to have published the first edition at his own cost, as well), and it is possible that careful analysis comparing Apes's text to a great many others contemporary with it might discover certain stylistic gestures of the sort we frequently assume to imply the unique individual himself. It is possible: but my own readings of Apes and of some—not a very great many— other texts of the period do not reveal such gestures. Rather, the voice that sounds everywhere in Apes's text seems to mirror very closely a voice to be heard commonly in the early nineteenth century, the voice of what I have called salvationism. Such a voice on these shores typically expresses what Sacvan Bercovitch has called the "sacral view of America" (1977, 17), effecting a "leap from secular into sacred history"— a "leap," as I should say, that denies secular history altogether. For if events in time are only variants of Biblical originals, if all human actions can be understood only in relation to God's will, as the salvationist view would have it, then we live not history but myth—the monomyth, in Joseph Campbell's term, a monomyth which in William Apes's autobiography is expressed in relentless monologue.

Apes is proud to acknowledge his Indian ancestry—
although he is much opposed, here, to the term "Indian;" for
him, "The proper term which ought to be applied to our nation, to distinguish it from the rest of the human family, is that
of '*Natives*' " (1829, 21) But even his understanding of what it
means to be a "Native" is filtered through Christian perspective. The "natives of this country," Apes explains, "are the
only people under heaven who have a just title to the name,
inasmuch as we are the only people who retain the original
complexion of our father Adam" (1829, 21). His pride in his
ancestry, in this instance—as in another I shall mention—thus
derives from no indigenous, Pequot sense of these matters—
although, to be sure, its Christian reference may not be entirely
orthodox either. Alluding to his Pequot forebears, Apes earlier
had noted his grandmother's relation to "the royal family"
(1829, 8). He quickly announces, however, that "I do not make
this statement in order to boast of my origin, or to appear great
in the estimation of others" for "in fact of myself, I am nothing
but a worm of the earth . . ." (1829, 8). Once again Apes
proclaims a sense of self, if we may call it that, deriving entirely
from Christian culture.

The voice that Apes achieves in his autobiography echoes
that of his Puritan predecessor Daniel Gookin, the biographer
of the Native converts Joseph, Black James, the well-docu-
mented Hiacoomes, and other "praying Indians" of Massachusetts in the Pilgrim century; or, in the eighteenth century, Cotton Mather and Samson Occom among others.[8] Nor is it a

---

8. Let me offer the following as examples of what I take to be salvationist
language in William Apes:
  Surrounded by difficulties and apparent dangers, I was resolved to seek the
  salvation of my soul with all my heart—to trust entirely to the Lord, and if I

very different voice from that of Apes's contemporary, Catherine Brown, a "Christian Indian of the Cherokee nation," as her biographer, Rufus Anderson of the American Board of Missions refers to her. Anderson's biography of Brown, which was already in its third edition the year Apes's autobiography appeared, includes many of her letters as well as numerous

---

> failed, to perish pleading for mercy at the foot of the throne. I now hung all my hope on the Redeemer . . . (1829, 44)
>
> There was not only a change in my heart but in every thing around me. The scene was entirely altered. The works of God praised Him and I saw in him every thing that he had made . . . (1829, 44–45)

Examples of similar language can be found on almost every page in Gookin. I will let one stand for many:

> and the Lord was graciously pleased to hear and answer their prayers, and shortly after gave the woman safe deliverance to a daughter; which the father named by a word in the Indian language, which signified in English, Return. (22)

This last is quoted from the *Historical Collections of the Indians of New England*. The name, Return, was chosen because Hiacoomes and his wife (the story refers to them) "are, through God's grace, *returning* back . . . with our faces set towards God, heaven and happiness," and because Mrs. Hiacoomes, in danger for her life as a consequence of her difficult labor, is *returned* to her husband. Gookin wrote some time between 1677 and 1687 (the year of his death); his book was not published until 1792. Cotton Mather on the Indians (1702) sounds like this:

> It is not among the English only, but among the Indians also, that our Glorious Lord Jesus Christ hath been glorify'd in doing of Wonders. And altho some of those Wonders have been mention'd elsewhere, but more of 'em have been faultily bury'd in such Oblivion that they are never like to have any mention at all in this World, yet I am able to furnish . . . a Collecion of Remarkables. . . . It is possible that some of the Americans may be the posterity of those Canaanites who, after the Wars of Canaan, set up their Pillars in Africa. . . . But behold, how Jesus the Saviour had follow'd them, and conquer'd them with his Glorious Grace. (vi, 62)

In somewhat less extreme fashion, this is also the mode of Jonathan Edwards and his son-in-law, David Brainerd, on the Indians in the first half of the eighteenth century, and of Samson Occom, both in his autobiographical writing and in his most famous work, "A Sermon Preached at the Execution of Moses Paul, an Indian."

entries from her journals.[9] If we seek to compare these two Christian Indians, we must note that the one writer is Pequot and the other Cherokee; the one male, the other female; one had neither safety nor security from his family relations, whereas the other was the devoted and obedient daughter of loving parents—the list of differences could easily be lengthened. And yet both speak with a similar voice, defining themselves exclusively in relation to salvationist discourse: if there is a Cherokee dimension to Brown's text and to her sense of herself (for all of Anderson's editing) or a Pequot dimension to Apes's, these are not apparent to me. In Apes's case, indeed, there is the implication that when the Native lost his land, he lost his voice as well.

It is not only the voices of Pequot and Cherokee relatives and friends—voices that, one may assume, must have played some part in the subjective formation of William Apes and Catherine Brown—which are suppressed in these texts, for we also hear virtually nothing of the secular, Anglo world of their time. Indeed, inasmuch as Apes's autobiography is con-

9. The extent of these gives the book some claim to autobiographical status: David Brumble's *Annotated Bibliography of American Indian and Eskimo Autobiographies* lists it as an autobiography. Nonetheless, Anderson's practice is typical of the manner of the eighteenth-century life-and-times biography also carried forward into the nineteenth century by Samuel Drake and B. B. Thatcher, among others. Brown's use of salvationist language is not only regular, as I have claimed of Apes's, but constant. Here is one example, for a letter of July 5, 1819:

I feel much indebted to you, but more particularly to that God who sent you here to instruct the poor ignorant Indians in the way that leads to everlasting life. Oh, my dear friends, may the Lord ever bless you, and make you the instrument of doing great good where he has called you.

You may pass through many trials; but remember beloved brother and sister, all our trials here will only make us richer there, when we arrive at our home. A few more days, and then I hope our weary souls will be at rest in our Saviour's kingdom, where we shall enjoy His blessed presence forever. (Brown, 55–56)

structed in terms of its author's progress to full permission to speak the language of salvationism, we may see it as documenting a struggle for monologism. It is Apes's wish to be the licensed speaker of a dominant voice that desires no supplementation by other voices. Just as the Puritans recorded no Indian song or story, regarding these, for the most part, as animal noise or the sounds of Satan, just as Anderson could blandly conclude that the Cherokee "had no literature" ("Not a book existed in the language. The fountains of knowledge were unopened. The mind made no progress" [14]),[10] so, too, could William Apes see no reason to register the various idiolects he encountered in his extensive travels—the speech of artisans and soldiers, drunkards and tradesmen, and the like. Representation of the speech of others comes predominantly in indirect discourse,[11] in which Apes, writing in retrospect from attainment to the position of mouthpiece of the Lord, translates fully and speaks for all others with no attempt to convey the sound of any voice other than the only

10. Anderson's comment directly echoes those heard from militant Christianizers for over two hundred years, whose eyes trained on heaven tended to miss a good deal here on earth. In fact, Sequoyah had just recently invented a written syllabary for the Cherokee language in which newspapers, if not yet books, were already being printed. A Cherokee war song, as I have noted, had been translated into English by Lt. Henry Timberlake in the eighteenth century. Anderson's use of the term "progress" might seem to align him with the secular partisans of natural law for whom progress was the key term. In fact, "progress" for Anderson as for all salvationists equates strictly with advances in Christian piety.

11. I have found only two occasions on which Apes directly reports— quotes—the speech of others. Both are highly charged. The first comes early in his life when he is pursued for punishment by a foster parent who says, " 'I will learn you, you Indian dog, how to chase people with a knife.' " (1829, 25). Much later, he quotes, again very briefly, some of those involved in denying him a preacher's license (1829, 110–113). Perhaps there is some greater degree of colloquialism allowed in the speech that is directly quoted: but that is about all I can conclude.

voice that came to count for him. Free indirect style, as James
Clifford has noted, "suppresses direct quotation in favor of a
controlling discourse always more-or-less that of the author,"
an author, it is necessary to add, himself formed by a specific
"controlling discourse" (1983, 137).

Contemporary with Apes's book is the earliest Indian autobiography, J. B. Patterson's *Life of Black Hawk* (1833), a text
which I shall not be able to align easily with strict monologue
or an openness to the dialogic. Here a dialectical approach
becomes particularly important. *Who* Black Hawk was, that
is to say, is not a question that can be answered by some
estimate as to whether we do or do not get the "authentic" or
"real" historical person. "Black Hawk" is—must be—only
the subject who emerges from this text, a collective subject
that includes the subjectivity of John Patterson (he, of course,
is nowhere mentioned or referred to in the text) foremost
among other participants in the making of this Indian self.
That there are other representations of Black Hawk, as I shall
remark later, is something that can only complicate our sense
of the matter; ultimately, we hear not so much Black Hawk's
voice as Black Hawk's voices. (And for all that, we do not
have transcripts of the sessions between Black Hawk and the
mixed-blood translator, Antoine LeClair, or drafts of Patterson's manuscript.)

In the first quarter of the nineteenth century, Christian salvationism as a dominant discourse in relation to the Indian was
increasingly superseded by the language of what Roy Harvey
Pearce, as we have seen, broadly defined as the discourse of
savagism. To review this matter briefly here, savagism derived
from a theory of universal history which substituted the secular category of scientific law for the Christian will of God. A
vague and self-justifying form of social Darwinism, this domi-

nant ideology (from perhaps 1830 or so until as recently as 1934) claimed as a necessity of nature the accession of Indian savagery to white civilization. As Pearce carefully demonstrated some thirty-five years ago, "the history of American civilization . . . [was] conceived of as three-dimensional, progressing from past to present, from east to west, from lower to higher" (1967, 49) and that "history" took the fate of the Indian as its major illustrative instance. In actual practice, of course, indigenous people submitted not to the superior values of civilization but to its superior numbers and technology: still, the history of white America's push westward in the nineteenth century was with few and brief exceptions a history of Euramerican triumph and Native American defeat.

The proposition that Indians could not as Indians survive found, so far as I can tell, no argument. Disagreement set in, however, in the attitude to be taken in the face of this "fact." Many westerners, some Christians, and all those who thought of Native people as wild beasts, varmints, or minions of the Devil could only rejoice at the thought of their being tamed or terminated by their rational superiors. Others—easterners, often some Christians, and any of broadly romantic bent—thought of Indians as savages, to be sure, but noble savages whose passing, however inevitable, was yet to be lamented.

In May of 1830, at the urging of President Andrew Jackson, Congress passed the Indian Removal Act into law. This provided for the removal of all Indians on lands east of the Mississippi to its west bank (or wherever) at the discretion of Congress. With this encouragement, white settlers encroached upon the traditional territory of the Sauk-and-Fox, leading, in 1832, to the so-called Black Hawk War, a fifteen-week affair in which large numbers of Illinois militia (the young Abraham Lincoln among them), together with detachments of federal troops, decimated and demoralized Black Hawk's band of resisters sufficiently to induce the old Chief's surrender. After months of imprisonment, Black Hawk was taken to meet President Jackson himself, and then on tour through the east. Finally, after another brief detention, he was returned to his people on the Rock River. It was at this time, according to Antoine LeClair, government interpreter for the Sauk-and-Fox, and translator for Black Hawk and Patterson, that Black Hawk requested his life story be written.

Just as William Apes assimilated the heteroglossia of craftsmen and merchants, Natives and whites, common soldiers and officers, pious and profane into the single strict monologue of salvationism, so, too, did J. B. Patterson, a youthful Illinois newspaperman pressed into service as Black Hawk's editor, assimilate the many languages of militiamen and regular army officers, of settlers, traders, bureaucrats, "progressive" Indians and conservatives into a single perspective and practice. The perspective is that of savagism and the practice is that of nineteenth-century American historiography (so far as syntax and diction or "style" are concerned, and, as well, standards for citation, documentation, and the like). There is no more variety in the speech of the many actors in Black Hawk's narrative, as Patterson has Black Hawk report it, than there was in William Apes's presentation. And, indeed, Patterson's Black Hawk, like Apes himself, usually represents the speech of others indirectly, assimilating what they actually may have said to that common period diction that is given as his own.

And yet, it would be mistaken to call the *Life of Black Hawk* a fully achieved monologic text. Very differently from what we seem to find in William Apes, there are gestures in Patterson's book that noticeably validate a certain alterity or difference, a relinquishment of full translation that yields, if not quite an Other voice yet still an Other viewpoint. For one thing, the very choice of the autobiographical form with its insistence that, however he may speak, it is nonetheless the Indian himself (the Indian as Indian, that is to say, not the "civilized" or Christianized Indian) who does speak—that no one else is required to speak for him—acknowledges a possibility that simply had not been permitted before. Formally, too, in point of structure, we may note both a presence and an absence at the opening of Black Hawk's story that hold Western biographical convention in abeyance and allow what Native equivalents may have existed a certain play.

I am thinking here of David Brumble's important observation that while the experiences of childhood are a virtual requirement for Western autobiography, such experiences are largely irrelevant to Native American personal narrative in the various forms tribal people generally and particularly developed to speak of what they as individuals had done. Patterson's Black Hawk begins by stating the year (1767) and place ("at the Sac Village, on the Rock river") of his birth, but, instead of offering details of his childhood and youth, he shifts immediately to a story about a prophecy to his great-grandfather of the coming of a white man. This story continues with accounts of dreams and special powers until it is linked specifically to the history of Sauk-and-Fox encounters with the French and the British. This opening is worth comparing to that of William Apes's story, in which Apes begins with his birth, turns back to the origins of his grandfather and father, and then details (briefly, to be sure) the horrendous circumstances of his childhood, up through his sixth year when he is finally sent to school "for six successive winters" (1829, 16), at which point the first chapter concludes. Learn-

ing to read and to write and being exposed to Christian doctrine are the noteworthy events of Apes's early years. For
Black Hawk, however, "Few, if any, events of note transpired
within my recollection, until about my fifteenth year" when
he "distinguished [him]self by wounding an enemy," thus to
be "placed in the ranks of the Braves!" (46).

Of course, we do not know whether Black Hawk actually
did begin his story with what Patterson offers as the first
chapter; all the accounts we have of the composition of Indian
autobiographies agree that Native narrators tell personal history in ways that are not closely conformable to Western
notions of appropriate beginnings. Still, to begin with visions, dreams, prophecy, and the granting of special powers
seems consistent with what we know of Native American
narrative modes, while to speak of the "realistic" details of
one's childhood is the mark of Western narrative influence.
Patterson throughout Black Hawk's story includes references
to dreams, gestures that may indeed point to a certain defer-
ence to the Native view of what is important to personal
narrative—although I must continue to insist that we simply
do not know how much these inclusions represent what
Black Hawk "really" said.[12] Patterson, like all editors of Indian autobiography even to the present moment, followed

---

12. These latter in particular are problematic as ostensible markers of authenticity and deferral to difference, because, although Black Hawk himself may have
chosen to speak of these important things, we also know that Native narrators
speaking to Native audiences frequently just assume familiarity with these materials and so allude to them without providing details. The details, in this light, may
be present because Black Hawk was asked for them, although, to be sure, he
might have proffered them himself for the benefit of the white audience he knew
he was addressing. Because Patterson would have seen himself as a historian
rather than a type of what we now call an ethnographer, one whose task was
precisely the elicitation of such details, I would guess that cultural material, so far
as it is present, probably was Black Hawk's voluntary contribution.

what Brumble refers to as the Chronological Imperative, or-
ganizing the narrative, that is, in linear, temporal sequence:
still, at least we can imagine that Corn Woman, dreams, and
prophecies are as much involved in Black Hawk's sense of
himself as the "experiences" of childhood.[13]

From beginnings we may move to endings and consider
what Patterson's structuring of the story, its *terminus ad quem*,
might imply. I have elsewhere explained more fully why I
take the structure of Indian autobiographies to be, finally, the
responsibility of the Euramerican editor rather than of the
Native American subject.[14] I have also suggested that from
the point of view of the dominant culture (which is, indeed,
here criticized but never seriously called into question), Black
Hawk's life story may be read as a comedy, the (sad) story of
civilization's inevitable progress and its triumph over savagery. From the Indian point of view this story is, to be sure,
what we would call a tragedy—but even recognition of and
sympathy for the Indian point of view can do no more than to
make the story sad to sympathetic whites who, despite their
sadness, cannot share the Indian point of view without a virtual abandonment of their own. Black Hawk's final concilia-

---

13. Further references to dreams occur on pp. 81 and 112; legends appear on
p. 88 and pp. 93–94 of Jackson's edition of *Black Hawk*.

14. See *For Those Who Come After*, passim. My sense of this matter needs to
be squared with David Brumble's observation that in *Crashing Thunder*, the
autobiography of the Winnebago, Sam Blowsnake, it was not the editor, Paul
Radin, who determined its form, for "The form of Blowsnake's autobiography
is all his own" (1988, 123). I am persuaded by Brumble's account—so far as
Crashing Thunder is concerned. For in that book, the essentially comic form I
attribute to Radin happens to be consistent with the essentially confessional form
Blowsnake himself adopted from other converts to peyotism. My sense is that
this agreement in choice of emplotment on the part of Native American subject
and Euramerican editor is more nearly the exception rather than the rule—and
that the editor's preference, when differences exist, is likely to prevail.

tory words to the whites come too late; the offer of Indian friendship is irrelevant to a power that does what it likes, whether the Indians accommodate or no. And thus Patterson's *Black Hawk* is a text that fits comfortably enough within the monologue of savagism for all that it pushes against the limits of that discourse; although it permits the Indian subject to speak in his "own" voice, it substantially translates that voice.

Lucullus Virgil McWhorter met the Nez Percé warrior Yellow Wolf in 1907, midway through the period when the United States looked to solve its Indian problem through the process of Americanization. With the "close" of the "frontier" in 1890, it was as if the Indian had dropped out of history; from that point on, for the Native to survive could only mean, as one Commissioner of Indian Affairs put it, that the American Indian would have to become the Indian American. Abandoned by history and soon, apparently, to lose his distinctive culture, the Indian became the privileged subject of science, of a new, professional, academically based anthropology. Ethnographic "salvage" became the order of the day, an urgent effort to preserve as artifact and text what could not— as these anti-evolutionist anthropologists seemed to agree with their evolutionist fellow citizens—be preserved as living lifeway.

McWhorter did not publish Yellow Wolf's story, however, until 1940, by which time a new federal policy toward the Indian had been established. The key legislation in this instance was the Wheeler-Howard or Indian Reorganization Act of 1934, passed at the urging of John Collier, FDR's Commissioner of Indian Affairs. With Wheeler-Howard, the government officially recognized the dignity and worth of Native cultures and committed itself to their preservation,

rather than to their destruction through Americanization.
McWhorter's sympathy for the Indians and his bitter doubts
about the values of "civilization" are expressed from the
first, in the Dedication to *Yellow Wolf: His Own Story,* which
reads:

> To the shades of patriotic warriors, heroic women, feeble age, and help-
> less infancy—sacrificed on the gold-weighted altars of Mammon and
> political chicanery, 1863–77, are these pages most fervently inscribed.
> (n.p.)

McWhorter centers Yellow Wolf's life story, as Patterson had
done with Black Hawk's, on an Indian "war," in this case, the
famous flight of the Nez Percés in 1877. McWhorter does not
claim, however, that it was Yellow Wolf who asked to tell his
story in order to set the record straight, acknowledging that it
was he who proposed the formal project of an autobiographical collaboration. In this, McWhorter's practice is rather like
that of his contemporaries, the early anthropological editors of
Indian autobiography, among them Paul Radin and Truman
Michelson, who pressed possible informants for their life stories. Unlike the anthropologists, however, McWhorter was
more interested in history than in personality-and-culture;
and, unlike them in this as well, McWhorter—as the Dedication quoted above indicates—pretended to no purely objective, "scientific" stance.

In 1877, the Nez Percés had been ordered to exchange the
million or so acres they held in what is now eastern Oregon
for a twelve-hundred-acre reservation in Idaho. Although
Young Joseph, their principal peace chief, sought to comply, a
series of events led him along with Looking Glass and other
traditional Nez Percé leaders to resolve on an escape to Can-

ada. The flight of the Nez Percés took four months and covered thirteen hundred miles, ending a mere thirty miles short
of the Canadian border where Joseph surrendered to Colonel
Nelson Miles. Yellow Wolf, twenty-one years old in 1877 and
an active participant in the entire campaign, did not come in
with Joseph but slipped off, managing to cross into Canada
with Chief White Bird and his band.

McWhorter casts Yellow Wolf's story as an autobiography
but from the outset he makes apparent his understanding that
Yellow Wolf's "own" story cannot be his alone, that it cannot, I mean to say, come into being as a purely private enter-
prise. For one thing, there is the presence and voice of
McWhorter himself to consider, the whole question of the
kind and degree of participation of the editor of an Indian
autobiography. J. B. Patterson, for example, did not attempt
to dramatize his own place in the production of Black Hawk's
narrative, allowing the autobiographical "I" to mask his participation. Patterson's procedure in this regard became standard practice both for the amateur, historically-minded Indian
autobiographers of the nineteenth and twentieth centuries as
well as for the professional, social-scientifically oriented Indian
autobiographers of the early twentieth century, all of whose
texts present themselves as what they are not, the monologue
of a single speaker. In contrast, almost like the dialogically
sophisticated ethnographer of today, McWhorter begins each
of his chapters with a headnote indicating the circumstances of
the narration to follow, dating and placing the story of the
making of the story, and he interrupts Yellow Wolf's monologues within the various chapters, to speak directly in his own
voice, now to comment on Yellow Wolf's tone or narrative
manner, now to explain that Yellow Wolf is speaking in direct
response to a question McWhorter has posed, or in acknowl-

edgment of a request to follow up some earlier matter. In this regard, McWhorter never lets us forget that Yellow Wolf's story results from a dialogue in the field, that it is the cross-talk of two men, representatives of two cultures—and representatives as well of two modes of cultural transmission, the one oral, the other textual.[15]

McWhorter's practice insists upon the fact that what we perceive as written was in actuality spoken, and he regularly notes shifts in tone, pauses, or changes in diction on Yellow Wolf's part, refusing to erase the inevitable gaps and fissures of the actual narrative event to produce the illusion of the unified, seamless textual object. A sense of the actual process of cross-cultural encounter itself, much in the way Dennis Tedlock has urged, has not been erased from the final text. Still, McWhorter's primary concern is not the rhetorical and affective force of Yellow Wolf's narration, nor its status as Otherness and Difference; what is wanted foremost is historical accuracy. For all his sympathy with the Nez Percés, McWhorter writes Yellow Wolf's autobiography not even to dramatize a powerful sense of personal self, but, rather, to record the public *truth*. McWhorter's manner of approaching this truth is also dialogic, for he will include in the narrative not only his own and Yellow Wolf's voices but a great many other voices, among them the voices of those, like General O. O. Howard and Colonel Nelson Miles, who were the adversaries and conquerors of the Nez Percés, and whose sympathy

15. In these regards McWhorter might be compared to Dr. Thomas Marquis, editor of *A Warrior who Fought Custer,* the autobiography of the Cheyenne, Wooden Leg. Marquis includes himself less fully then McWhorter and only by way of footnotes that supplement and comment on Wooden Leg's remarks, yet this is more than the anthropologists of the period do. Like McWhorter, Marquis was an amateur and interested in historical truth rather than in culture.

to them and to their cause was by no means uncomplicated or assured. McWhorter's book contains notes and appendices (to individual chapters as well as to the text in its entirety) which quote widely and at length from the published and unpublished testimony of participants in and eyewitnesses to the events in question. There are also citations from official government reports, from the published and unpublished letters and documents of Army officers, and from responses to McWhorter's own specific queries. These texts multiply the languages of *Yellow Wolf: His Own Story,* each of them serving, as Bakhtin remarked of the many languages of the novel, as ". . . a point of view, a socio-ideological conceptual system of real social groups and their embodied representatives" (1981, 411). Yellow Wolf's story is the story of his time and his world in all its multiplicity, and L. V. McWhorter does not seek to reduce the heteroglossia of that world to a single, univocal language. (Nonetheless, as Brumble has remarked, McWhorter not only followed the Chronological Imperative but explicitly coaxed Yellow Wolf to speak of his childhood: at least McWhorter allows us, right within the text, to recognize that he has done so.)

Of course, McWhorter did not learn to admire and respect novelistic many-languagedness from his great Russian contemporary; he did, however, discover it as a value much prized by the Indians. In a headnote to the second chapter, describing his first interviews with Yellow Wolf, McWhorter recalls how he was

surprised to see Yellow Wolf and interpreter Hart walking up from the river, accompanied by Two Moons, Roaring Eagle, and Chief David Williams, all of the Joseph band. These men came and sat through each day's session, mostly in silence, but there was an occasional short confer-

ence held in their own language. It was not until afterwards that I
learned it was customary to have witnesses to what was said. The
listeners, should they detect error, intentional or otherwise, in statements, were privileged to make corrections. (34)[16]

This was the custom not, to be sure, for autobiography as
such, which did not exist, but for the telling of *coup* stories,
which were always at one and the same time private and
public, original and augmentative in both content and form,
the New World's equivalent, as one might say, of novelized
discourse, or, better, instances of that storytelling which presents the collective self.

Monologue and dialogue, then, may be traced in Native
American autobiography from the first examples of autobiography by Indians and Indian autobiographies to the most recent instances of both forms. In every case, as I have tried to
suggest, the tendency toward monoglossia or heteroglossia
cannot be—as Bakhtin made it easier for us to see—the result
of a merely idiosyncratic or purely personal choice. For the
single voice on which the monologist settles is never his or
hers alone, but is derived from a social hegemony, as the
many voices that the dialogist might represent are always the
voices of social others. Monologue and dialogue, then, are

---

16. Marquis encountered the same practice in his work with Wooden Leg. He
concludes his "Author's Statement" noting,

> The principal story-teller's statements of essential facts have been amalga-
> mated with those of his fellow tribesmen who fought as companions with
> him. Groups of them, with him as the leader, took the author many times into
> assemblage. Thus all points of importance have been checked and corrobo-
> rated or corrected. The helpers have been Limpy, Pine, Bobtail Horse, Sun
> Bear, Black Horse, Two Feathers, Wolf Chief, Little Sun, Blackbird, Big
> Beaver, White Moon, While Wolf, Big Crow, Medicine Bull, the younger
> Little Wolf, and other old men, as well as some old women and a few Sioux,
> all of whom were with the hostile Indians when Custer came. (ix)

terms that indicate a method and also name an end—just as the Formalists' central concept, *ostranenie,* "defamiliarization" or making strange, was both technological and teleological at once. To attempt to present many voices in one's text has the result of legitimating those voices; to present one language alone is to send a warning to all other languages to beware.

iv.

To bring these reflections nearly to the present, I should like to offer some comments on Leslie Marmon Silko's *Storyteller* (1981) in relation to the questions of monologue and dialogue I have raised by reference to Bakhtin and to current anthropological theory.

Merely to consider *Storyteller* among Native American autobiographies might be thought to require some explanation, inasmuch as the book is a collection of stories, poems, and photographs as much as it is a narrative of its author's life. Of course a variety of claims have been made recently for the fictionality of autobiographies in general, the autobiography being recognized not only as the West's foremost genre oriented toward the expression of the self, but, too, its most deeply dialogic genre in which a conversation between *historia* and *poesis,* documentation and creation, let us say, is always in progress. And some of these claims might easily be instanced as providing justification for classifying *Storyteller* as an autobiography.

Indeed, to justify the book's classification as an autobiography in this way would not be mistaken; it would, however, be to treat it exclusively from a Western perspective, and so to fail to acknowledge that traditional Native American literary forms did not—and, in their contemporary manifestations usually do not—seem to be as concerned about keeping fiction and fact or poetry and prose quite so distinct from one another as the West has been.

From the Western point of view, of course, to the extent that Silko's book is permissibly classified as an autobiography, it would seem to announce by its title, *Storyteller,* the familiar pattern in which one discovers who one is as an individual by discovering what one does socially, the pattern of identity in vocation. This is useful enough as a way to place Silko's text; still, it has been a very long time in the West since the vocational storyteller—different from the speaker of the word of God in this—has had a clear and conventional social role.[17] In Pueblo culture, to be known as

17. An important reference here, I think, is to Walter Benjamin whose beautiful "The Storyteller," wavers between secular-historicist and religious-timeless perspectives on this matter (as on so many others). Benjamin conceives of storytellers both in relation to artistic and artisanal practices and "the secular productive forces of history" (87) but also in relation to such things as "death": "Death is the sanction of everything that the storyteller can tell. He has borrowed his authority from death. In other words, it is natural history to which his stories refer back" (94). Native American stories also straddle these two perspectives referring both to the immediate and concrete as well as to the remote and mythic. Compare Silko

> Pueblo oral tradition necessarily embraced all levels of human experience. . . .
> Thus stories about the Creation and Emergence of human beings and animals
> into this World continue to be retold each year. . . . The "humma-hah" stories
> related events from the time long ago when human beings were still able to
> communicate with animals and other living things. But, beyond these two
> preceding categories, the Pueblo oral tradition knew no boundaries [. . . , so
> that] Accounts of the first Europeans in Pueblo country or of tragic encoun-
> ters between Pueblo people and Apache raiders were no more and no less
> important than stories about the biggest mule deer ever taken or adulterous
> couples surprised in cornfields and chicken coops. (1986, 87)

Native American storytellers, predictably enough, can also see themselves voca-
tionally, now in relation to their legendary similarity to their predecessors, now
in relation to their inevitable historical difference from them. My focus on the
social dimension of Native American storytelling is an attempt to see these two
perspectives as integrated—but a study (for example) of Walter Benjamin and
Native American narrative would help me (and others) with these matters.

a storyteller is to be known as one who participates in a traditionally sanctioned manner in sustaining the community; for a Native American writer to identify herself as a storyteller today is to express a desire to perform such a function. In the classic terms of Marcel Mauss, person, self, and role are here joined.

Silko dedicates her book "to the storytellers as far back as memory goes and to the telling which continues and through which they all live and we with them." Having called herself a storyteller, she thus places herself in a tradition of tellings, suggesting what will be the case, that the stories to follow, Silko's "own" stories, cannot strictly be her own; nor will we find in them what one typically looks for in post-Rousseauian, Western autobiography—or, as Bakhtin would add, in poetry—a uniquely personal voice. There is no single, distinctive, or authoritative voice in Silko's book nor any striving for such a voice (or style); to the contrary, Silko will take pains to indicate how even her own individual speech is the product of many voices.[18] *Storyteller* is presented as a strongly polyphonic text, in which the author defines herself—finds her voice, tells her life, illustrates the capacities of her vocation—in relation to the voices of other storytellers Native and non-Native, tale tellers and book writers, and even to the voices of those who serve as the (by-no-means silent) audience for these stories.

It is Silko's biographical voice which commences *Storyteller* but not by speaking of her birth or the earliest recollections of childhood, as Western autobiography usually dictates. Rather,

18. Cf. Silko, "Traditionally everyone, from the youngest child to the oldest person, was expected to listen and to be able to recall or tell a portion, if only a small detail, from a narrative account or story. Thus the remembering and retelling were a communal process" (1986, 87).

she begins by establishing the relation of "hundreds of photographs taken since the 1890s around Laguna" that she finds in "a tall Hopi basket" to "the stories as [she] remembers them" (1): visual stories, speaking pictures, here, as in the familiar Western understanding, will also provide a voice. And Silko's relation to every kind of story becomes the story of her life. (It is interesting to note, however, that there is no developmental or evolutionary dimension to the story of Silko as storyteller: unlike Western autobiographies of artists, that is, she makes no attempt to dramatize *stages* in the recognition or choice of an artistic vocation; certainly she does not explain the reasons, however retrospectively perceived, that may have led her to do what she does.)

Dennis Tedlock has made the important point that Zuni stories are fashioned in such a way as to include in their telling not just the story itself but a critique of or commentary on those stories, and Silko's autobiographical story will also permit a critical dimension, voices that comment on stories and storytellers—storytellers like her Aunt Susie, in *Storyteller,* who, when she told stories, had "certain phrases, certain distinctive words/she used in her telling" (7). Both Aunt Susie and Aunt Alice "would tell me stories they had told me before but with changes in details or descriptions. . . . There were even stories about the different versions of stories and how they imagined these different versions came to be" (227). Silko's own "versions" of stories she has heard from Simon Ortiz, the Acoma writer whom Silko acknowledges as the source of her prose tale, "Uncle Tony's Goat," and her verse tale, "Skeleton Fixer," also introduce "certain phrases" and "distinctive words" that make them identifiably her own—yet these and all the other stories are never presented as the final or definitive account: although they are intensely associated with

their different tellers, they remain available for other tellings.[19]
"What is realized in the novel," Bakhtin has written "is the
process of coming to know one's own language as it is perceived in someone else's language . . ." (1981, 365), and so,

19. And, indeed, there are other tellings, most noticeably those by Silko
herself: many of the stories in *Storyteller,* that is, have appeared elsewhere, some
of them in several places, but all seem to have slight variations. Of course, it may
be that Silko is just trying to get the most mileage she can out of what she's done,
a practice not unknown both to fiction writers and essay writers, Native and
non-Native. But in the context of Native American storytelling, repetition of the
"same" story on several different occasions is standard procedure, "originality"
or noticeable innovation having no particular value. It should also be noted that
the retellings of Silko's stories are not exact reprintings. For example, "The Man
to Send Rain Clouds," as it appears in Kenneth Rosen's anthology of the same
name and in *Storyteller,* have slight differences. In Rosen's anthology there are
numbered sections of the story (one to four), while there are only space breaks in
Storyteller (no numbers). In the first paragraph of the Rosen version, Levis are
"light-blue" while in *Storyteller* they are "light blue"; "blue mountains were still
deep in snow" (3) in Rosen while in *Storyteller* "blue mountains were still in
snow" (182). If we turn to the story called "Uncle Tony's Goat" in both books,
we find differences in the endings. In Rosen, the story ends this way:
Tony finished the cup of coffee. "He's probably in Quemado by now."
    I thought his voice sounded strong and happy when he said this, and I
looked at him again, standing there by the door, ready to go milk the nanny
goats. He smiled at me.
    "There wasn't ever a goat like that one," he said, "but if that's the way he's
going to act, O.K. then. That damn goat got pissed off too easy anyway."
(99–100)
The ending in *Storyteller* goes:
"He's probably in Quemado by now."
    I looked at him again, standing there by the door, ready to go milk the
nanny goats.
    "There wasn't ever a goat like that one," he said, "but if that's the way he's
going to act, O.K. then. That damn goat got pissed off too easy anyway."
He smiled at me and his voice was strong and happy when he said this. (18)
The differences in the first example may not amount to much, while those in the
second might suggest a slight change in emphasis; a systematic study of the
differences in Silko's retellings (something I have not attempted to do) might tell
us something about her development as a writer—or might not be all that substantial. My point here is that Silko's retellings in writing, whether she is aware

too, to know one's own language as bound up with "someone else's language." Any story Silko herself tells, then, is always bound up with "someone else's language"; it is always a version, and the story as *version* stands in relation to the story as officially sanctioned myth as the novel stands to the national epic. Silko's stories are consistent with—to return to Bakhtin—attempts to liberate "cultural-semantic and emotional intentions from the hegemony of a single and unitary language," consistent with a "loss of feeling for language as myth, that is, as an absolute form of thought" (1981, 367).

Stories are transmitted by other storytellers, as Silko writes early in *Storyteller,*

> by word of mouth
> an entire history
> an entire vision of the world
> which depended upon memory
> and retelling by subsequent generations.
> . . . .
> . . . the oral tradition depends upon each person
> listening and remembering a portion. (6–7)

But the awareness of and respect for the oral tradition, here, is not a kind of sentimental privileging of the old ways. Indeed, this first reference to the importance of cultural transmission by oral means comes in a lovely memorial to Aunt Susie who, Silko writes,

---

of this or not (and it is always possible that different versions come into existence as a result of the demands of different editors rather than as a result of Silko's own determinations), tend to parallel what we know of the oral retellings of traditional narrators.

> From the time that I can remember her
> . . . worked on her kitchen table
> with her books and papers spread over the oil cloth.
> She wrote beautiful long hand script
> but her eyesight was not good
> and so she wrote very slowly.
>
> . . . .
>
> She had come to believe very much in books. (4)

It is Aunt Susie, the believer in books and in writing, who was of "the last generation here at Laguna,/that passed an entire culture by word of mouth." Silko's own writing can be seen as a kind of frontier on which two modes of cultural transmission meet when it is explicitly compared to oral telling by a neighbor. Finding Silko's "Laguna Coyote" poem in a library book, Nora remarks,

> "We all enjoyed it so much,
> but I was telling the children
> the way my grandpa used to tell it
> is longer."

To this critical voice, Silko responds,

> "Yes, that's the trouble with writing . . .
> You can't go on and on the way we do
> when we tell stories around here.
> People who aren't used to it get tired." (110)

This awareness of the audience is entirely typical for a Native storyteller who cannot go forward with a tale without the audience's response. As Silko writes,

> *The Laguna people*
> *always begin their stories*
> *with "humma-hah":*
> *that means "long ago."*
> *And the ones who are listening*
> *say "aaaa-eh"*[.] (38)

These are the stories, of course, of the oral tradition. Silko invokes the feel of "long ago" both in the verse format she frequently uses and in the prose pieces, although perhaps only those sections of the book set in verse attempt to evoke something of the actual feel of an oral telling.

It is interesting to note that there are two pieces in the book that echo the title, one in prose, the other set in loose verse. The first, "Storyteller," is an intense and powerful short story that takes place in Alaska. The storyteller of the title is the protagonist's grandfather, a rather less benign figure, it seems to me, than the old storytellers of Silko's biographical experience; nonetheless, the stories he tells are of the traditional "mythic" type. The second, "Storytelling," is a kind of mini-anthology of (I think) five short tales of women and their (quite historical, if fictional) sexual adventures. The "humma-hah" (in effect) of the first section goes,

> You should understand
> the way it was
> back then,
> because it is the same
> even now. (94)
> [aaaa-eh]

The final section has its unnamed speaker conclude,

My husband
left
after he heard the story
and moved back in with his mother.
It was my fault and
I don't blame him either.
I could have told
the story
better than I did. (98)

In both these pieces ("Storyteller" and "Storytelling") we find
a very different sense of verbal art from that expressed in the
West in something like Auden's lines in the poem on the death
of Yeats, where he writes that "poetry makes nothing happen."
In deadly serious prose and in witty verse, Silko dramatizes her
belief, in common with all Native people, that stories—both
the mythic-traditional tales passed down among the people
and the day-to-day narrations of events—do make things happen. The two pieces refer to very different *kinds* of stories
which, in their capacity to produce material effects, are nonetheless the same.

Among other identifiable voices in Silko's texts are her
own epistolary voice (to call it that) in letters she has written
to Lawson F. Inada and James A. Wright, or the voices of
Coyote and Buffalo, as well as of traditional figures like
Whirlwind Man, Arrowboy, Spider Woman, and Yellow
Woman—some of whom appear in modern day incarna-
tions. In stories or letters or poems, in monologues or dialogues, the diction may vary—now more colloquial and/or
regional, now more formal—or the tone—lyrical, humor-
ous, meditative—yet always the effort is to make us hear the
various languages that constitute Silko's world and so her
sense of human agency, or her *self*. If we would say with

Bakhtin that "The primary stylistic project of the novel as a genre is to create images of languages" (1981, 366), or, with the retreat from an imperializing realistic mode in ethnography, say with Kevin Dwyer that anthropology "is a wager that destroys the notion of an isolated and independent self" (273), then *Storyteller* is a clear instance of novelized, of dialogic discourse.

v.

The texts I have examined thus far have been presented in such a way as might seem to suggest a definite historical shift from monologism to dialogism in the writing of Native American autobiography, as if William Apes had operated according to a fashion now superceded by the mode of Leslie Silko; as if J. B. Patterson's construction of the *Life of Black Hawk* had rendered obsolete by the procedures of L. V. McWhorter in *Yellow Wolf.* This is not so: the autobiographies of N. Scott Momaday, on the one hand, and Joseph Brant's collaboration with Jim Whitewolf, or Thomas Mails' work with Frank Fools Crow, on the other, stand to indicate that monologism or the desire for same is alive and well in contemporary Native American autobiography, whether in Indian autobiography or autobiography by Indians.

What is worth remarking, however, is how extremely difficult it seems to be to write as an Indian (even as an Indian minister of Christ, or a self-conscious modernist Indian artist) without some measure of polyphony entering one's text. For all that the Indian author of an autobiography may wish to privilege a single perspective and a single stylistic practice, it usually turns out that there are, nonetheless, traces of other voices, even, it may be, other voices of the author herself, if not actually in the text then in the margins. To the extent that this is true (I offer some illustration of why I think it may be true in just a moment), it seems tempting to attribute it to the historical formation of the Native American as subject, to her collective sense of self, and to the persistence within the European-derived autobiographical form of traditional Native American narrative forms—which, as I have tried to indicate in the discussion of *Storyteller,* also tend to the collective, mixed, or heteroglossic.

But just as it seems difficult for the Native person to appropriate the authority of one voice alone, so, too, is it difficult for the non-Native editor of an Indian autobiography to write for (even, sometimes, with) his subject without being pulled toward a dominant, univocal discursive manner. For all that non-Native editors may sympathize with and be open to Native voices, the necessity of accommodating their texts to the conventions that determine what the dominant culture can take seriously as history or social science in the realm of truth, exerts considerable pressure against the sound of any substantial difference. This tendency is very likely also attributable to the historical formation of the Euramerican as subject, but as well, to the formation of disciplines in the cultures of the West. In what follows, I offer examples of the persistence of (some degree of) dialogism in ostensibly monologic autobiographies by Indians, with some further reference to the resistances to (degrees of) dialogism in Indian autobiographies.

Let us begin with William Apes whose autobiography, I have claimed, is militant in its attempt to subsume all voices to the single voice of Christian salvationism. Four years after the publication of *A Son of the Forest* (1829; hereinafter abbreviated *ASOF*), Apes, now "a preacher of the gospel" (20) who refers to himself as "The Missionary," published the *Experiences of Five Christian Indians of the Pequod Tribe* (1833;

(abbreviated as "Experience"). This is an anthology of biography and autobiography made up of brief life histories of Hannah Caleb, Sally George, and Anne Wampy written "By the Missionary," as well as a self-written account by Apes's wife, Mary ("Experience of the Missionary's Consort, Written by Herself"). It begins with the "Experience of the Missionary," that is, of Apes himself. This curious volume also has appended to it an eight-page text—a pamphlet, or sermon, as it were—called "An Indian's Looking Glass for the White Man."

Apes's "Experience" does not make reference to the earlier autobiography, promising, instead, a third autobiographical volume "should the Lord spare my life, a book of 300 pages, 18 mo. in size; and there, the reader will find particulars respecting my life" (4). In most respects, to be sure, this second autobiography simply duplicates, in condensed fashion, Apes's first—although there are some minor variations of detail. For example, Apes now gives his birthday as the "30th day of January," 1798, instead of the thirty-first as in *ASOF* (4), or places an incident in his fourteenth year (14) that had formerly been assigned to his fifteenth (*ASOF*, 43); he remembered getting only a cold potato for dinner in *ASOF* (10), whereas he now recalls that potato for breakfast ("Experience," 4); and so forth. More substantially, it might be noted that whereas in 1829, he found the term Indian a misnomer if not an outright slur, in 1833 he uses it without comment, and uses it regularly in referring to himself (e.g., "Experience," 1, 7–9) as the "self-taught Indian youth," the "little Indian boy," or the "poor little Indian boy." (And then there is the appended "Looking Glass," in whose title the term appears, with no irony, as well.)

Apes's very first paragraph, however, refers to Indians with reference to the title of his earlier book. He invokes the plight of

those poor children of the forest, who have had taken from them their once delightful plains, and homes of their peaceful habitations; their fathers and mothers torn from their dwellings and they left to mourn, and drop a tear, and die, over the ruins of their ancient sires. ("Experience," n.p.)

This has occurred, writes Apes, as the result of "deception and power, assisted with the fiery waters of the earth— Rum." We have here rather stronger language than what Apes formerly allowed himself, and he uses it as part of an indictment of the whites' virulent race prejudice against Native people. Contrary to what he experienced as a child, Apes notes, white children have "not a nation to hiss at" them only for the color of their skin ("Experience," 5). In reference to the tribulations of his early life, Apes says,

Had my skin been white with the same abilities and the same parentage, there could not have been found a place good enough for me. But such is the case with depraved nature, that their judgment for fancy only sets upon the eye, skin, nose, lips, cheeks, chin or teeth, and sometimes the forehead and hair; without any further examination the mind is made up and the price set. ("Experience," 8)

"Now, if my face had been white," he writes a page later, "it would have been a town talk [that he was not taken to church of a sabbath]. But as it was an Indian face, no matter whether it was dirty or poor, or whether I had clothing or not" (9–10). This sort of criticism is repeated several times more (e.g., 17, 19). And this gives the clue, perhaps, to why Apes's book concludes the way it does, with the "Indian's Looking Glass."

For the central concern of that text is race prejudice. Or, put another way, the "Looking Glass" prominently adds the voice of social justice to the voice of salvationism, integrating the two. Let me quote Apes's extraordinary opening to this text at some length, for it is little known, I think, and deserves more attention than it has received. Apes begins,

Having a desire to place a few things before my fellow creatures who are travelling with me to the grave, and to that God who is the maker and preserver both of the white man and the Indian, whose abilities are the same, and who are to be judged by one God, who will show no favor to outward appearances, but will judge righteousness. Now I ask if degradation will not be heaped long enough upon the Indians? And if so, can there not be a compromise; is it right to hold and promote prejudices? If not, why not put them all away? I mean here amongst those who are civilized. (54)

Acknowledging "that this is a confused world and I am not seeking for office" (55), Apes puns upon the folly of "the black inconsistency" of race prejudice "which is ten times blacker than any skin that you will find in the Universe" (55). "If black or red skins, or any other skin of color," he continues,

is disgraceful to God, it appears that he has disgraced himself a great deal—for he has made fifteen colored people to one white, and placed them here upon this earth. (55)

The argument builds in intensity, and the diction and syntax, as well as the punctuation, come dangerously close to sliding away from "good" style: "What then is the matter now," Apes asks, "is not religion the same now under a colored skin as it ever was? If so I would ask why is not a man of color respected . . . [?] Jesus Christ and his Apostles never

looked at the outward appearances" (57). Apes goes on in this
vein, marching directly up to the dreaded question of inter-
marriage and criticizing "the disgraceful act in the statute
law" of Massachusetts levying a fifty pound fine upon "any
Clergyman or Justice of the Peace that dare [*sic*] to encourage
the laws of God and nature by a legitimate union in holy
wedlock between the Indians and whites" (59). The irony that
was absent or invisible formerly in Apes here is pointedly and
consistently aimed: "But . . . I am not looking for a wife,
having one of the finest cast" (59). "By what you read, you
may learn how deep your principles are. I should say they
were skin deep" (60). At last, he concludes,

> Do not get tired, ye noble-hearted—only think how many poor Indians
> want their wounds done up daily; the Lord will reward you, and pray
> you stop not till this tree of distinction shall be levelled to the earth, and
> the mantle of prejudice torn from every American heart—then shall
> peace pervade the Union. (60)

Perhaps it is not too much to suggest that Apes, here, looks
forward to the concerns and discourse of the pre-Civil War
period—for this passage sounds like what is rhetorically more
common in 1853 than in 1833; surely it is not too much to
suggest that it looks back to Apes's "Experience" where the
"poor little Indian boy" was both literally (Apes suffered a
great deal of brutality as a child) and figuratively in much
want of having his "wounds done up daily." And this strong
emphasis on Native American suffering as a result of Euramerican race prejudice appears to be very different from the
emphasis of Apes's first autobiography.

But, then, it may not be so very different, on another look.
For, although the language here is certainly less guarded and
more willing to allow anger at injustice to sound, a return to

A Son of the Forest reveals more than one might first have
noticed of at least a version of just this sort of thing. The first
paragraph of *ASOF,* for example, did describe the *betrayal* of
King Philip and the Pequods, referring to acts of "injustice"
to an "oppressed nation." In 1829 it was not first Rum, but,
rather, "having their daughters claimed by the conquerors"
(*ASOF,* 8) that Apes singled out as productive of a "more
intense and heart corroding affliction" imposed upon his dis-
possessed people. Criticism of the whites for the introduction
of "ardent spirits" (*ASOF,* 14) among the Indians does not, in
fact, occur until several pages later, nor is that criticism ever
developed into the full-blown critique of racism to be found
in Apes's writing of 1833. Apes's conversion and his exhortation of white and red to a Christian life is so much in the
forefront of *ASOF* that his social criticism may tend to go
unnoticed. Yet—and this is my point—it is definitely there:
and it cán be seen with great clarity the moment one rereads
ASOF through the glass of Apes's subsequent autobiography
as given in the *Experience.*

Or for that matter, rereads it through any of his succeeding
work: his *Indian Nullification of the Unconstitutional Laws of
Massachusetts Relative to the Marshpee Tribe: or the Pretended Riot
Explained* (1835), a text which details what has to be called his
political engagement on behalf of the Mashpees (for which
Apes served time in prison); and his *Eulogy on King Philip,* the
text of a sermon preached in 1836. In this latter text, Apes
calls Philip "the greatest man that was ever in America; and so
it will stand, until he is proved to the contrary, to the everlasting disgrace of the pilgrims' [*sic*] fathers." (55–56) Apes's
again and again attacks racism as the affliction equivalently (if
differently) suffered by all people of color. Apes goes so far as
to say,

Let the children of the pilgrims blush, while the son of the forest drops a tear, and groans over the fate of his murdered and departed fathers. He would say to the sons of the pilgrims, (as Job said about his birth day,) let the day be dark, the 22d of December, 1622; let it be forgotten in your celebration, in your speeches, and by the burying of the Rock that your fathers first put their foot upon. . . . We say, therefore, let every man of color wrap himself in mourning, for the 22d of December and the 4th of July are days of mourning and not of joy. (1836, 20)

These strong words, first spoken in Boston, to the descendants of the Pilgrims, saw print and even a second edition, in 1837—after which, rather mysteriously, Apes seems to disappear from public record; no date or place is known for his death. While I would still claim that the voice of salvationism is, indeed, the dominant voice of Apes's fullest and best known (for all that, it is little known) autobiography, it should be clear that reading it back through Apes's later work reveals that that is not the only voice.

The Native American writer most committed to hegemonic monologue, to the all-encompassing voice of lyric or epic, romantic or modernist art-speech in his writing has always seemed to me N. Scott Momaday. Momaday is not only the best known and most celebrated contemporary Native American writer, recipient of a Pulitzer Prize for fiction (1969), but, for Silko's work to date, the presumptive groundbreaker or forefather. Her *Ceremony* (1977), it is said (with some justice), is heavily dependent upon his *House Made of Dawn* (1968); her *Storyteller* (1981) perhaps no more than a rerun of his *The Names* (1976). And, so far as Native American autobiography is concerned, there is also Momaday's earlier *The Way to Rainy Mountain* (1969) to consider. This latter text, it has been claimed, offers three different voices in its tripartite arrangement of its materials into (I take here Alan

Velie's description) "a legend or story, a historical anecdote or observation, and a personal reminiscence" (Velie, 24). Moreover, inasmuch as *The Names* precedes *Storyteller* in its use of family photographs, quotation, and —if not poems and stories, at least—stream of consciousness meditations, "poetry" if one would call it that—it would appear that this text as well requires attention from anyone interested in the development of dialogic autobiography and the collective self.

Yet what I find everywhere in Momaday's work is a determination toward what Bakhtin calls "poetry" in its most extreme "epic" sense, to the establishment, that is, of a single authoritative voice, with its own "unique" or "personal" style, sufficiently distinctive to subordinate all other voices, everywhere translating them into the terms congenial to it. Critics may debate whether Momaday's tone in the two autobiographies is more accurately described as elegiac or simply lyrical: what one cannot miss is that whatever the name appropriate to that tone it rarely varies. There is very little in the way of wit or humor, no gossip or scatology, decidedly no self-criticism or criticism by others permitted to sound. But how could there be for a writer who opens *The Way to Rainy Mountain* by calling his reflections on the end of his people's traditional culture "idle recollections, the mean and ordinary agonies of human history" (1). History, for Momaday is only interesting as the stuff of myth, "agonies," I dare say, uninteresting so long as they remain "mean and ordinary."

Let me quote the third of the three parts of the very first section of *The Way to Rainy Mountain* by way of illustrating some of the comments above. This is the "personal" section, following upon the "legendary" section which portrays the "coming out" or emergence of the Kiowa, and then the "historical" section (in my view once again "legendary" inasmuch as Momaday has no historical sense whatever), explaining the origin of the name, "Kiowa." Here, Momaday, speaking, it would seem, in his "own," "personal" voice, says,

I remember coming out upon the northern Great Plains in the late Spring. There were meadows of blue and yellow wildflowers on the slopes, and I could see the still sunlit plain below reaching away out of sight. At first there is no discrimination in the eye, nothing but the land itself, whole and impenetrable. But then smallest things begin to stand out of the depths—and each of these has perfect being in terms of distance and of silence and of age. Yes, I thought, now I see the earth as it really is; never again will I see things as I saw them yesterday or the day before. (19)

Navajo autobiographies in which the protagonist recalls lonely times in the hills with the flocks often convey some degree of the isolation Momaday notes in this passage; autobiographical texts from the Plains document the aloneness felt at moments by the youth engaged in vision quest. But I have seen no Native American autobiography that ever took such aloneness-with-the-landscape as definitive or instrumental in the shaping of a world view or personal self. For most Native Americans, it could not be this sort of casual—if highly charged—random and unprepared moment *alone* that could show "the earth as it really is." In any case, the category "as it really is" in itself is more Western than Native American, as is that of "perfect being" (which may, as well, echo Buddhist teaching). For that matter, the notion of the land as "impenetrable" is quite foreign to indigenous conceptions: who could or would imagine *penetrating* the land— except, as Annette Kolodny has shown, a fairly typical American (not Native American) male.[20] For all of this,

20. See *The Lay of the Land.*

what I want most to point up is the commitment to a tone of high portentousness: everything in Momaday begs for an upper case letter; and every sentence in Momaday, since day-to-day temporal "agonies" are of no interest, is capable of the "Yes" of mythic affirmation.

What is true of *Rainy Mountain,* is true as well of *The Names:* there is everywhere the predominance of Momaday's distinctive lyric/epic art-speech. In this regard it is interesting to note that whereas the photographs in Silko's autobiographical text appear without captions (they are identified at the end of *Storyteller* but there are no markings along the way to tell the reader that they will be identified, let alone to tell the reader just what names Silko herself would give to these pictures), Momaday has seen fit to provide captions for his photos. Here, too, there is the determination to full control; the photos may speak as they will to their viewers, but they may do so only in the presence of Momaday's own cues as to their content or meaning. Here is a passage from *The Names,* one, I ask the reader to believe, I chose at random: it was in the center of the page to which I simply opened the book in search of an illustrative passage.

Gallup is a rough-edged town of dubious character and many surfaces of rich color. It is a place of high tensions and hard distinctions. I once heard someone say that Gallup is the last frontier town in America; there is a certain truth to that, I believe. On a given day you can see in the streets of Gallup cowboys and Indians, missionaries and miscreants, tradesmen and tourists. Or you can see Billy the Kid or Huckleberry Finn or Ganado Mucho—or someone who is not impossibly all these worthies in one, Everyman realized in some desperate notion of himself. (70)

Momaday writes well, let us grant, or, more exactly, his writing is readily assimilable to a tradition of elaborated prose celebrated in American literature at least from Whitman, Faulkner, and Thomas Wolfe to its degenerated continuation in Jack Kerouac. This, then, is a *friendly* and *familiar* sort of passage for the literary reader—although to say so is to adopt that florid fondness for alliteration (the last paragraph of the Introduction to *The Way to Rainy Mountain* has given us "a long and legendary way": but examples are too abundant to document)[21] that brings high tensions in tandem with hard distinctions, missionaries with miscreants, and tradesmen with tourists, among other "worthies" (a perfect pairing for "miscreants," the two archaisms balancing and so creating a mild, altogether bookish pleasantry). Whoever it may be who actually populates the town of Gallup, these people are best understood by way of literary and legendary typology, from Everyman to Billy the Kid—or whomever. In any case, no one of them, like Silko's Aunt Susie, gets to speak with his own "certain phrases/ certain distinctive words."

Obviously Momaday is free to choose whatever stylistic manner he pleases. My intent here is simply to establish that his texts seek to fix that manner univocally; his writing offers a single, invariant poetic voice that everywhere commits itself to subsuming and translating all other voices. If this assessment is at all correct, then it should be clear that however much Leslie Marmon Silko may appear to be reproducing Momaday's work with a different content, any reproduction on her part represents a radical revision, for, as I have at-

---

21. The passion for alliteration is apparent in *House Made of Dawn* as well: "Later, when their *ch*ores were done, the *ch*ildren of the town would run out to see, to stand at the fences and *ch*eer and *ch*ide . . ." (66). "She ar*ch*ed her throat and her eyes glanced upward to the dark *c*eiling and *s*ource of *s*o much *s*ound . . . She could hear only the *r*oar of the *r*ain . . . across the *r*oad and *r*umble and *r*ush of the *r*iver . . ." (70–71), followed by "*m*ean and *m*yriad fears," "*f*ood and *f*ires of the *f*east," etc. (71).

tempted to show earlier, Silko's autobiographical writing is as firmly oriented toward dialogue and polyphony as Momaday's is toward monologue.

For all of this, not even Momaday can achieve the representation of himself as a Native American without allowing other voices than his own a certain trace. However he may want to translate all speech into Western art-speech, his texts, in much the same way as Silko's, remain possible only in relation to the speech of others. Just as a full reading of William Apes's *A Son of the Forest* must manage to hear the socially oppositional voice of Apes's "Experience," along with the voice of salvationism, so, too, must a full reading of Momaday's two autobiographies manage to hear other voices—however, in this case, faintly. In *The Way to Rainy Mountain,* I can at least note specifically the voices of James Mooney and George Catlin,[22] the one representing the perspective of late nineteenth- and early twentieth-century ethnographic "science," the other of nineteenth-century art.

Here is the first section of the first part ("The Setting Out") of *The Way to Rainy Mountain:*

You know, everything had to begin, and this is how it was: the Kiowas came one by one into the world through a hollow log. They were many more than now, but not all of them got out. There was a woman whose body was swollen up with child and she got stuck in the log. After that, no one could get through, and that is why the Kiowas are a small tribe in number. They looked all around and saw the world. It made them glad to see so many things. They called themselves *Kwuda,* "coming out." (17)

22. Both Mooney and Catlin are named in the text, but there is no cue to the reader that they are being closely paraphrased.

Under the heading—it is not the first—"Genesis and Migration," Mooney's *Calendar History of the Kiowa Indians* offers the following:

> According to Kiowa mythology, which has close parallels among other tribes, their first ancestors emerged from a hollow cottonwood log at the bidding of a supernatural progenitor. They came out one at a time until it came to the turn of a pregnant woman,[23] who stuck fast in the hole and thus blocked the way for those behind her so that they were unable to follow, which accounts for the small number of the Kiowa tribe. (152–153)

Mooney's preceding heading, "Tribal Names," had said of the Kiowa, "Ancient names used to designate themselves are *Kwu'da* and afterward *Tepda,* both names signifying 'coming out,' perhaps in allusion to their mystic origin" (152). Momaday's second section takes up the matter of naming:

> *They called themselves* Kwuda *and later* Tepda, *both of which mean "coming out." And later still they took the name* Gaigwu . . .(18)

going on to describe the hand sign for the Kiowa as "*indicated . . . by holding the hand palm up and slightly cupped to the right side of the head and rotating it back and forth from the wrist.*" To this we may compare Mooney: "The tribal sign, a quick motion of the hand past the right cheek, they explain as referring to a former custom of cutting the hair on that side on a level with the ear" (152). Momaday's conclusion to this second

23. Compare Momaday, here: "There was a woman *whose body was swollen up with child,* and she got stuck in the log" (1970, 17; my emphasis). Is this an artistic "improvement" of Mooney, a making visible/vivid what was formerly abstract? Or is it part of Momaday's insistent sexism—a subject I have never seen engaged but one that is well worth some discussion.

segment—" *'Kiowa' is thought to derive from the softened Co-manche form of* Gaigwu"—is from Mooney's first sentence (of "Tribal Names"), "Kiowa . . . is from the softened Comanche form of the name by which they call themselves, Ga'igwu'." Momaday does not indicate any reference to Mooney here.

Let me document here the single allusion I am aware of to George Catlin's vision and voice. In the second part of *The Way to Rainy Mountain*, "The Going On," the second section of chapter 15 says:

> *The artist George Catlin traveled among the Kiowas in 1834. He observes that they are superior to the Comanches and Wichita in appearance. They are tall and straight, relaxed and graceful. They have fine classical features, and in this respect they resemble more closely the tribes of the north than those of the south.* (71; author's italics)

For some reason I cannot grasp, Momaday begins a new, a third section to complete this subject. I quote it, necessarily I think, in its entirety:

> *Catlin's portrait of Kotsatoah is the striking figure of a man, tall and lean, yet powerful and fully developed. He is lithe, and he knows beyond any doubt of his great strength and vigor. He stands perfectly at ease, the long drape of his robe flowing with the lines of his body. His left hand rests upon his shield and holds a bow and arrows. His head is set firmly, and there is a look of bemused and infinite tolerance in his eyes. He is said to have been nearly seven feet tall and able to run down and kill a buffalo on foot. I should like to have seen that man, as Catlin saw him, walking towards me, or away in the distance, perhaps, alone, and against the sky.* (72; author's italics)

Now we must hear Catlin in his own voice:

> The Kioways are a much finer looking race of men, than either the Camanchees or Pawnees—are tall and erect, with an easy and graceful

gait—with long hair, cultivated oftentimes so as to reach nearly to the ground. They have generally the fine and Roman outline of head, that is so frequently found at the North,—and decidedly distinct from that of the Camanchees and Pawnee Picts. (74)

Kots-a-to-ah, the "smoked shield," Catlin writes,

is another of the extraordinary men of this tribe, near seven feet in stature, and distinguished, not only as one of the greatest warriors, but the swiftest on foot, in the nation. This man, it is said, runs down a buffalo on foot, and slays it with his knife or his lance, as he runs by its side! (75)

What Catlin specifically called Kotsatoah's Roman features become for Momaday his "classical" features—classically Indian? I think not; the classic for Momaday seems more likely to remain strictly Roman. That Kotsatoah has a look of "infinite and bemused tolerance" in his eyes is pure Momaday, not Catlin, as is the placement of Kotsatoah "alone, and against the sky," a reflex gesture of Momaday's romantic mythicism. Was Catlin (as has been suggested of Edward S. Curtis) also a romantic mythicizer? Perhaps; the question is too large for consideration here. But whatever Catlin was or was not, what he saw and described, and how he wrote was different from Momaday's vision and description: and that difference, I am suggesting, functions in Momaday's text, where a voice from nineteenth-century American art, as also a voice from nineteenth-century American "science," continues to be heard, however slightly, however faintly.[24] Still,

24. For all that Momaday has certainly tried to obscure or translate differences into his own distinctive "poetic" style. Unlike Silko, his desire is precisely—I repeat, here, the quotation I offered earlier from Bakhtin—to produce a "feeling for language as myth, . . . as an absolute form of thought."

Momaday insists upon the last word in his book; just as his first word, this will come in a piece of formal verse.

In *The Names* Momaday reuses and revises some of the material from *The Way to Rainy Mountain* (hereinafter abbreviated *WRM*), with the effect, as I have noted in the case of Silko, that we may recall its status as no more than a version (for all the trappings of univocal authority). The 'Prologue" to *WRM,* for example, has as its epigraph a prose paragraph that is identified as a "Kiowa folk tale" (1). That is no doubt correct; but the actual words here are a direct quotation of the first section of the first part of *WRM* ("You know, everything had to begin."), which, as I have shown, derives from James Mooney's written prose rather than from the oral presentation of any Kiowa storyteller. Momaday moves further from what Mooney or the Kiowa themselves might make of this with his gloss, beginning, "They were stricken, surely, nearly blind in the keep of some primordial darkness . . . ," and concluding, "They could at last say to themselves, 'We are, and our name is *Kwuda*' " (1). We are quite far here, "surely," from anything the Kiowa or James Mooney might actually have said to themselves or to anyone else: but this is N. Scott Momaday.

Momaday's commitment to a controlling monologue rests as much as anything upon his notion, as stated in *WRM,* that

A word has power in and of itself. It comes from nothing into sound and meaning; it gives origin to all things. By means of words can a man deal with the world on equal terms. And the word is sacred . . . (*WRM,* 42)

Although the Gospel according to John may agree that the "word gives origin," inasmuch as "In the beginning was the

Word," this is hardly what Native American cultures have believed nor is it what Momaday's own practice reveals. Words have power; they may indeed be sacred. But they do not come from "nothing"; "nothing" is yet another category of the West whose Native American equivalents would be hard to specify. Nor is the power of a word purely autonomous ("in and of itself"). What power there is in Momaday's own words, for example, comes from their relation to the words of others—Mooney, Catlin, Euramerican artists, even Momaday's own earlier words, as well as the words of a great many Kiowa people living and dead. What is fascinating to me is the way in which Momaday's autobiographies attempt to assert the independent word and the single voice while yet demonstrating, along with most Native American autobiographies, that words are always interdependent, that other voices always sound.

vi.

J. B. Patterson chose the autobiographical form for Black Hawk but this did little to produce for him a voice different from that of savagist historicism generally: the only gesture toward difference comes, as I have already noted, in Patterson's selection and arrangement of the materials that probably derive from Black Hawk himself. This at least suggests an Other perspective, if not actually an Other voice. Still, just as Apes wrote his autobiography twice, so, too, did Patterson write Black Hawk's twice. For there is an 1882 version of the *Life,* now for the first time called the *Autobiography of Black Hawk,* and Black Hawk, to be sure, is in places represented as speaking somewhat differently from the way he did in 1833.[25]

---

25. Donald Jackson notes some of these differences along with five instances of material added to the 1882 text, in pp. 29–30 of his Introduction.

Unlike the two autobiographies *by* William Apes, however, the differences in the two autobiographies *of* Black Hawk finally yield only sameness. Indeed, we can add more representations of Black Hawk to Patterson's two and still find only the same voice all over again. We can do this because Black Hawk was of interest to Americans for more than fifty years, and his life, in particular those parts of it relating to the Black Hawk "war," came to be represented in a variety of texts. Thus, to the extent that these give us other views and voices of Black Hawk, they might serve, as I have claimed for William Apes's "other" autobiography, to dialogize Patterson's monologic texts. But this does not happen: other representations of Black Hawk's voice largely replicate Patterson's. It might be concluded, therefore, that Patterson must have actually captured the "authentic" voice of Black Hawk. More likely, as I think, is that Patterson, along with his fellow historians, amateur and professional, all quite thoroughly translate Black Hawk's "authentic" voice (whatever we may imagine that to be—and we can only imagine it) into the dominant discourse for dealing with Indians. As Roy Harvey Pearce long ago showed in specific regard to the Indian, as Edward Said more recently showed for the "Oriental," it is precisely the achievement of a hegemonic discourse to produce a kind of blanketing effect, to insist upon the minimalization of difference as a primary condition for coherence and comprehensibility.

Writing in the *Journal of the Illinois State Historical Society* in 1927, John H. Hauberg mentions a recent meeting of the Society at which the speaker "exhibited a collection of two hundred volumes, by many authors, every one of which carried stories of Black Hawk and his Indians, and these were but a fraction of the books bearing on this historic subject" (265). It would, of course, be valuable to examine these two hundred texts (although Hauberg does not provide their titles), along with any others that may have followed, in order to see how Black Hawk is represented as speaking in each. I cannot claim to have done this; indeed I have only examined a mere four books dating from 1834 to 1913 which center on "Black Hawk and his Indians" to consider the sameness or difference in the representation of Black Hawk as speaker. I have studied John A. Wakefield's *History of the War Between the United States and the Sac and Fox Nations of Indians* . . .(1834), Benjamin Drake's *The Life and Adventures of Black Hawk: With Sketches of Keokuk, the Sac and Fox Indians, and the Late Black Hawk War* (1838), N. Matson's *Memories of Shaubena* . . .(1878), and Charles M. Scanlan's *Indian Creek Massacre and Captivity of Hall Girls . . . during the Black Hawk War, 1832* (1913). Wakefield, Drake, Matson, and Scanlan all differ in their opinion of the justice of the Indians' resistance to white settlement, as they differ in other regards; for all of that, their representations of Black Hawk's voice turn out to be remarkably similar to Patterson's and to one another.

Of the texts under consideration, the only full-scale biography is that of Benjamin Drake, published in 1838. Wakefield's book appeared only a year after Patterson's and so is very close in time to the events he considers; it is presented specifically as a "history." Matson's attention to Black Hawk occurs in a biography or personal reminiscence of Shaubena, a Pottowatamie chief who refused to join Black Hawk in war against white encroachment. Matson, who is concerned to justify "progress" and "civilization," has great affection and respect for Shaubena, and these color his perception of Black Hawk. And Scanlan is a professional author (*Scanlan's Rules of Order, Law of Hotels,* etc.) who now turns to the

dramatic and commercial possibilities of captivity and Indian
war narratives, these two being the earliest genres of literature developed on these shores, providing an indigenous
model, perhaps, of that mix of public and personal reportage
most common before the professionalization of history writing in America. All of these are western writers, at least to
the extent that their books were published in Cincinnati,
Milwaukee, Rock Island, and Chicago.

The first thing to be observed is that, in terms of perspective, each of these writers sets Black Hawk and the "war"
which bears his name firmly in relation to the discourse of
savagism, differing, as I have said, only in regard to a sense of
satisfaction or sadness that the Indian must disappear. It is *that*
sense which determines which, among minor events or inci-
dents, are included or left out, as it determines the different
versions of events that appear. For the most part, so far as my
limited investigations reveal, this practice doesn't bear substantively on the reader's understanding—although sometimes it might well.[26] An encounter, for example, between

26. Thus it may make a difference in one's view of these events, for
example, whether Black Hawk *surrendered* or was *captured* to end the "war." In
1833, Patterson had Black Hawk go to a Winnebago village (after the whites
massacred an Indian party heavily made up of women and children trying to
cross the Mississippi) and say "that I intended to give myself up to the
American war chief, and *die,* if the Great Spirit saw proper. . . . I then
started, with several Winnebagoes, and went to their agent, at Prairie du
Chien, and gave myself up" (39). Patterson in 1882—in his "History of the
Black Hawk War" appended to the *Autobiography* writes that "Black Hawk
and a few of his people left for the lodge of a Winnebago friend, and gave
himself up" (187). This is very different from John Wakefield's account which
I must quote at some length:

  The reader will recollect that I have, in a preceding chapter, given the
  substance of a talk between Gen. Atkinson and Gen. Street, agent for the
  Winnebagoes, and several Winnebago Chiefs. . . . In this talk, Gen. Street
  told the principal chiefs that if they would bring in the Black Hawk and the

Black Hawk and General Gaines appears very differently in
Benjamin Drake's biography from the account in Patterson's
autobiography of Black Hawk.[27] Both of these men were

Prophet, it would be well for them, and that the government of the United
States would hold them in future as friends. . . .

Accordingly, on the 27th of August, these two Winnebago chiefs [Decorri
and Cheater] returned, bringing with them the Black Hawk and the Prophet,
the principal movers and instigators of the war. . . . I will give the reader the
substance of their talk with General Street and Col. Taylor, which will go to
show how vigilant, and with what perseverance, these Winnebago chiefs
acted to take these prisoners. (96–97).

Wakefield is exceedingly hostile to the Indians' cause. (Something which may
also explain his reference to the Indian Agent Joseph Street as General Street.
Atkinson was a General in the United States Army; Street may well have been
General in the militia or some such—I confess to not having mastered the distinctions of rank in the various volunteer and professional military divisions of
nineteenth-century America—but he is not referred to by that rank in Patterson's
text—nor in Donald Jackson's notes.) Still, Benjamin Drake, in 1838, writing
soon after Patterson (1833) and Wakefield (1834), and extremely sympathetic to
the Indians' cause, takes Wakefield's account, not Patterson's, in his biography of
Black Hawk (he also refers to Agent Street as a General):

When the fortunes of Black Hawk became desperate, his few straggling
allies, from other tribes, not only deserted him, but joined his enemies. It is to
two Winnebagoes, Decorie, and Chaetar, that the fallen chief is indebted for
being taken captive. On the 27th of August, they delivered Black Hawk and
the Prophet to the Indian agent, General Street, at Prairie des Chiens. (Drake,
171, 1851 edition)

Drake follows with direct quotation of Decorie's speech and that of General
Street. He gives no source, but the text is very close to Wakefield's, although not
only spellings—and of these not only spellings of Indian names, which one
expects, but of places (Prairie du Chien/Prairie des Chiens, among others)—but
details and constructions vary (in Wakefield, Decorri says "we," referring, it
would seem, to himself and Cheater; in Drake, Decorie says "I," with no reference to Chaetar, etc.). Drake gives no source for the speeches.

27. Patterson's 1833 version is of outrage and anger on the part of both
parties (cf. 111–112, with its rare use of direct quotation in virtually sticho-
mythian fashion, as well as the fullest complement of exclamation points), while
Drake's 1838 rendition seems softened considerably (cf. 107). As in the example
cited above, one might take the different presentations of the "same" material
here as evidence for variant interpretations. Yet the majority of differences I have
discovered are not easily seen as differences to any substantive point. Rather,

generally sympathetic to the Indians, so it is no easy matter to
say why each gave a different account: were different "facts"
presented to each?

---

they seem to represent opinion as to what best represents "good" style—good,
here, being understand as accommodation to an *a priori* model of appropriateness
for a particular form of discourse. Small alterations in what are offered as strictly
reprintings seem to be the norm in American historiography before the 1870s
when the influence of German methodological rigor begins to be felt on these
shores. Let me give a single example, which, however, I believe to be representative of the very many possible.

N. Matson gives a speech of Black Hawk's in direct quotation—he does not
give a source for this—as follows:

"I was born at the Sac Village, and here I spent my childhood, youth and
manhood. I like to look on this place with its surrounding of big rivers, shady
groves, and green prairies. Here is the grave of my father and some of my
children; here I expected to live and die and lay my bones by the side of those
near and dear unto me; but now in my old age I have been driven from my
home, and dare not look again upon this loved spot." Here the old chief's
utterance was choked by a flood of tears, and covering his face with a blanket,
he remained for a few moments weeping in silence. After wiping away his
tears he continued, . . . (98, 101)

Scanlan's 1913 account offers the same scene and quotes the same speech. Consistent with its period's apparently more rigorous standards of attribution in history
writing, Scanlan, on p. 19, footnotes the speech as coming from *Memories of
Shaubena* p. 98, which is correct. But compare this "*quotation*" to what Matson
acutally wrote:

"I was born at the Sac Village, and here I spent my childhood, youth and
manhood. I like*d* to look on this place with its surrounding*s* of big rivers,
shady groves [. . .] and green prairies. Here *are* the grave*s* of my father and
some of my children. *H*ere I expected to live and die and lay my bones *beside*
those near and dear *to* me; but now in my old age I have been driven from my
home, and dare not look again upon this loved spot.

*The old chief choked with grief and tears flowed down his cheeks. Covering his face
in his blanket, he remained silent for a few moments. Then* wiping away his tears,
he continued: . . . (18–19; emphasis mine)

Wakefield has certainly stayed close to Matson, but he hasn't *quoted* him; rather,
he's revised him very slightly, revising, thereby, Black Hawk himself. And
Matson, of course, did not say where his own translation of Black Hawk's
words—Black Hawk spoke hardly any English, so this must be a translation—
came from. All the writers I have examined, from Patterson in 1833 and 1882 to
Scanlan in 1913 do this sort of thing.

In similar fashion, all these authors quote abundantly but treat their published sources in the same way they seem to have treated their oral sources, that is, with a good deal of casualness. For example, Scanlan quotes from Matson, even given page references: but if one looks up the quotations in Matson, one discovers that Scanlan has altered the material as a matter of regular course. Patterson does this to himself, revising, in 1882, where he is ostensibly reprinting. Commitment to verbatim quotation (or an approximation thereto for oral sources)[28] seems not to have been typical of American historiography in general until the 1870s and the influence of German historical method. (It should be noted that Hauberg, quite a responsible author, so far as I can tell, as late as 1927 offers substantial quotation from Black Hawk—material, that is, presented inside quotation marks—without providing references for his sources.)

Next, it is to be observed that each author not only writes in relation to a discursive perspective but in accordance with an established stylistic practice. As each would be taken seriously as *historian*—reporters and chroniclers of events, compilers or students of the public documentary record—so does he accommodate a standard period diction, editing the speech of others (when quoted directly) in the direction of this standard or submitting the speech of others to a standardized indirect discourse. Thus each speaker in a text presented under the sign of History sounds pretty much the same. By way of

28. No speech of Black Hawk's, so far as I am aware, has entered, even marginally, American culture in general. The case is very different in regard to a speech of Tecumseh in 1810 from which the phrase, "The earth is my mother," became almost common currency, as it is with the speech Chief Seathl is supposed to have made in 1855. The important studies of Sam Gill and, earlier, Rudolf Kaiser show the extraordinary latitude nineteenth-century journalists and historians permitted in their reporting of Indian speech.

contrast, we may briefly take note of the work of an easterner on a visit to the west, John Treat Irving, Jr., whose text is not offered as public history but as private observation. Irving's *Indian Sketches Taken During an Expedition to the Pawnee Tribes* (1833) is exactly contemporaneous with Patterson's *Life of Black Hawk,* and includes, in its reportage, the monologue of a Tennesseean named Wolf, "a tall, gigantic fellow" (perhaps he might be worthy of comparison to his Native contemporary Kotsatoah!). Upon Irving's party encountering some Indians, Wolf is represented as offering the following remarks:

"You see them ar Ingens; well, them is Sacs and Foxes. I know 'em, for I *fit* agin 'em when Black Hawk led 'em on. And now I think on't: it's dreadful aggravating to see how the folks at east'ard are honouring that ar rascal for killing and murdering the whites, while we who *fit* agin him to prevent it, a'int taken no notice on; its monstrous aggravating. But that a'int nothing to the *pint.* (50)

And so forth. This would, of course, be no more than an approximation of Wolf's speech, Irving making notes when and as he could. But clearly the attempt is to give the idiosyncratic—regional, personal—dimension of this speaker's talk which is interesting to Irving, and, so, he hopes, to his readers (probably *eastern* readers, for the most part) back home. There is no need for these informal "sketches" to accommodate Wolf's language (or that of anyone else) to a standard of "good" historical style.[29] By way of contrast, Matson's book offers, to be sure, only his "memories," but to the extent

29. This problem does arise, however, for Western autobiographers who want to be taken seriously as public figures. Some, like David Crockett of Tennessee, ruefully admit to having their speech edited some, while others, like Kit Carson and Sam Houston, eschew regional flavor. See my "American Autobiography: The Western Tradition" for a fuller account.

that these are marshaled for the purpose of defending the ongoing advance of "civilization," one can pretty well understand
his desire to edit out the distractions of any speech deviating
from the "civilized" norm. In these regards, it would have
been interesting to see what J. T. Irving might have done with
the speech in English of an Indian—or, had the opportunity
somehow arisen, to work with an Indian autobiographical subject and an interpreter.

In any case, non-Native representations of Native people
for the historical record, whether these are sympathetic or
unsympathetic representations, tend to be pulled in the direction of period perspective and period style. Exceptions to this
generalization may well exist but I have not come upon them.

What is true for Patterson and the other speakers for Black
Hawk is even true for an Indian autobiographer like L. V.
McWhorter. His text, as I have claimed, is strongly dialogic,
yet it cannot abandon an unquestioning Western sense of autobiographical form (with McWhorter's insistence on including
something of Yellow Wolf's childhood, noted above), as it
cannot envision a distinctive manner for Yellow Wolf's speech.
I would only add further that the curious contradiction in
McWhorter's book between full commitment to a plurality of
voices combined with an unexamined commitment to Western
forms may be taken as homologous with the contradictions of
the Collier Indian Reform program generally. I mean only to
point to what continues to have painful effects, the fact that
John Collier's promotion and administration of the Wheeler-
Howard, Indian Reorganization Act of 1934, legislated the
preservation of Native cultures by means of Western parliamen-
tary institutions. Indians, after Wheeler-Howard, might hope
to influence the federal government not to interfere with traditional lifeways, but such influence was contingent upon a will-

ingness to present the Indian case in "American" forms. This is
not to condemn McWhorter or Collier, both of whom deserve
admiration at least for their courage. It is, however, to note
again the difficulty of achieving a genuine dialogism, textual or
institutional, from the outside, on the part of one trained in
Western discourse and committed to it in however revisionist
or radical a fashion.

It remains now to suggest what all of this may mean for
our understanding of language and of social organization.

vii.

Native American autobiographies, I have claimed, are interesting both for the model of the self and the model of the
text they propose, the first of these more nearly collective, the
second more nearly dialogic than what has been typical of
Euramerican autobiography. Collective selves and dialogic
texts imply particular kinds of semantic and social theories.
Let me review these as I see them in relation to Native American autobiography and the canon of American literature.

In regard to the understanding of language and the nature
of communication, a commitment to dialogism, on the one
hand, may be seen as a recognition of the necessity of an
infinite semantic openness, where the inescapable possibility
of yet some further voice is crucial inasmuch as that voice
always must alter or ambiguate any relatively stable meaning one might claim to understand. Attempts to stabilize
meaning, in this view, always smack of a tendency to totalitarianism, with a (typical although mistaken) identification
of textual authority (based on epistemological totalization)
and sociopolitical authority.

On the other hand, commitment to dialogism may be seen
as a type of radical pluralism, a more relativized openness,

concerned to state meanings provisionally in recognition of the legitimate claims of otherness and difference. Norms, here, are decidedly established but these are not seen as denying—the denial enforced by legitimated violence—the proposal of alternatives.

My own reading suggests that most of those committed to deconstructive, postmodern, or, as I should say with Fredric Jameson, schizophrenic models of polyphony do, in fact, simply project their view of textuality on to the social. Thus James Clifford—who is more careful about this sort of thing than many—refers to Bakhtin as envisioning "a carnivalesque arena of diversity," and "a *utopian* textual space" (1983, 135; my emphasis). Although spaces are not places—utopia, is, after all, *ou topos,* no place—this textual utopia is as close as we get to a postmodernist, dialogical model for worldly politics. It is, as a model, a category of pure abstraction, an image out of time as well as place, one oblivious to material conditions of historical possibility: and diversity as the limitless freeplay of social praxis is not easy to institute.

Here is the moment to see whether we can at least tentatively define some form of democratic and egalitarian principle of community that would be the social equivalent of a dialogic pluralism as distinct from an infinite openness. In this regard, it should be noted that traditional Native American examples of communal organization need further study; although I am not ready to suggest that the Pueblo, in its current forms, or the Plains camp circle (let us say) as once it was, will directly contribute models for a harmonious world-community to come, those like myself who are interested in the literary forms developed by Indians will need to pay more attention to Indian social forms as well.

I will suggest as a social alternative to dialogism as quotidian carnival and polymorphous diversity, what Paul Rabinow has called *cosmopolitanism*. "Let us define cosmopolitanism," Rabinow writes,

as an ethos of macro-interdependencies, with an acute consciousness (often forced upon people) of the inescapabilities and particularities of places, characters, historical trajectories, and fates. (258)[30]

What is necessary, here, is to avoid "reify[ing] local identities or construct[ing] universal ones"; this, as Rabinow notes, requires a rather delicate "balancing act," one that has not thus far met with conspicuous success anywhere in the world. Local identities socially can, of course, seem very attractive; currently, to reify one's Blackness, Jewishness, Italianness, or, to be sure, Indianness (among other locally available identifications) has seemed to some a hedge against an unprecedented explosion of diversity and complication. The temptation to construct universal identities seems less a threat just now, although, as I have noted earlier, the attempt to assert Western male values as Human does certainly persist.

Cosmopolitanism, then, is the projection of heterodoxy not to the level of the universal, but, rather, to the level of the "inter-national." I shall take this matter up from a literary

---

30. Rabinow also notes that his conception "attempts to be highly attentive to (and respectful of) difference, but is also wary of the tendency to essentialize difference" (258). This is consistent with Allon White's desire, quoted earlier, to align Bakhtin with "an ultimate political perspective of humanity as unity-in-difference," rather than "A politics of pure difference" (233). Bakhtin writes, "It is quite possible to imagine and postulate a unified truth that requires a plurality of consciousnesses, one that cannot in principle be fitted into the bounds of a single consciousness, one that is, so to speak, by its very nature *full of event potential* and is born at a point of contact among various consciousnesses" (1984, 81) The problem, as I have noted, is that Bakhtin also says rather different things on this subject. Still, this is the side of him I have chosen to take as determining.

point of view in the next chapter. Here, I want to comment briefly on the major objection I know to heterodoxy as authorizing a social rather than merely a textual order as this is stated by Steven Sangren.

Sangren makes the point that heterodoxy best makes sense as an adversary to orthodoxy; and, indeed, I have taken the term in exactly this way in proposing a principle for the canon. Heterodoxies, according to Sangren, are order-questioning ideologies rather than order-affirming ideologies (which is what orthodoxies are). Thus, he claims, heterodoxies are

socially less robust . . . because they cannot legitimate any conceivable cultural or social order. They make *social* (as opposed to textual or philosophical) sense only in opposition. (410)

I think this is unduly narrow. If one takes the heterodox not as an absolute commitment to difference unending but, instead— as I have several times noted—to difference within a normative context, then it may yet be that heterodoxy can be a social, not only a textual, principle, one authorizing a cosmopolitan world order. For all the apparent irony of proposing that the highly place-oriented and more or less homogenous cultures of Native Americans might help teach us how to be cosmopolitans, that is exactly what I mean to say. But here let me take the example of *Storyteller*.

Storyteller, I have claimed, is open to a wide range of voices. What keeps it from entering the poststructuralist, postmodernist, or schizophrenic heteroglossic domain is its commitment to the equivalent of a normative voice. For all the polyvocal openness of Silko's work, there is always the unabashed sense of the value of Pueblo tradition as a reference point. Now, unlike the Judeo-Christian tradition, Native

American tradition has not been exclusivist; thus "Pueblo tradition" is more nearly a norm than an orthodoxy. (I leave it to others to work out further the correlations between oral tradition and norm, textual tradition and orthodoxy.) This may be modified, updated, playfully construed: but it serves as a focal point that cannot be ignored; whatever one understands from any speaker is to be understood in reference to *that*. Here—to open an issue I shall not be able to pursue—we find dialogic as dialectic (not, it seems, the case in Bakhtin); meaning as the interaction of any voiced value whatever with the continuing—if modified and modifiable—voice of the Pueblo storyteller (who, with whatever modifications, carries forward a *version* of the traditional point of view). Some parallel sense of the situated normative value of a vital tribal (social, collective, communitarian) tradition will likely be present in any Native American autobiography that acknowledges its doubly dialogic determination. (And, as I have tried to show, even the insistently monologic examples of the genre still show traces of other voices, other stories, that at least complicate any desired identification with a single discursive voice.)

If my account of *Storyteller's* semantics, or theory of meaning—and, by extension, the semantics of other Native American autobiographies and all dialogically oriented texts—is at all accurate, then it would follow that its political unconscious is more easily conformable to Rabinow's cosmopolitanism, as I have glossed it, than to a utopianized carnival. Thus I would align a commitment to dialogism with that reading of Bakhtin and of dialogical anthropology that insists upon human and cultural diversity as the way things "really" are, an empirical commitment, and as well to the way things ought to be, an ethical and political commitment. Textual and social production and reproduction are not identical, to be sure; but they may on occasion materialize according to the same principles.

For all that one may desire a future cosmopolitan community of diverse values, it is still necessary to work toward it from the local communities that actually exist in the present, with their distinctly local values. To be sure, one must not reify these values, but one must not ignore them either. It seems to me that the way to the cosmopolitan in social terms is through the local, from thence to the national—where heterodoxy is acknowledged as legitimate within the political boundaries of nation-states—and after, to some concretely imaginable cooperation on an international scale leading to the cosmopolitan community, heterodoxy legitimated globally. To be sure, this is to offer a conceptual paradigm—an image, a vision—not a political program; and to imagine the cosmopolitan polyvocal polity in this way is also utopian—but perhaps only in the sense that it does not as yet exist. To imagine it may also be to make a contribution to its existence.

5. Local, National, Cosmopolitan Literature

I have claimed that the canon of American literature must substantially include the literary production of Native American and Afro-American peoples quite as well as those of the Euramerican peoples whose culture came to dominate the United States. *That,* for good historical reasons, is what American literature, as a national literature, should, empirically, be. But what of the theoretical status of "national literature" itself, not only as an empirical but as a conceptual category? How might we define national literatures in relation to, on the one hand, local, or regional, or ethnic literatures (the appropriate designation is not immediately apparent), and, on the other, to an international, or—as I shall further attempt to define this as the horizon of these considerations—to a cosmopolitan literature? If it is a heterodox canon that is wanted for American literature, how would such heterodoxy stand in relation to and/or itself define a cosmopolitan or world-literary canon?

In these regards, it might suddenly appear as though formalist critics, New Critical or New Rhetorical, did not and do not ignore or scorn national literary production, as I earlier accused them of doing, so much as they consciously choose to promote only those texts that could be accommodated to the wider context of international, or, more exactly, *Western* literary production. To the extent that this may be true, it must be said that their notion of Western internationalism is defined independently of any actual sociotemporal reference, as if one actually could read universally and eternally, avoiding the "mean and ordinary" details of time and place to pass directly to the highest levels of generalization—as if literary language, rhetorically considered, were a matter of figures only, independent of real occasions. Still, if one wishes to discredit this version of an international (or, again, a Western) literature, it is necessary to offer some alternative in its place.

A current visibility to such matters has recently been provided by Fredric Jameson's discussion of what he has called (reluctantly, it would seem, and in full awareness of the problematic nature of such a category) "third world literature":[1] Jameson also considers what he calls national literature, first and second world literature, and world literature, as well. He does not in this essay, as he does not elsewhere, make reference to Native American literature—which might, of course, be considered among third world literatures. Such consideration, admittedly, would then make it difficult to include Native American literature in the national canon of *American* literature, the most powerful of first world literatures! These questions are fruitfully complicated in Jack Forbes's interesting polemical essay, "Colonialism and Native American Literature: Analysis," in the *Wicazo Sa Review,* an essay that takes up some of the same issues as Jameson's, albeit from a very different perspective.

Before going any further, it seems important to note that, whatever its value, Forbes's essay will not have the circulation (and so it will not have the influence) of Jameson's. Socializing the classic Jakobsonian paradigm, Forbes himself remarks that "*we must also view literature* not as a series of artistic or creative

1. See "Third-World Literature in the Era of Multinational Capital."

acts only, but *as a social transaction,* a transaction involving the process of dissemination as well as reception by a specific audience" (1987, 23), and the same point must be made—made or reiterated—for the social circulation of criticism. Professor of Anthropology at the University of California, Davis, Jack Forbes is a mixed blood of Powhatan-Lenape-Saponi background. He has published fiction and poetry as well as scholarly articles, autobiography, and a book-length study of Indian policy in the Nixon administration[2] that was singled out for blame by the venerable Wilcomb Washburn of the Smithsonian Institute—who damningly dubbed Forbes "a redoubtable warrior of the radical left" (1987, 93). The very fact that Forbes has chosen to publish this piece in *Wicazo Sa,* as I hope to show, is an illustration of his thesis concerning Indian literature—and its (his) dilemma.

For *Wicazo Sa* is a journal whose purpose is "to serve as a publishing outlet and . . . resource for Native American scholars and readers" (n.p.). Edited by Elizabeth Cook-Lynn, it comes out of the Native American Studies Center of Eastern Washington University, Cheney, Washington, and circulates among a readership quite different from the readership of *Diacritics, Critical Inquiry, New Literary History,* and *Social Text,* the places where Jameson is most often to be found.[3] Understandably, the modes of discourse usual to the articles in *Wicazo Sa* are also different from the continentally influ-

2. See *Native Americans and Nixon: Presidential Politics and Minority Self-Determination, 1967–1972.*

3. Some comparative circulation figures may be of interest. As of November 1988, Elizabeth Cook-Lynn told my research assistant, West Moss, that *Wicazo Sa* had just under 500 subscriptions and rent out over 100 complimentary copies. *Diacritics* has a circulation of 1350; *Social Text* about 2000; *New Literary History,* 2079; and *Critical Inquiry,* 4000. PMLA has a circulation of some 30,000 copies, including library sales. For comparison sake, circulation figures for the *Reader's Digest,* subscription and newsstand sales, as of June 30, 1988, were 16,964,226.

enced discourse of the journals of high theoretical criticism.
Yet Forbes has something important to offer to the developing discussion of these matters, and theorists would do well
to read him (as Indianists—to reiterate a point of some importance to me—would do well to read the theorists).

Further to anthropologize our own discourse and place it in
the appropriate contexts of knowledge/power, let me cite, as
of more than anecdotal interest, some of the historian Robert
Berkhofer's recent recollections. Berkhofer writes,

When I entered the field of American Indian history as a graduate student in the 1950s, I was told by a noted historian of the United States's
past that Indian history was not part of American history. If I persisted
in writing a dissertation on Protestant missionaries to the American
Indians from the 1770s to the 1860s, he said, I would never gain acceptance in my chosen profession of American history. (35)

Although Berkhofer completed the dissertation and requested
that it be listed in *Dissertation Abstracts* "under American religious history, it was placed under the anthropology heading.
The anonymous classifier knew . . . that anthropologists, not
historians, studied Indians" (35). The situation, Berkhofer
says, is better today in the field of history. In the field of
literature and cultural studies, however, as I have remarked
earlier, improvement seems only negligible; the subject of the
past history and present practice of Native American literatures, as well as the theoretical questions that consideration of
that literature can acutely focus still remain at a tangent to or
at a considerable distance from the circles where cultural and
social values are determined and major careers established
(perhaps, now, this is true *even* for anthropologists).

Forbes begins with the question, "*What is a national or ethnic
literature?*" (1987, 18) as a way of considering, "What is Indian

Literature?" His answer insists upon the local constitution of such literature, which he says can only be "determined by the particular culture, from an internal perspective, and by the forms which are current within that culture." "*The crucial element,*" Forbes continues, "*is whether the work is composed or written to be received by a particular people. Is it internal to the culture?*" Focusing, thus, first on the "primary audience," and then on the author—"*Native American literature must consist in works produced by persons of Native identity and/or culture . . .*" (19)—he concludes that most of what would fit his criteria for contemporary Indian literature tends to be not what Western culture would call "literature" at all so much as the discourse appearing in "Indian published periodicals" (20)[4]—poetry and

---

4. Forbes, for example, names *Akwesasne Notes* as one of the specifically Indian periodicals he has in mind. In "An Open Letter on Recent Developments in the American Indian Movement/International Indian Treaty Council" (1980), the Cherokee poet, painter, and activist Jimmie Durham writes that *Akwesasne Notes* was founded in 1969 by "a white man named Jerry Gamble (who gave himself the Indian name of 'Rarihokwats')" and that throughout its history, at least to 1980, it "has been mainly written, produced and read by white people, who carried on the tradition of white romantics defining Indian culture." Durham nonetheless acknowledges *Akwesasne's* influence "among some urban Indians, and in determining how the left and counterculture see the Indian struggle" (4). A suspicious fire on January 8, 1988, nearly destroyed *A.N.* According to Joseph Bruchac (quoted in the March, 1988, ASAIL NOTES), they "lost everything . . . all their back issues, the plates for their books, the works" (2). If Swann's criterion of acceptance by other Native Americans (see n. 5, just below) is to apply to journals as well as to individuals, the June 6, 1988, benefit for *Akwesasne Notes* in New York certainly testifies to the devotion of "representatives of the New York City Native American Community" (Program Notes: n.p.) to the journal. Forbes's claim that the journals he lists "*are* read by Indians" (1987, 20) might be supported by the circulation figures I've managed to obtain for some of these. *Akwesasne Notes* reports a circulation of 10,000, the same figure given by the *Yakima Nation Review* out of Toppenish, Washington. *Talking Leaf,* published by the Indian Center, Inc., in Los Angeles, claims a circulation of 6000. *Wassaja: the Indian Historian,* more nearly a professional journal than these others, has a circulation of 82,000.

fiction, some of the time, to be sure, but most often nonfic-
tional, topical writing. Forbes also notes, as I have earlier, the
ongoing production of traditional oral literature—this almost
never circulated much beyond the boundaries of its actual
performance. He is well aware that this definition of Indian
literature excludes the work of those considered by the dominant Euramerican culture to be the most notable contemporary Native American authors; nonetheless, it is the oral and
periodical literature that is for him the only discourse being
produced today that may appropriately be called *Indian* literature because these alone are primarily for an Indian audience
by authors whose primary self-identification is Indian, working in forms historically evolved by or at least currently most
readily accessible to that primary audience.

Forbes's is a pretty restrictive definition—and one replete
with problems. First is the problem of defining the producer
of Indian literature as an Indian on the basis of her Indian
"identity or culture." While this is somewhat more useful
than N. Scott Momaday's hopelessly vague definition of an
Indian as the "idea a man [sic] has of himself," it is still less
than rigorous. For one thing, an Indian "identity" cannot be
used to define an Indian until the concept of "identity" itself
has been defined. Forbes occasionally has recourse to the racial sense of identity, as, for example, in his references to
Indians as not currently "a free and independent race of people" (19). But in the contemporary American world such
reference is not only largely useless (e.g., a great many Indians, as a great many others, are persons of mixed racial origins), but obnoxious (e.g., it can tend to distinguish different
percentages of "blood," ranking each a "higher" or "lower"
type, depending on the context of concern). In the end, then,
it would seem that Indians must be *culturally* Indian, with

such cultural "identity" not a wholly random or arbitrary choice (e.g., the Indian person having *some* actual heredity link to persons native to America).[5] Yet Forbes does not indicate (this would be no easy task) what one has to do to be culturally Indian: one does not, for example, have to understand or speak a Native language.

Then there is the problem of just how "internal to the culture" the forms of the journalistic discourse Forbes nominates as the major part of a strictly Indian literature actually are. For, regardless of their producers' and their audiences'— but here one might want to say their *consumers'*—identities (let us say they will indeed both be "Indian"), these texts are, in actual fact, thoroughly saturated by the most degraded forms of the dominant culture. Even more, I suspect a sociological study of this subject would reveal that, so far as circulation is concerned, more Native Americans read the *National Enquirer, TV Guide,* car and motorcycle publications, and movie or assorted popular culture magazines than read some of the Indian periodicals Forbes mentions. (More non–Native Americans read these periodicals than read the *American Poetry Review* or *Fiction* magazine, but most definitions of American literature are not set up in such a way that this statistic is crucial.) This is, to be sure, the consequence, as Forbes notes, of the fact that any consideration of Indian literature today— texts written by and read by Native people—must take into

5. Citing the absurdity of the Bureau of Indian Affairs' standard for enrollment in a tribe, that "one must possess one-quarter Indian blood," inasmuch as there is no chemical analysis for "Indian blood," Brian Swann reasonably decides that "Native Americans are Native Americans if they say they are, if other Native Americans say they are and accept them, and (possibly) if the values that are held close and acted upon are values upheld by the various native peoples who live in the Americas" (1988, xx). Loose as this is, it is about the best one can do for a contemporary working definition.

account the historical status of Indians as a colonized people. The positive side of this—for Indians, like other colonized peoples, do not merely suffer their condition passively but actively respond to it with energy and ingenuity—has to do with the language mix often to be found in these periodicals, where Native language articles often coexist with articles in standard English and, as well, with writing in that curiously fascinating hybrid called "Red English."⁶ I will come back to this later.

So far as the category of an Indian literature—and along with it the general category of local literature—may be useful, it would seem to be necessary to define it pretty exclusively by reference to the ongoing oral performances of Native people. These, too, are aware of the standards and productions of dominant culture, aspects of which they may, indeed, incorporate (so that to speak of an Indian literature is in no way to go in search of some pristine, aboriginal purity of form and content). Nonetheless, inasmuch as they are spoken/sung rather than written in a Native language, and controlled by traditional forms "internal to the culture," oral performances seem the best representatives of what might be meant by an Indian literature. I am unable to say what the circulation of such literature among Indians might be, although, as with Euramerican literature, numbers do not, here, determine importance in any absolute way. The circulation of oral Native literature among non-native Americans, predictably enough, has not been very great, nor has this literature very often been taken up as a source of analysis and imitation by students of

6. I take the term from Anthony Mattina, most particularly. He has defined it as an "English dialect," and a "pan-Indian phenomenon, with various subdialects" (1985, 9), and defended it as an option for translators in his Introduction to *The Golden Woman*.

literature and by non-Native artists. Outside Indian communities it has attracted the attention predominantly of social scientists. A clear statement of the problems and possibilities here has been given by Larry Evers and Felipe Molina in their recent study of Yaqui deer songs. I have quoted them to somewhat different purpose in my Introduction, but I trust it will not be amiss to cite them again here. Evers and Molina write,

In all, we work for two goals: for the continuation of deer songs as a vital part of life in Yaqui communities and for their appreciation in all communities beyond. Most of the time these goals coincide. (8)

Just what form that "appreciation" may take in "communities beyond" Yaqui communities remains, of course, to be seen. The work that Evers and Molina are doing, however, is absolutely essential if there is to be any chance at all for traditional, local, Indian literary expression to influence the literature of the dominant culture.

The ongoing production of traditional Indian literature, of course, is not limited to the United States. For it is not only possible but necessary, as Forbes writes, to "*regard the Americas as a single unit for literature study,*" and thus to see that "*Native American literature is an international body of literature*" (1987, 18), "*hemispheric in dimension*" (1987, 23). It seems then that we have Native American literature, on the one hand, as what I have called a local literature—as ethnic, or national literature, in Forbes's account—but also as an *international* literature, on the other, at least so far as the Americas may mark an inter-national site for the circulation and reception of locally produced Indian literary expression. Forbes does not consider Indianness, ethnicity, nationality, and international-

ity beyond the Western hemisphere, or as these might connect
with the literary production of indigenous people elsewhere;[7]
he offers no concept roughly equivalent to what is conveyed
by the term "third world literature," a global conception en-
compassing the national literatures of the recently independent third world states.

Indeed, Forbes never takes the term "national" as having
reference to nation-states at all, perhaps because such reference is entirely non-Indian. His understanding of the national
equates the term, as I see it, with a certain traditional American understanding of the *tribal,* as in Chief Justice John Mar-
shall's well-known description of Indian sociopolitical units
as "domestic dependent nations." But Forbes does not either
speak of tribes or the tribal, perhaps now (I can only guess at
this) to avoid the divisive question of the political implications of tribalism and nationalism.

Here we may return to Fredric Jameson, and suggest that
his essay may not mention literature by Native Americans as
available for inclusion in the category "third world literature"
precisely because, as we shall note in a moment, he finds third
world literature to be marked by nationalism, something
Eurocentric thinkers tend to distinguish rigorously from the
tribalism that marks the literature of Indians. Jameson posits
the categories of first, second, and third world literature, of
national, and of world literature. World literature, according
to Jameson, is a category that has yet to be reinvented (largely

7. Some sense of indigenous peoples' self-conscious awareness of themselves
as such may be had from the "Declaration of Principles adopted by the Indigenous Peoples Preparatory Meeting, held at Geneva, 27–31 July 1987," Annex V
of the *Study of the Problem of Discrimination Against Indigenous Populations,* a Report
of the Working Group on Indigenous Populations on its fifth Session, sponsored
by the United Nations Economic and Social Council.

as a result of the thrust of current cultural studies); he says little else about it. National literatures are constituted by a national sense, or, what may or may not amount to the same thing, by a sense of nationalism. Thus national literatures are not necessarily present (not prominent or dominant) in all nation-states, nationalism having been largely discredited and/or abandoned in the first and second world states;[8] national literatures are, however, characteristic of the newly independent states of the third world. These latter are defined by—no doubt their nationalism is fueled by—an experience, the experience of imperial and colonial domination; this in contrast (as Aijaz Ahmad has pointed out)[9] to the definition of first and second world states that are to be known by their modes of production, not by their historical experience. Of course this definitional discrepancy can be corrected, at least in theory, by specifying the mode of production of third world countries (no harder and no easier to do, when, once again, one descends to specific details, than indicating that of first or second world countries), or by identifying the typical experience of first and second world countries (imperial dominance? national humiliation at the end of colonialism? there are difficulties here, too, at the level of specifics).

In this particular essay, what seems to interest Jameson most about third world literature is not its production, circulation,

---

8. I have some trouble with this particular generalization inasmuch as I recall vividly American reaction to such things as the hostage situation in Iran during the Carter administration and the jingoistic response to the invasion of Grenada during the Reagan administration, not to mention the ABC coverage of the 1984 Olympics with its unrelenting orientation toward nothing but the accumulation (or failure to accumulate same) of medals for the United States. I tend to think that these are instances of first world nationalism, of however a degraded and anachronistic type.

9. In "Jameson's Rhetoric of Otherness and the 'National Allegory'."

and reception (locally, nationally, internationally), but, rather, its thematic content. Whoever the third-world literary author may be, whatever the nature of her primary audience, she produces texts that "are necessarily . . . allegorical" (1986, 69), that are to be read as "national allegories," so that—in this, unlike the most typical case in the first world—*"the story of the private individual destiny is always an allegory of the embattled situation of the public third world culture and society"* (1986, 69). In third world literature, libidinal and political investments are thus typically joined in ways unusual in first and second world literature. (It would seem to no useful point, here, to focus on Jameson's use of "necessarily" and "always," as these may well mark a determinism he might not wish to defend; his argument is sufficiently suggestive as an heuristic.)

Jameson does not discuss questions of form or language in third world literature, except for a fascinating equation (presented, alas, only in passing) between the difficulty for the Chinese intellectual in the period "shortly after the founding of the Chinese Communist Party" (75) or the African intellectual "after the achievement of independence" of discovering "political solutions . . . present or visible on the historical horizon" (75) and "the possibility of narrative closure" (76). The texts Jameson analyzes from Lu Xun and Ousmane Sembene indicate that the forms of third world literature he has foremost in mind are narratives based upon realist paradigms—these, now, like nationalism, somewhat outmoded in the West. The forms of third world literature, then, as Jameson appears to think of them here, are not national (or ethnic) in Forbes's sense of being internal to the culture or cultures of formerly or currently colonized peoples. Rather, they resemble the sort of writing Forbes explicitly excludes from the category of Indian literature, writing of the sort done by Momaday and Silko and

Forbes himself, writing influenced in very substantial degree by the central forms and genres of Western, or first world literature. Forbes has no name for this kind of text; Jameson's "third world literature" might do except for the fact that, as I see it, it tends to obscure the importance of local, internal, or Indian modes of literary expression *within* texts that externally appear to fit the Western typology of "novels," "poems," and "short stories." Let me call this kind of mixed breed literature *indigenous literature.*

Indigenous literature I propose as the term for that form of literature which results from the *interaction* of local, internal, traditional, tribal, or "Indian" literary modes with the dominant literary modes of the various nation-states in which it may appear. Indigenous literature is that type of writing produced when an author of subaltern cultural identification manages successfully to merge forms internal to his cultural formation with forms external to it, but pressing upon, even seeking to delegitimate it. (The parallel term for the literature of other minority populations not historically indigenous to the territory of the nation-states in which they reside, as this is also marked by traditional/local modes of expression interacting with the modes of the dominant culture, might, I suppose, be *ethnic literature:* I mention this for the sake of a certain comprehensiveness, with no wish, however, to intervene just here in the current debates as to the empirical or theoretical constitution of an ethnic literature, or, indeed, to comment even on the usefulness of the term. Ethnic literature, for example, does not seem to me the best way to categorize Afro-American literature; but I must leave greater wisdom on this matter to others.) Indigenous literature exists not only in the Americas, of course, but globally, inasmuch as what I have said for Native Americans can be said for natives of the Philippines and Japan, of Basques in Spain, and Welsh in Britain; indigenous literature is a term that can probably apply to much of the recent production of African writers, as well. These need study in themselves and comparatively, that is, study as indigenous literatures in relation to one another and in relation to the various *national literatures* of which they are a part.

This is to say that I would define the term *national literature,* in contradistinction to Forbes and Jameson, as the *sum* of *local* (traditional, "Indian"), *indigenous* (mixed, perhaps "ethnic"), and *dominant* literary productions within the territory of the given national formations. Any national literary *canon,* therefore, will be a selection from all the available texts of these various kinds, and it may thus be thought to stand as the heterodox, collective autobiography of any who would define themselves in relation to a particular *national* identity—literature as a kind of multivoiced record of the *American,* for example.

An *international literature,* then, becomes the *sum* of these *national* literatures, in actual practice no doubt the sum of the national canons of these nation-states. The categories of national and international literature as so defined carry a commitment to dialogism and heterodoxy, and the movement from one to the next—as I believe, the *progression* from one to the next, this latter term denoting a moral and political position—is a movement to a wider and more comprehensive sense of what literature can do and be. But inasmuch as I have projected international literature as no more than the sum of national literatures, some further category, one that involves interaction and mutual influence, not only mere addition, is necessary. One might call this category, after Jameson's suggestion, *world literature;* I prefer to call it *cosmopolitan literature.*

A cosmopolitan literature would be constituted not only by the simple sum but by the complex interaction of national literatures. Such a literature of course does not yet exist—nor can it fully exist short of a cosmopolitan world order. In the meantime, it may be useful to work toward it on the theoretical as well as on the material level, reading the social and the cultural in tandem, as I tried to do in the last chapter. The concept of a cosmopolitan literary canon may seem as utopian as that of a cosmopolitan world order, the polyvocal polity; but it, too, I will repeat, is utopian only to the extent that it is not yet imminent. The project of a cosmopolitan literature is not to overthrow the Tower of Babel but, as it were, to install a simultaneous translation system in it; not to homogenize human or literary differences but to make them at least mutually intelligible. As Allon White has written in relation to Bakhtin,

> Though our current fashion is to prioritize difference, and rightly, in the struggle against the false universalism and essentialism which has so oppressed all those who do not conform to the European, white, male, heterosexual shape which "Man" is evidently supposed to have, nevertheless, an ultimate political perspective of humanity as a unity-in-difference, a complex of co-existing and mutually understanding cultures, is just as important to any radical politics. (233)

It seems to me that the achievement of human "unity-in-difference" in practice not only in theory may well depend upon whether cultural variation can ultimately be treated—to refer to the metaphor I mentioned in passing in the Introduction—as a matter of the analog (more/less, louder/softer, hotter/colder, etc.), rather than the digital (on/off, either/or, etc.). While it is important to avoid the mistake of

poststructural deconstructionism, which digitalized the analog functions of communication and meaning, it is important as well to recognize that some cultural practices may
not merely be the variants of others but their negatives or
opposites.[10] It is not yet clear, as I noted in regard to Yaqui
deer songs, just *how* certain literatures can—*if* they can—
interact with others, whether some mediation or "translation" can be effected to permit such interaction. While I take
such interaction, the cornerstone of that polyphonic cosmopolitanism I have imagined, as a salutary thing, others, with
different moral and political values, may disagree.

For it is certainly the case that local, Indian literature is
quite sufficient unto itself, adequate, that is, to the purposes
of its performers and its immediate audiences. Why should
outsiders intrude upon it and try, as it were, to carry it away?
Scholars, like missionaries and settlers and mercantile capital-
ists before them, after all, have their own history of violence
and expropriation. Isn't culture best left to those who are of
it? As a matter of practical fact this simply will not be. But as
a matter of principle, ought it to be? Let me quote Dell
Hymes on this subject. Hymes writes,

10. In this regard, I am in substantial disagreement with students of Native
American literature like Karl Kroeber and Jarold Ramsey who have claimed that
(this is Kroeber) a "reader can rewardingly apply to traditional Indian narratives
the kind of critical attitude he brings to other literatures" (1981, 9), or (this is
Ramsey) that "the most valuable ethnographic resources we can turn to on behalf
of modern Indian writing are the transcribed oral-traditional literatures of the
tribes or groups in question" (1983, 189). Their universalist premise is that art is
art everywhere and that any sensitive person of goodwill can always appreciate
art. Like most extreme universalisms, this position slights the particular cultural
codes that make art recognizable as art with considerable differences from people
to people. It happens also to be the case that their own practice in interpretation
frequently runs counter to their stated principles, as I have tried to show in my
"Identity and Difference in the Criticism of Native American Literature."

A world in which knowledge of each people was owned exclusively by that people itself would be culturally totalitarian. Just as it is indefensible to have an anthropology in which only outsiders know, and insiders are only known, so it is simply to reverse that inequity. None of us is able to stand outside ourselves sufficiently to know ourselves comprehensively. (1987, 42–43)

Hymes operates here as a secular critic concerned to achieve a knowledge which all humankind may equally share. Such knowledge as it may be contained in traditional Native American literatures requires study both by "insiders," familiar with them "naturally," as their own, and by "outsiders," familiar with them "culturally," as subject/objects of study. Only to the extent that such persons can find terms to effect the mediation and translation I have referred to above, conveying both their similarity to and difference from the literature of the dominant culture, will they be available for inclusion in the national canon and in any cosmopolitan canon.

Still, as Heisenberg's principle showed the case to be with the mass and velocity of particles at the atomic level, so, too, is it with the presentation of oral materials at the textual level: for every gain there is a certain loss. A nearer approach to authenticity is likely to take us further from comprehensibility, while the privileging of comprehensibility cannot help but sacrifice some of the strangeness and difference of Other cultural production. For all of this, I take the ongoing work of scholars like Donald Bahr, Richard Bauman, William Bright, Regna Darnell, David Guss, Larry Evers, Dell Hymes, Leanne Hinton, M. Dale Kinkade, David MacAllester, Anthony Mattina, Joel Sherzer, Dennis Tedlock, and a number of others, as extremely promising. But, again, that is because I desire the interaction of traditional Indian literatures with the other literatures of the

United States, and desire their interaction with Western and other world literatures in the interest of producing a cosmopolitan canon. It is as a consequence of this desire that I turn next to some local/"Indian" and indigenous/mixed examples of Native American literature, considering them in relation to the questions I have raised thus far in this chapter.

On the local level, consider first the ongoing performances of traditional singers like Vincent Lewis (Tohono o'odham), Guadalupe Molina and Don Jesus Yoilo'i (Yaqui), Frank Mitchell (Navajo), among others; and traditional storytellers like Peter Seymour (Colville), Andrew Peynetsa (Zuni), Nick Thompson (Apache), and Yellowman (Navajo) among many, many others. Their performances, as I have already said, seem to me the best candidates for a specifically American *Indian* literature. Like Western literature in its generalized, pre-nineteenth-century sense, these performances, in cultural context, are not necessarily oriented functionally toward pedagogy *and* pleasure, teaching *and* delighting. Some songs are specifically for curing, marked by a strictly *functional* "dominant"; some stories are largely anecdotal, to be funny. But a very great many performances, sung or spoken, are precisely literary in the post-nineteenth-century sense. "Yaqui deer songs," Felipe Molina and Larry Evers write, "tell a continuing story of life and death in the wilderness world of the Sonoran desert" (8), which is paralleled by life "in that mythic, primeval place called by Yaquies *sea ania,* flower world" (7). And these songs are also "regarded by Yaqui people . . . as containing some of the most aesthetically pleasing Yaqui language spoken or sung" (10–11). As Anthony Mattina says of Colville stories, they "contain principle by principle the secrets of how to be Colville—what it means to have been preceded in life by Coyote, by the other animals of their land, and by the birds of their sky, and by the fishes of their waters" (1985, 16). As Mattina also points out, unless the storyteller manages to give pleasure—to keep interest alive—the audience (most of these tales being told at night) responds by simply falling asleep, children first, others after. Barre Toelken has quoted the Navajo storyteller Yellowman as saying, "If my children hear the stories, they will grow up to be good people; if they don't hear them, they will turn out to be bad" (80). For all the seriousness of this storytelling business, however, as Toelken notes, the Coyote stories told by Yellowman nonetheless make "everyone laugh" (80). So far as traditional narrative is concerned, something of this sort—that they are instruments of socialization and that they are pleasurable—can be said of a great many of them as they function in the cultural maintenance system of Native peoples throughout the United States (and, no doubt, of the Americas overall).

I want to ask of these traditional songs and stories, following Jameson's lead, whether they show sufficient similarity in their concerns, if not their forms, so that one might generalize and claim them "allegorical" in relation to some specific theme. I have a tentative suggestion to make that I hope will prove useful, but this is not to imply that local, Indian literature is as homogeneous a body of work as Jameson (unintentionally, I believe) implied "third world" or "national literature" to be. Thus I could not even tentatively specify a commonality of theme among Indian song types; there simply are not yet enough individual and comparative studies to allow for that. Story types, concerning which a great deal of work has recently been done, are also many and complex; nor are genres and subgenres uniform from tribe to tribe.

Among the Western Apache, for example, Keith Basso counts "four major and two minor genres. . . . The major genres include 'myths' . . . 'historical tales' . . . 'sagas' . . . and stories that arise in the context of gossip" (1984, 34). Coyote stories, however, are one of the minor genres, along with "seduction tales." Thus it would seem that Coyote stories are *not* to be classed among "myths" for the Western Apache—although they might well be so classed among Yellowman's Navajo people. Among the Swampy Cree, Howard Norman writes, "Wesucechak is the . . . Trickster" (1987, 402), one of the " 'human-like' beings" (403), like Coyote—or Mink, or Raven—about whom many stories exist. "Narratives concerning Wesucechak are categorized as atuyookao" (403), or legends of a hero. But these may concern "a time before the earth was in its present, definitive state (many Cree refer to this as 'before people'), . . . be contemporaneous with *otowemak,* ancestors . . ." (403), or involve life today. Are all of these to be considered myth? only the first type? the first two?

If the possibilities are so complex among story types with which we are relatively familiar, they become even more so when we turn to types we know less well, stories such as those Norman has collected as Swampy Cree "Windigo tales," for example. These can be told formally as "part of 'announced' performances" (Norman, 1982, 21), in the way that myths are frequently told, but they also exist in anecdotal, informal variants. What Keith Basso has called Apache "sagas," a major literary genre, are literally "*nit'eego nagoldi . . .* 'to tell of pleasantness' . . ." (1984, 34): do other peoples have parallel forms or transforms of this kind of telling? Then there are stories like that told by Peter Seymour, which Mattina has transcribed. Dealing with kings, restaurants, and printed notices, this is an instance, in Donald Bahr's view, of a "genre that we would call 'folktale' rather than 'myth' " (1988, 83), a genre that may be a subcategory of the possibly broad grouping of tales that make up what Bahr terms "Red Literature" (1988, 83). Bahr himself has recently reread a group of Yuman myths formerly studied by the great Alfred Kroeber as what he calls "romances." And, in "The Bible in Western Indian Mythology," Jarold Ramsey has examined stories that show similar borrowings from Euramerican culture, for all that they are incorporated into ancient forms; these stories are probably best *not* thought of as "mythology" at all. Similarly, in South America, David Guss has collected stories among the Yekuana of Brazil, which, entirely traditional in motif and manner, nonetheless take up the origin of the tape recorder.[11] Examples of this sort could easily be multiplied—although it is likely we would in the end conclude with Alan Dundes that "myth and folktale are not structurally distinct genres. . . . The distinction between them is wholly dependent upon content criteria [e.g., setting, time, and dramatis personae] or totally external factors such as belief or function" (in Wiget, 1985: 3) that differ from tribe to tribe. Thus the attempt "to find some clear and universal criteria for distinguishing different types of narratives," as Andrew Wiget has written, has been—and I would add, will probably remain—an "ever-elusive goal" (1985, 3).[12]

For all that, I would still chance a return to the question, in the manner posited by Jameson for "third world" or "national literature," whether there might be for large numbers of traditional stories, whatever their particular genre, some single dominant theme. And I will answer, in a tentative way, Yes,

11. See "Keeping it Oral."
12. Wiget's chapter on "Oral Narrative," in his *Native American Literature*, probably offers the best brief summary of these matters.

suggesting that they may be read as *tribal allegories* whose central concern is *kinship relations*.

Consider, first, the southwestern myths of Yuman peoples which Alfred Kroeber, near the end of his life, analyzed at length, only to conclude that they "revel in acmes of purposeless contradictions," show "deliberate or artistic incoherence," and treat as inconsequential "ordinary rules of satisfaction and moral proportion" (in Bahr, MS, n.p.). Donald Bahr's rereading of these stories as "romances," which I noted just above, sees them as concerned with "the theme of unbridled willfulness." Thus, Bahr writes, "I reject Kroeber's perception of deliberate artistic incoherence because I find the myths coherent." In a more generalizing fashion, Bahr adds that, "Myths are essentially about genealogical deformations or abnormalities. They are cosmic soap operas, they are family histories about times when there were no families." This, for him, is "the coherence behind what [Kroeber] misperceived as incoherence." and, as I should say, perhaps the central theme of myth narratives generally.

As one more piece of evidence in support of this hypothesis, let us consider a myth from the northwestern Clackamas Chinook, called, in its most recent translation by Dell Hymes, "Seal and Her Younger Brother Lived There." Jarold Ramsey's essay, "The Wife Who Goes Out like a Man, Comes Back as a Hero: The Art of Two Oregon Indian Narratives," summarizes the commentary on this story by Melville Jacobs, who first transcribed it, and by Hymes who retranslated it (and explained its verbal form) and alludes to others—Alan Dundes, Frank Kermode, J. Barre Toelken—who have referred to it, offering, as well, his own interpretation of it. Short of summarizing this material, let me say only that all the readings, however much they may differ—and Ramsey finds

those by Hymes and Jacobs "mutually exclusive" (1983, 80)—
have in common the familial focus of the story. All of them
might be said to read it as a family history about the time when
there were no families. This would seem to be true as well for
the second Oregon narrative Ramsey's essay considers, one
translated by Leo. J. Frachtenberg from a 1903 narration,
called "The Revenge Against the Sky People."[13]

To the extent, then, that Native American myth narrative
presents some form of tribal allegory, it is as with Jameson's
national allegory: libidinal investments are most certainly tied
to kinship responsibilities and the individual destiny bound
up with that of the larger social unit, tribe *or* nation. Whether
it is an adventuring male or female, or some newly arrived
relative by marriage who is the protagonist, the story will
have a bearing upon how kin are to behave toward one another so that not merely survival, but a good life as defined by
the particular culture can be maintained. (It should be said, if
only parenthetically, that the tribal allegory also always importantly includes or implies the issue of right relation to
supernaturals—"Above Beings," or "gods"—a dimension absent from the generally secularized national allegories.)

The value of these generalizations, of course, lies in their
claim to provide an overview, accommodating the apparently
disparate details of a wide range of texts to a pattern of sameness. That is also the danger of these generalizations, inasmuch as they can only be achieved by a certain suppression of
difference. Anthony Mattina is no doubt correct in saying
that "ethnography, the study of different cultures, attracts
more nominalists than universalists," while "literature . . .

---

13. One might add here Keith Basso's gloss on a historical tale told by Mrs.
Annie Peaches, that it "deals with the harmful consequences that may come to
persons who overstep traditional role boundaries" (1984, 37) as these relate specifically to parents and in-laws.

[attracts] more universalists than generalists" (1985, 6), but perhaps modern cultural studies will be the field that attracts those committed to dialogue and a dialectical relation between the particular and the general.

It is at this point that, having said this much (or little) about the themes of Native American local narrative, I ought to consider their forms. Jameson's observation, noted earlier, that the theme of political solutions to third world problems tends to manifest itself formally in problems of narrative closure, is an attempt to establish a relationship between a typical theme and its (typical) formal expression as this relationship appears historically in a particular literary category, that of third world literature. Can we correlate the typical theme of Indian narrative as I have specified it to any typicality of form?

I must answer, speaking only for myself, Not now, not yet. For one thing, we don't know what traditional story telling sessions were actually like; we don't even know what a "real" telling even of some stories we have on tape or in translation (e.g., a telling to a culturally prepared audience, which, as we've noted with Silko, and can confirm with reference to many others, means an audience prepared to respond) would have been like. We certainly do know that narrators telling a story to an anthropologist or linguist, an audience of one, would react to that fact, sometimes offering just a bare outline or summary as the "whole" story. Even for a culturally prepared audience, narrators always modified and adjusted their tellings. Coyote stories, for example, could be longer or shorter, the episodes multiplied or not, so that it becomes difficult to speak of form with these narratives. The revival of traditional storytelling among contemporary Indians provides much material for study—which is currently progressing.

For all of this, questions of form in Native American narrative are in any case contingent upon questions of format, the necessity to translate not only one language into another but one medium (speech, the voice) into another (writing, the text). Anyone who would present these materials for study has the problem not merely of what words to offer by way of translation of one language to another, hoping to convey (at least not entirely obscure) the linguistic structure of what is said, but also of what transcriptional strategies—what layout on the page—to offer so as to convey (at least not entirely obscure) the immediate and dramatic feel of oral performance. Much has been done in both these regards, yet it must be said that there is no way to translate and present Indian oral performance in any completely satisfactory way, inasmuch—as I have tried to show elsewhere—every fullness here entails its inevitable emptiness, presence its inevitable absence.[14]

Those in any regard familiar with Native American literatures will be aware of the debates that have raged and continue to rage over these matters. They will be aware, too, of the major contributions to these debates over the last twenty years of Dell Hymes and Dennis Tedlock foremost among others. So far as these can be summarized—and I don't want, here, too much to go over ground others have already covered—one might speak of the particle-pause argument, Hymes attempting to indicate dramatic structure in a narrative by means of linguistic markers in the text (Hymes for the most part working not from actual performances or tapes but from transcriptions of earlier recorders), Tedlock attempting to indicate dramatic effect by dynamic shifts (volume changes, or vowel lengthening, rising or falling pitch; Tedlock works from tape recordings he has made).[15] William

14. See my "Post-Structuralism and Oral Literature."
15. My summary hardly begins to do justice to the transcriptions of Hymes and Tedlock. Still, for what use it may be to those unfamiliar with their work, let

Bright has noted that there appears to be, in point of fact, a high correlation/correspondence between the two methods,

---

me offer some (truncated) illustrations. Here is just the opening of Hymes' translation of Louis Simpson's "The Deserted Boy":

> [I. The people and the boy.]
> i/A(1) Now then they told a boy,
>   "Now let us go for reeds."
>   Long ago the boy was mean.
> (2) Now then they said,
>   "Now you will take him for reeds."
> (3) Now then they told them,
>   "You shall abandon him there." (1981, 145)

Pertinent to the concerns of this book as a whole are Hymes's introductory comments to his translation. He writes,

> The Northwest states have done little for Native American literature. If they are ever to be recognized as homes of authors of world reputation, it will be in large part because of what we can know of the art of Louis Simpson, of Victoria Howard (a Clackamas), of Charles Cultee (a Kathlamet and Shoal-water Chinook), and others like them. (1981, 144)

Here is an example of Tedlock's mode of transcription, from near the conclusion of the tale, "The Girl Who Took Care of the Turkeys":

> YEE-E-E-E HU^{LI}HU^{LI}HU^{LI} TOK TOK TOK TOK
> THE ONE WHO WAS DANCING HEARD HIM.
>   LHA^{PAA}——
> HE FLEW BACK to the place
> where they were penned, and
> the girl ran all the way back.
> When she got to the place where they were penned, they
>   sang again, they sang and FLEW AWAY, GOING ON
> until they came to what is now Turkey Tracks,
>   and they glided down there. (1978, 72)

Let me also give a very brief excerpt from the "Guide to Reading Aloud" that Tedlock places before the actual story transcriptions themselves.

O——n he went.	Hold vowels followed by dashes for about two seconds.
KERSPLASHHHHHH	Hold repeated consonants for about two seconds
aaaaaaAAAAAAH	Produce a crescendo when a repeated vowel changes from lower case to capitals.
l$_{a_{a_{a_{a_a}}}}$ ta	Produce a glissando for ascending or descending vowels. (1978, xxxiii)

which others (Bright, Kinkade, Sherzer, Toelken, et al.)
have adopted and/or adapted. There is no doubt that the
work of Hymes and Tedlock has revolutionized this field.
What also seems to be the case is that their procedures,
powerful as they are, are not inevitable. If Hymes privileges narrative structure linguistically marked by particles
(etc.); if Tedlock privileges performative dynamics marked
by pauses (etc.)—orientations toward the language and toward the speaker—then we might also instantiate Mattina's
orientation toward the translator, which privileges neither
the linguistic structure of the original nor its delivery in
performance but, rather, the translator's feel for what an
"Indian" version in English might be like. Mattina's commitment to "Red English" versions of Native narrative provides another option for understanding the particular artistry of local, Indian literatures in addition to the major
initiatives of Hymes and Tedlock.[16] In each case, we have a
transcriptional and translational "solution" that may serve
as a type of mediation between the local and the national,
rendering the former in terms more or less comprehensible
to the latter.

16. I give as an example the conclusion to Mattina and deSautel's translation
of Seymour's "The Golden Woman":

He said: "This here is the Golden Woman. Maybe you've heard about her
in a story, in some other country that I never seen where she popped out of the
water. That's your daughter-in-law, that's the one I married. Right now we're
married. I was the one that.got her and then I brought her and then we got
married and then we came back."

Now I'm going to walk away. The one I'm teaching [reference is to Mattina],
I'm teaching him, and then we wanted fairy tale stories, and then I told him:
"All right, I'll tell you about this Golden Woman." And now it's two weeks
and I'm talking all this time, and it's just now that I ended the story. Now I
quit talking. (52)

I will conclude with a turn to some North American examples of indigenous literature, at least to remark their occasional thematic relation to the tribal allegory concerned with kinship relations I have ascribed to the myth-narrative part of traditional Indian literature. Here, perhaps because the influence of the Euramerican tradition tends to loosen the constraints that traditionally allied particular themes to particular genres, it seems reasonable to move back and forth among the types of literature the West defines as not so much song, story, and oratory, but more nearly poetry, fiction, and autobiography. What attachments to kinship concerns may mean formally for a given poem, story, novel, or autobiography remains to be worked out.

Let me return to Wendy Rose's "What My Father Said." Perhaps it will not be amiss to quote it in its entirety.

What My Father Said

when lightning danced
west of the mesa
was this: that for us
among the asphalt
and black shadowed structures
of the city
there is some question
about living our lives
and not melting back
to remembered stone, to adobe, to grass,
innocent and loud, sweetly singing
in the summer rain
and rolling clouds.

Begin, he said, by giving back;
as you eat, they eat
so never be full.

Don't let it get easy.
Remember them
think of those ones
that were here before,
remember
how they were hungry,
their eyes like empty bowls,
those ribs sticking out,
those tiny hands.

Your grandmother is singing
that as your feet fold
and your apron wrinkles
kneeling by the stove
you may hear your clan
in the sound of stirring,
find magic stored
in the bottom
of the basket.

Remember the spirits
lying in the scrub,
remember the spirits
in the tree tops huddled,
remember to speak,
to smile, to beckon,
   come and eat
   come and eat
   live in my tongue
   and forget
   your hunger.

"[A]s you eat, they eat," says the speaker's father, "Remember them"; think of grandmother; "you may hear your clan," as well as the spirits in the tree tops. To live is to live familially, tribally. A great many Native American poets develop themes of this nature, as a look through Duane Niatum's recent *Harper's Anthology of 20th-Century Native American Poetry* will show. It will also show that this theme is by no means ubiquitous, replaced in a great many instances by concerns more typical of the dominant culture.

The same is probably true of indigenous fiction. Ralph Salisbury's "The Sonofabitch and the Dog," as I noted earlier, presents an individual protagonist whose adventures may serve as an allegory of Native people's experience throughout the Americas, inasmuch as Native people often were forced, like the narrator, to seem crazy and dumb to the dominant culture if they were to survive. Native Americans, like the unnamed narrator of Salisbury's story, might well survive as Indians, but not quite or not yet as people free of the colonial experience. If Salisbury's story is a tribal allegory, however, it is a tribal allegory of posttribal experience, where no kin are present. Still, some of the best-known centemporary Native American novels—I am thinking, here, of Momaday's *House Made of Dawn* and Silko's *Ceremony*, of James Welch's *Winter in the Blood*, and Louise Erdrich's *Love Medicine*—are very much concerned with the tribal as it can indeed be experienced in terms of the family.

Given the dominant culture's insistence upon singling out the individual, and requiring separation from the familial nexus for the achievement of a unique identity, the Native American autobiographer committed to his or her Indianness has sometimes found it necessary to discover metaphors for family, to shift from the tribal allegory concerned with kinship relations to part-to-whole relations *of one sort or another* (e.g., *not* strictly of the individual to his kin). That Native American autobiographers have adopted this synecdochic mode (part-to-whole) rather than the metonymic mode (part-to-part) of modern Western autobiography seems evidence of the persistence of traditional forms of self-conception among educated and sophisticated contemporary Indian writers,[17] whatever distance they may feel from the "cosmic soap opera" of traditional, mythological family orientations.

Some of these indigenous texts, as well as some of the textualizations of local, Indian literature ought to be included in the canon of American literature so that they might illuminate and interact with the texts of the dominant, Euramerican culture, to produce a genuinely heterodox national canon.

17. See my "Native American Autobiography and the Synecdochic Self."

Conclusion

That the question of the canon occupies us at all today is, I believe, a legacy of the 1960s. For all the many "missed revolutions"—the phrase is from Paul Goodman (231 ff.)—of that currently maligned decade, at least the cultural revolution then "demanded" by students and faculty is one that has not yet or completely been "missed," remaining a matter of ongoing contest both within the academy and beyond. Not only does PMLA come belatedly to a special issue on the canon, but articles on the subject have appeared in *Newsweek* and *TIME* magazine, the *Wall Street Journal,* and the *New York Times,* among other less widely circulated "print media" of general interest. The popular articles I have seen tend, for the most part, either to bewail or at best worriedly acknowledge the continuing process of alterations in the liberal arts curricula of the highest academies of the empire. The wailing as well as the worry are related to the fact that such alterations are being made on explicitly ideological and political grounds, which politicization of what is conventionally taken to be an area for esthetic evaluation only (i.e., literature is to be treated strictly in terms of its excellence or lack of excellence, independent of its "ideas," or its "content"), as in the breathtaking illogic of Lynne Cheney, William Bennett's successor at the National Endowment for the Humanities, presumably explains why the numbers of students majoring in English or philosophy or history is now

down! The pressures of the job market beyond the under-
graduate major, the incommensurability of salaries (even for
those who get good jobs) in publishing or teaching with
those in business or engineering or law are largely irrelevant
to Cheney's Adam-Smith world of free and independent
individuals making purely rational choices. But even if such
a world existed, it would not necessarily be the case that
students were turned off by the notion that literary studies
were, in another term from the 1960s, somehow "relevant"
to the world they live in.

Meanwhile, it happens that the traditional Western Civilization courses, those of the putatively apolitical and purely ap-
preciative kind approved by the Bennetts, and Cheneys, and
Allan Blooms, as Cyrus Veeser has pointed out in a letter to
the New York *Times,* "are the offspring of a government-
sponsored propaganda course instituted during World War I"
called "War Issues": "At the war's end, the Columbia College
faculty and deans took War Issues as a model for an innova-
tive course called Contemporary Civilization" (A22). Whether
students today are actually offered, or required to take, a
course in Western or Contemporary Civilization or instead
must define such categories as the sum of their courses of
study, their view of the civilization of the West will nonetheless
depend upon what they have read in those courses, by what
have been offered to them as the canonical texts. And, as
Veeser correctly concludes, "defining civilization is very much
a political act" (A22).

Once upon a time, of course, civilization was what *we* had
while others had only culture, or rather, cultures, for a great
number of those could exist while there could be only one
civilization. Today, culture and civilization are used more or
less synonomously. For all of that, in the literary world of the

West, "our" work always takes precedence over "theirs," not, of course, because it is more "civilized"—one knows better than to say such a thing!—but because it is more complex, more subtle: more excellent. Just as we have religion while they have superstition, so, too, do complexity and subtlety in their highest degree belong pretty exclusively to the writing of the West. The Rest have charm and energy and naturalness, in their writing, but that doesn't provide a very great deal to work with for our highly developed critical capabilities. Thus, the most complex and subtle of our critics, the critical theorists, have until recently been little attracted to the cultural production of people on the margins of "civilization"; their attention has been to Nietszche and Rousseau and Proust; to Faulkner and Eliot and Pound: the great stretch was to Herman Melville and William Carlos Williams.

This situation has now begun to change—at least, as I noted earlier, in regard to work by Afro-American writers, by women, and by gays and lesbians. It is changing, too, for work by Native American writers—but changing less, and changing, as I think, too slowly. Let me repeat my contention that we will never comprehend American civilization or culture (not to say American society) until we comprehend the European component of it in historical relation to the Afro-American and the Indian, and, increasingly, in relation to those cultural others whose Otherness is nonetheless deeply American. And we will never see these Other cultural productions properly in their relation to the European until we learn to recognize the particular forms of their subtlety and complexity. Primitive means complex, Jerome Rothenberg insisted— also in the 1960s. And work over the last twenty years has documented this assertion.

While there are other values beside complexity and subtlety

worth celebrating, still, so far as our material situation makes these important for our cultural situation, those I have called Indianists can show the theorists just how complex and subtle the oral tradition and its written affiliates can be. And the theorists, to be sure, can show Indianists some further ways to articulate complexity. Indianists have not been able to ignore theory, its *cachet,* if not its actual power, having become so considerable in the academy over the past ten years. But their relation to it has generally been scornful and dismissive. Meanwhile, the theorists, as I have said more than once, have simply not been much interested in what the Native American specialists know. This is not a good situation and it has been one of the purposes of this book to bring some of the knowledge of these disparate groups together.

With Walt Whitman, I believe poetry—literature—can be "good health" to us, and "filter and fibre" our blood. For all that there is no fixed entity that may eternally, essentially, autonomously stand as literature, still, as I have tried to show, literary discourse historically and in the aggregrate can be differentiated from other types of discourse. There is much to be learned from Terry Eagleton's witty analysis of the sign in the London Underground that announces, "Dogs must be carried on the escalator" (1983: 6) as potentially a "literary" text. Eagleton shows that these words can in fact be read so that they conform to various definitions of literary discourse in regard to ambiguity, overdetermined signification, and the like. I agree, and can add an example of my own from a recent cross-country drive: "Seat Belts Must be Worn." But to read either of these texts as literary requires that we remove them from their temporal and spatial milieus, remove them, indeed, from any normative context—and then go on to take single sentences as paradigmatic of extended discursive con-

structions. Some philosophers of language and many deconstructionists revel in this sort of thing; cultural critics, of
whom Eagleton is one of the best, should not. So I think it
still makes sense to speak of literature as a term with specifiable reference if not independent existence.

In just the same way, I have tried to say that for all my
suspiciousness of the received canon of American literature, I
believe in the concept of the canon. Meanwhile, to speak of
revising the canon, it should be repeated, does not mean
simply to install a "new canon" of one's own to replace the
old, as in the D. C. Heath Company's "Newsletter" proposing "New Canon Authors" and "New Canon Syllab[i]" (4).
Even in the unlikely case that a majority of teachers suddenly
began to have their students read "new canon authors," that
would still not make those authors canonical, only current;
and currency is not canonicity—if, that is, one takes the term
seriously.

The canon, as I have tried to show, must arise through the
responsible exercise of principles of exclusivity and inclus-
ivity. Representing a selection from among the most technically interesting and morally and politically admirable of
texts—these qualities, as I have said, sometimes in conflict—
the canon is a fragile construction, always open to question
and to change, even as it seeks a certain permanence and
imperviousness to question. The canon cannot be made in a
day nor reconstructed overnight, but to say this is hardly to
turn one's responsibility for what is read and taught over to
the slow-grinding millstones of Time. What we come to see
as the canon of American literature can help us define who we
are as Americans and, as Americans, to place ourselves in the
cosmopolitan world of peoples and nations. Different canons,
different definitions and placements: that is why J. Hillis

Miller, William Bennett, Allan Bloom, and E. D. Hirsch, among others, continue to contest these matters with the reconstructionists. And that is why I have tried to insist upon the relations between the textual and the social, for all that the textual and the social are not mirror images of one another. To read Native American literature, to take pleasure in it and try to understand it, can be an end in itself, like going to a museum or a concert. It can also engage us in a struggle for the values that determine our lives.

About five miles outside the town of Why, Arizona, in a Tohono O'odham (formerly Papago) Indian village, there is a poet currently at work on a body of material which promises to be of particular interest. A. C. doesn't write his songs out, nor does he sit down to compose them in the various ways familiar to the West; rather, he dreams them, consistent with one of the Papago models of cultural production. And lately, his wife says, he has been dreaming a lot, regularly, maybe even too much. My friend, the anthropologist Donald Bahr, who took me to meet this singer, described his understanding of what A. C. is doing in a way that reminded me of what T. S. Eliot defined as the relationship between "tradition" and the "individual talent." Indeed, it may be that A. C.'s current practice provides even a better illustration than any Eliot could give of the relation between the traditional and individual, inasmuch as the European tradition to which Eliot made exclusive reference was far more diverse than he tended to allow. And A. C.'s tradition, while hardly simple, seems still a bit less variegated (but maybe not).

This is to say that many of the images in A. C.'s songs, as Bahr has pointed out to me, are familiar in Papago cosmology and occur in the prose narratives that we call their "my-

thology." But some of the images are very much A. C.'s own
and seem to be invoked to dramatize themes of personal importance to him. He is particularly concerned with death,
perhaps because just now (summer 1987) he has liver and
kidney trouble, or perhaps generally. When he sings his
songs, the melodies are recognizable as more or less standard
Papago melodies for this kind of song, but his songs are long,
much longer than what is traditional, nor do they fall clearly
into the known Papago dreamsong categories. A. C.'s language will probably also prove both traditional and personal,
historically predictable and humanly, individually unpredict-
able: but this we can only guess, for Bahr has managed to
record only one of these songs nor has he yet done more than
an initial working-through of the language. A. C. is a Papago
speaker, and his songs are in the Papago language; but he is
wild for words, a lover of tongues, as in the West, too, we
often think great poets are. For fun he will improvise what he
calls (saying the words in English) an "unknown language"
which is probably made up of nonsense syllables—although
these seem to have some of the clicks and gutturals of Apache
and Navajo speech. A. C. also knows English and Spanish,
but these do not, at least so far as is immediately apparent,
influence the songs he dreams.

So we have here a body of original traditional poetry being
produced by someone fascinated with languages and preoccu-
pied with death. He lives in a Tohono O'odham village, but
he is not oblivious—how could he be—to the Anglo world
that surrounds him. He hears its music, too (actually, we
heard *reggae* music coming from a house nearby), and he also
is very much interested in the music of the Yaqui Indians to
which he listens on cassettes, the oral tradition appropriating
those technologies congenial to it. It is a local, Indian poetry

that he is making, but he is making it in a world where a good many of the rules are made by the whites. His is an Indian poetry that responds to that fact, even as it continues to draw form and content from materials that were around long before the whites came.

Maybe Bahr will record some more of these songs and translate them. If he does—and if he doesn't, there isn't anybody waiting in line to take over the task—then they will be available for celebration and study, for the sheer pleasure anyone may take in them, and for what we may learn from them. Might they then take some place in the national canon of American literature, or somehow bear upon it? Might they even one day enter into relation with the cosmopolitan canon of the world's literature? I, for one, hope so.

Works Cited

Ahmad, Aijaz. "Jameson's Rhetoric of Otherness and the 'National Allegory.' " *Social Text* 17 (1987): 3–25.

Apes, William. *Eulogy on King Philip, as Pronounced at the Odeon in Federal Street, Boston, by the Reverend William Apes, an Indian. January 8, 1836.* Boston, 1836; rpt. Brookfield, Mass.: Lincoln Dexter, 1985.

———. *The Experiences of Five Christian Indians: Or the Indian's Looking Glass for the White Man.* Boston: James B. Dow, 1833.

———. *Indian Nullification of the Unconstitutional Laws of Massachusetts, Relative to the Marshpee Tribe, or, The Pretended Riot Explained.* Boston: Jonathan Howe, 1835.

———. *A Son of the Forest: The Experience of William Apes, a Native of the Forest.* New York: Published by the Author, 1829.

Astrov, Margot, ed. *The Winged Serpent: An Anthology of American Indian Prose and Poetry.* New York: Fawcett, 1973 [1946].

Auerbach, Erich. *Mimesis.* Princeton, N.J.: Princeton University Press, 1953.

Aupaumut, Hendrick. *A Narrative of an Embassy to the Western Indians, from the Original Manuscript of Hendrick Aupaumut, with Prefatory Remarks by Dr. B. H. Coates.* Pennsylvania Historical Society Memoirs II, pt. 1 (1827 [1791]): 61–131.

Austin, Mary. *The American Rhythm: Studies and Reexpressions of Amerindian Songs.* Boston: Cooper Square, 1930 [1923].

———. Introduction to *The Path on The Rainbow: An Anthology of Songs and Chants from the Indians of North America,* ed. George W. Cronyn. Chapman, 266–275.

———. "The Path on the Rainbow." *Dial* 31 (May 1919): 569–570.

Bahr, Donald M. "Dream Songs." *Dictionary of Native American Literature,* ed. Andrew Wiget et al. Westport, Conn.: The Greenwood Press, forthcoming.

———. "Kroeber's Romances." Unpublished MS.

———. Review of *The Golden Woman: The Colville Narrative of Peter Seymour,* tr. Anthony Mattina and M. deSautel. *American Indian Quarterly* 12 (1988): 83–86.

Baker, Houston A., Jr. *Modernism and the Harlem Renaissance.* Chicago: University of Chicago Press, 1987.

Bakhtin, Mikhail. *The Dialogic Imagination: Four Essays by Mikhail Bakhtin,* ed. Michael Holquist. Austin: University of Texas Press, 1981.

———. *Problems of Dostoevsky's Poetics,* ed. and tr. Caryl Emerson. Minneapolis: University of Minnesota Press, 1984.

Barthes, Roland. "To Write: An Intransitive Verb." Macksey and Donato, 134–144.

———. "Reflexions sur un manuel." *L'Enseignement de la litterature,"* ed. Serge Doubrovsky and Tzvetan Todorov. Paris: Plon, 1971.

———. *The Pleasure of the Text.* New York: Hill and Wang, 1975.

Bartlett, Lee. "Gary Snyder's *Myths and Texts* and the Monomyth." *Western American Literature* 17 (1982): 137–48.

Basso, Keith, "Speaking with Names." *Cultural Anthropology* 3 (1988): 99–130.

———. "Stalking with Stories: Names, Places, and Moral Narratives among the Western Apache." In *Text Play and Story: The Construction and Reconstruction of Self and Society;* ed. Edward Bruner, 19–55. Washington, D.C.: American Ethnology Society, 1984.

Baym, Nina. "Melodramas of Beset Manhood: How Theories of American Fiction Exclude Women Authors." In *The New Feminist Criticism: Essays on Women, Literature, Theory,* ed. Elaine Showalter, 63–80. New York: Pantheon, 1985.

Benjamin, Walter. "The Storyteller: Reflections on the Works of Nikolai Leskov." In *Illuminations,* ed. Hannah Arendt, 83–110. New York: Schocken, 1969.

Bercovitch, Sacvan. "Foreword." In Charles M. Segal and David C. Stineback, *Puritans, Indians and Manifest Destiny.* New York: G. P. Putnam's Sons, 1977.

———, ed. *Reconstructing American Literary History.* Cambridge: Harvard University Press, 1986.

———, and Myra Jehlen, eds. *Ideology and Classic American Literature.* Cambridge: Cambridge University Press, 1986.

Berkhofer, Robert F., Jr. "Cultural Pluralism versus Ethnocentrism in the New Indian History." Martin, 35–45.

Bevis, William. "American Indian Verse Translations." Chapman, 308–323.

Black Hawk. *Black Hawk: An Autobiography,* ed. Donald Jackson. Urbana: University of Illinois Press, 1955 [ed. J. B. Patterson, 1833].

Bridgman, Richard. "The American Studies of Henry Nash Smith." *The American Scholar* 56 (1987): 259–268.

Brown, Catherine. *Memoirs of Catherine Brown a Christian Indian of the Cherokee Nation,* ed. Rufus B. Anderson. Philadelphia: American Sunday School Union, 1824.

Bruchac, Joseph. Letter to ASAIL Notes (March 1988).

Brumble, H. David. *American Indian Autobiography.* Berkeley, Los Angeles, London: University of California Press, 1988.

———, *An Annotated Bibliography of American Indian and Eskimo Autobiographies.* Lincoln: University of Nebraska Press, 1981.

———. "A Supplement to *An Annotated Bibliography of American Indian and Eskimo Autobiographies.*" *Western American Literature* 17 (1982): 242–260.

Bruns, Gerald. "Structuralism, Deconstruction, and Hermeneutics." *Diacritics* 14 (1984): 12–23.

Burlin, Natalie Curtis, ed. *The Indians' Book: An Offering by the American Indians of Indian Lore, Musical and Narrative, to Form a Record of the Songs and Legends of Their Race.* New York: Dover, 1968 [1907].

Carrithers, Michael, Steven Collins, and Steven Lukes, eds. *The Category of the Person: Anthropology, Philosophy, History.* Cambridge: Cambridge University Press, 1985.

Castro, Michael. *Interpreting the Indian: Twentieth-Century Poets and the Native American.* Albuquerque: University of New Mexico Press, 1983.

Catlin, George. *Letters and Notes on the Manners, Customs, and Conditions of North American Indians,* vol. 2. New York: Dover, 1973 [1844].

Chapman, Abraham, ed. *Literature of the American Indians: Views and Interpretations.* New York: New American Library, 1975.

Chona, Maria. *The Autobiography of a Papago Woman,* ed. Ruth Underhill. Memoirs of the American Anthropological Association, No. 46, 1936; rpt. as *Papago Woman,* New York: Holt, Rinehart, and Winston, 1979.

Clausen, Christopher. "Point of View: It Is Not Elitist to Place Major Literature at the Center of the English Curriculum." *The Chronicle of Higher Education,* January 13, 1988: 52–53.

Clements, William M. "Faking the Pumpkin: On Jerome Rothenberg's Literary Offenses." *Western American Literature* 16 (1981): 193–204.

Clifford, James. "On Ethnographic Authority." *Representations* 2 (1983): 132–43.

———. "Review Essay of Edward Said's *Orientalism.*" *History and Theory* 19 (1980): 204–223.

Clifford, James, and George Marcus, eds. *Writing Culture: The Poetics and Politics of Ethnography.* Berkeley, Los Angeles, London: University of California Press, 1986.

Consumer Reports. "Life at the Edge." June 1987: 375–378.

Crevecoeur, St. Jean de. "What Is an American?" In *Letters from an American Farmer.* New York: Boni and Liveright, 1925 [1782].

Day, A. Grove. *The Sky Clears: Poetry of the American Indians.* Lincoln: University of Nebraska Press, 1964 [1951].

D. C. Heath Company. *The Heath Anthology of American Literature Newsletter* 1 (1988).

DeLoria, Vine. "Introduction." *Black Elk Speaks,* ed. by John G. Neihardt. Lincoln: University of Nebraska Press, 1979.

de Man, Paul. "The Resistance to Theory." *Yale French Studies* 63 (1982): 3–20.

Densmore, Frances. *Chippewa Music.* Washington: Bureau of American Ethnology Publications, 1910.

Derrida, Jacques. "Like the Sound of the Sea Deep within a Shell: Paul de Man's War." *Critical Inquiry* 14 (1988): 590–652.

———. "Structure, Sign, and Play in the Discourse of the Human Sciences." Macksey and Donato, 247–264.

Drake, Benjamin. *The Life and Adventures of Black Hawk, with Sketches of Keokuk, the Sac and Fox Indians, and the Late Black Hawk War.* Cincinnati: H. S. and J. Applegate and Co., 1851 [1838].

Drinnon, Richard. *Facing West: The Metaphysics of Indian-Hating and Empire-Building.* Minneapolis: University of Minnesota Press, 1980.

Durham, Jimmie. "An Open letter on Recent Developments in the American Indian Movement/International Indian Treaty Council." Unpublished MS, 1980.

Dwyer, Kevin. *Moroccan Dialogues: Anthropology in Question.* Baltimore: Johns Hopkins University Press, 1982.

Eagleton, Terry. *Literary Theory: An Introduction.* Minneapolis: University of Minnesota Press, 1983.

———. "The Subject of Literature." *Cultural Critique* 1 (1985–1986): 95–104.

———. *Walter Benjamin, or Towards a Revolutionary Criticism,* London: Verso, 1981.

Eliot, T. S. "Tradition and the Individual Talent." In *The Sacred Wood,* 47–59. London: Methuen, 1920.

Ellis, John. "What Does Deconstruction Contribute to Theory of Criticism?" *New Literary History* 19 (1988): 259–280.

Erdrich, Louise. *Love Medicine.* New York: Bantam, 1984.

Evers, Lawrence J., and Felipe Molina. *Yaqui Deer Songs: Maasa Bwikam, A Native American Poetry.* Tucson: Sun Tracks-University of Arizona Press, 1987.

Ferguson, Priscilla, Philippe Desan, and Wendy Griswold. "Editors' Introduction: Mirrors, Frames, and Demons—Reflections on the Sociology of Literature." *Critical Inquiry* 14 (1988): 421–430.

Fiedler, Leslie A. "Literature as an Institution: The View from 1980." Fiedler and Baker, 73–91.

Fiedler, Leslie A., and Houston A. Baker, Jr., eds. *English Literature: Opening Up the Canon.* Baltimore: Johns Hopkins University Press, 1981.

Foley, Barbara. "The Politics of Deconstruction." *Genre* 17 (1984): 113–134.

Forbes, Jack. *Native Americans and Nixon: Presidential Politics and Minority Self-Determination, 1969–1972.* Los Angeles: University of California-American Indian Studies Center, 1981.

———. "Colonialism and Native American Literature: Analysis." *Wicazo Sa Review* 3 (1987): 17–23.

Fowler, David, et al. *The Letters of Eleazar Wheelock's Indians,* ed. James Dow McCallum. Hanover, N.H.: Dartmouth College Publications, 1937.

Fox-Genovese, Elizabeth. "Gender, Race, Class, Canon." *Salmagundi* 72 (1986): 131–43.

Franklin, H. Bruce. "English as an Institution: The Role of Class." Fiedler and Baker, 92–106.

Freud, Sigmund. "A Difficulty in the Path of Psycho-Analysis." *The Complete Psychological Works of Sigmund Freud,* vol. 17 (1917–1918), 137–144. Ed. James Strachey. London: Hogarth Press, 1955.

Gates, Henry Louis. *The Signifying Monkey*. New York: Oxford University Press, 1988.

Geertz, Clifford. "Common Sense as a Cultural System." *Local Knowledge: Further Essays in Interpretive Anthropology*. New York: Basic Books, 1983.

———. " 'From the Native's Point of View': On the Nature of Anthropological Understanding." Shweder and LeVine, 123–136.

———. "Ideology as a Cultural System." *The Interpretation of Cultures*. New York: Basic Books, 1973, 193–233.

———. "Thick Description: Toward an Interpretive Theory of Culture." *The Interpretation of Cultures*. New York: Basic Books, 3–32.

Gill, Sam D. *Mother Earth: An American Story*. Chicago: University of Chicago Press, 1987.

Golding, Alan C. "A History of American Poetry Anthologies." von Hallberg, 279–307.

Goodman, Paul. *Growing Up Absurd*. New York: Vintage, 1960.

Gookin, Daniel. *Historical Collections of the Indians of New England*. Salem, N.H.: Ayer Co., 1972 [1792].

Greenblatt, Stephen. *Renaissance Self-Fashioning: From More to Shakespeare*. Chicago: University of Chicago Press, 1980.

Greenway, John. *Literature among the Primitives*. Hatboro, Pa.: Folklore Associates, 1964.

Guillory, John. "The Ideology of Canon-Formation: T.S. Eliot and Cleanth Brooks." von Hallberg, 337–362.

Hauberg, John H. "The New Black Hawk State Park." *Journal of the Illinois State Historical Society* 20 (1927): 265–281.

Hymes, Dell. "Anthologies and Narrators." Swann and Krupat, 1987a, 41–84.

———. *"In Vain I Tried to Tell You"*: *Essays in Native American Ethnopoetics*. Philadelphia: University of Pennsylvania Press, 1981.

———. "Some North Pacific Coast Poems: A Problem in Anthropological Philology." *American Anthropologist* 67 (1965): 316–341.

Irving, John Treat, Jr. *Indian Sketches Taken During an Expedition to the Pawnee Tribes,* ed. John Francis McDermott. Norman: University of Oklahoma Press, [1833].

James, Henry. *Hawthorne*. Ithaca: Cornell University Press, 1963 [1879].

———. *The American Scene*. Bloomington: Indiana University Press, 1963 [1907].

Jameson, Fredric. "From Criticism to History." *New Literary History* 12 (1981): 367–375.

———. "Periodizing the '60s." Sayres, et al., 178–209.

———. *The Political Unconscious: Narrative as a Socially Symbolic Act*. Ithaca: Cornell University Press, 1981.

———. "Postmodernism, or the Cultural Logic of Late Capitalism," *New Left Review* 146 (1984): 53–93.

————. "Third-World Literature in the Era of Multinational Capital" *Social Text* 15 (1986): 65–88.

Jehlen, Myra. "Introduction: Beyond Transcendence." Bercovitch and Jehlen, 1–18.

Jennings, Francis. *The Invasion of America: Indians, Colonialism, and the Cant of Conquest*. New York: Norton, 1975.

Kaiser, Rodolf. "Chief Seattle's Speech(es): American Origins and European Reception." Swann and Krupat, 1987*a*, 497–536.

Kampf, Louis, Paul Lauter, and Richard Ohmann. "Note." *PMLA* 102 (1987): 374.

Keiser, Alfred. *The Indian in American Literature*. New York: Octagon-Farrar, Straus and Giroux, 1970 [1933].

Kelley, Donald R. "Horizons of Intellectual History." *Journal of the History of Ideas* 58 (1987): 143–169.

Kelly, Ernece B., ed. *Searching for America*. Urbana: National Council of Teachers of English, 1972.

Kolodny, Annette. *The Lay of the Land: Metaphor as Experience and History in American Life and Letters*. Chapel Hill: University of North Carolina Press, 1975.

Kroeber, Karl. "An Introduction to the Art of Traditional American Indian Narration." Kroeber, 1–24.

————, ed. *Traditional American Indian Literatures: Texts and Interpretations*. Lincoln: University of Nebraska Press, 1981.

Krupat, Arnold. "American Autobiography: The Western Tradition." *Georgia Review* 35 (1981): 307–317.

————. "Anthropology in the Ironic Mode: The Work of Franz Boas." *Social Text* 19/20 (1988): 105–118.

————. *For Those Who Come After*. Berkeley, Los Angeles, London: University of California Press, 1985.

————. "Identity and Difference in the Criticism of Native American Literature." *Diacritics* 13 (1983): 2–13.

————. "Native American Autobiography and the Synecdochic Self." *American Autobiography: Retrospect and Prospect*, ed. Paul John Eakin. Madison: University of Wisconsin Press, forthcoming.

————. "Post-Structuralism and Oral Literature." Swann and Krupat, 1987*a*, 113–128.

Lacan, Jacques. "Of Structure as an Inmixing of an Otherness Prerequisite to Any Subject Whatever." Macksey and Donato, 186–194.

Lauter, Paul. "History and the Canon." *Social Text* 12 (1985): 94–101.

Lawrence, D. H. *Studies in Classic American Literature*. New York: Viking, 1973 [1925].

Longfellow, Henry Wadsworth. *Hiawatha*. New York: Crown, 1969 [1855].

Lovejoy, Arthur O. *The Great Chain of Being.* Cambridge: Harvard University Press, 1936.

———. "Reflections on the History of Ideas." *Journal of the History of Ideas* 1 (1940): 3–23.

———. "Reply to Professor Spitzer." *Journal of the History of Ideas* 5 (1944): 204–219.

Lukes, Steven. "Conclusion," Carrithers, Collins, and Lukes, 282–301.

Lyotard, Jean-François. *The Postmodern Condition: A Report on Knowledge.* Minneapolis: University of Minnesota Press, 1984.

Macksey, Richard, and Eugenio Donato, eds. *The Structuralist Controversy: The Languages of Criticism and the Sciences of Man.* Baltimore: Johns Hopkins University Press, 1972.

Manuel, Frank. "Lovejoy Revisited." *Daedalus* 46 (1987): 125–147.

Marcus, George, and Michael M. J. Fischer. *Anthropology as Cultural Critique.* Chicago: University of Chicago Press, 1986.

Marcus, George, and Dick Cushman. "Ethnographies as Texts." *Annual Review of Anthropology* 11 (1982): 25–69.

Martin, Calvin, ed. *The American Indian and the Problem of History.* New York: Oxford University Press, 1987.

Mather, Cotton. *Magnalia Christi Americana: Or, The Ecclesiastical History of New England.* New York: Arno, 1972 [1702].

Matthews, F. H. "The Revolt Against Americanism: Cultural Pluralism and Cultural Relativism as an Ideology of Liberation." *Canadian Review of American Studies* 1 (1970): 4–31.

Matson, N. *Memories of Shaubena,* 3rd ed. Chicago: R. Grainger and Co., 1882 [1878].

Matthiessen, F. O. *American Renaissance: Art and Expression in the Age of Emerson and Whitman.* New York: Oxford University Press, 1941.

Mattina, Anthony, and M. deSautel, trans. *The Golden Woman: The Colville Narrative of Peter Seymour.* Tucson: University of Arizona Press, 1985.

Mauss, Marcel. "A Category of the Human Mind: The Notion of Person, the Notion of Self." Trans. W. D. Halls. Carrithers, Collins, and Lukes, 1–25.

Meiners, R. K. "Marginal Men and Centers of Learning: New Critical Rhetoric and Critical Politics." *New Literary History* 18 (1986): 129–150.

Midgley, Mary. "Sex and Personal Identity: The Western Individualistic Tradition." *Encounter* 62–63 (1984): 50–55.

Miller, J. Hillis. "Presidential Address 1986: The Triumph of Theory, the Resistance to Reading, and the Question of the Material Base." *PMLA* 102 (1987): 281–291.

Miller, Perry. *Errand into the Wilderness.* Cambridge: Harvard University Press, 1956.

Miller, Wayne Charles. "Toward a New Literary History of the United States." *MELUS* 11 (1984): 5–25.

Milner, Andrew. "Criticism and Ideology: Andrew Milner Interviews Terry Eagleton." *Thesis Eleven* 12 (1985): 130–144.

Momaday, N. Scott. *House Made of Dawn*. New York: Harper and Row, 1968.

———. *The Names*. New York: Harper, 1976.

———. "Personal Reflections." Martin, 156–161.

———. *The Way to Rainy Mountain*. New York: Ballantine, 1970 [1969].

Mooney, James. *Calendar History of the Kiowa Indians*. Washington, D.C.: Smithsonian Institution Press, 1979 [1895–1896].

Morris, Wesley. *Toward a New Historicism*. Princeton: Princeton University Press, 1961.

Nelson, Richard K. *Make Prayers to the Raven: A Koyukon View of the Northern Forest*. Chicago: University of Chicago Press, 1983.

Niatum, Duane, ed. *Carriers of the Dream Wheel: Contemporary Native American Poetry*. New York: Harper and Row, 1975.

———, ed. *Harper's Anthology of 20th Century Native American Poetry*. New York: Harper and Row, 1988.

Norman, Howard, "Wesucechak Becomes a Deer and Steals Language: An Anecdotal Linguistics Concerning the Swampy Cree Trickster." Swann and Krupat, 1987*a*, 402–421.

———, ed. and trans. *Where the Chill Came From: Cree Windigo Tales and Journeys*. San Francisco: North Point Press, 1982.

———, ed. and trans. *The Wishing Bone Cycle: Narrative Poems of the Swampy Cree*. New York: Stonehill, 1976.

Occom, Samson. "A Short Narrative of My Life." *The Elders Wrote: An Anthology of Early Prose by North American Indians,* ed. Bernd Peyer, 12–18. Berlin: Dietrich Reimer Verlag, 1982 [1768].

———. "A Sermon Preached at the Execution of Moses Paul, an Indian." New York: Association for the Study of Native American Literatures, 1982 [1772].

Ong, Walter J., S.J. *Interfaces of the Word: Studies in the Evolution of Consciousness and Culture*. Ithaca: Cornell University Press, 1977.

Ortiz, Simon, ed. *Earth Power Coming*. Tsaile, Ariz.: Navajo Community College Press, 1983.

———. "This Preparation." Sanders and Peek, 467.

Parrington, Vernon L. *Main Currents in American Thought,* 3 vols. New York: Harcourt, 1927–1930.

Patterson, J. B. ed. *The Autobiography of Ma-ka-tai-me-she-kia-kiak, or Black Hawk*. Rock Island, Ill., 1882.

Pearce. Roy Harvey. *The Continuity of American Poetry*. Princeton: Princeton University Press, 1961.

———. "From the History of Ideas to Ethnohistory." *Journal of Ethnic Studies* 2 (1974): 86–92.

———. *Gesta Humanorum: Studies in the Historicist Mode*. Columbia, Mo.: University of Missouri Press, 1987.

————. "Historicism Once More." *Historicism Once More: Problems and Occasions for the American Scholar*, 3–45. Princeton: Princeton University Press, 1969.

————. "Introduction." Nathaniel Hawthorne. *The Scarlet Letter*, v–xi. London: J. M. Dent, 1957.

————. "On the History of Ideas (III)." *History of Ideas Newsletter* 2 (1956): 2–4.

————. "The Metaphysics of Indian-Hating: Leather-Stocking Unmasked." *Historicism Once More: Problems and Occasions for the American Scholar*, 109–136. Princeton, N.J.: Princeton University Press, 1969.

————. *Savagism and Civilization: A Study of the Indian and the American Mind.* Baltimore: Johns Hopkins University Press, 1967; rpt. Berkeley, Los Angeles, London: University of California Press, 1988, with a Foreword by Arnold Krupat and a Postscript by the author.

Pike, Kenneth. *Language in Relation to a Unified Theory of the Structure of Human Behavior; 2d. ed.* The Hague: Mouton, 1967.

Program Notes. Akwesasne Benefit, June 6, 1988.

Rabinow, Paul. "Representations Are Social Facts: Modernity and Post-Modernity in Anthropology." Clifford and Marcus, 234–261.

Rahv, Philip. "Paleface and Redskin." In *Literature and the Sixth Sense*. 1–6. Boston: Holt, 1969 [1939].

Ramsey, Jarold. "The Bible in Western Indian Mythology." *Reading the Fire: Essays in the Traditional Indian Literatures of the Far West*. Lincoln: University of Nebraska Press, 1983, 166–180.

————. "From 'Mythic' to 'Fictive' in a Nez Perce Orpheus Myth." Kroeber, 25–44.

————. "The Wife Who Goes Out like a Man, Comes Back as a Hero: The Art of Two Oregon Indian Narratives." *Reading the Fire: Essays in the Traditional Indian Literature of the Far West*, 76–95. Lincoln: University of Nebraska Press, 1983.

Reising, Russell. *The Unusable Past: Theory and the Study of American Literature.* New York: Methuen, 1986.

Rexroth, Kenneth. "American Indian Songs." Chapman, 278–291.

Ridington, Robin. "Fox and Chickadee." Martin, 128–135.

Roethke, Theodore. "The Longing." *Collected Poems of Theodore Roethke*. Garden City, N.Y.: Doubleday, 1966.

Rose, Wendy. "What My Father Said." *The Halfbreed Chronicles and Other Poems.* Los Angeles: West End Press, 1985.

Rosen, Kenneth, ed. *The Man to Send Rain Clouds: Contemporary Stories by American Indians.* New York: Random House, 1975.

Rothenberg, Jerome. Pre-face. Norman, 1976, ix–xi.

————. "Total Translation: An Experiment in the Presentation of American Indian Poetry." Chapman, 292–307.

————, ed. *Shaking the Pumpkin: Traditional Poetry of the Indian North Americas.* Garden City, N.Y.: Doubleday, 1972.

————. *Technicians of the Sacred: A Range of Poetries from Africa, America, Asia, and Oceania.* Garden City, N.Y.: Doubleday, 1968.

Said, Edward. *Orientalism.* New York: Vintage, 1979.

————. *The World, the Text, and the Critic.* Cambridge: Harvard University Press, 1983.

Salisbury, Ralph. "The Sonofabitch and the Dog." Ortiz, 182–187.

Sanders, Thomas E., and Walter W. Peek, eds. *Literature of the American Indian.* New York: Glencoe, 1973.

Sangren, P. Steven. "Rhetoric and the Authority of Ethnography: 'Postmodernism' and the Social Reproduction of Texts." *Current Anthropology* 29 (1988): 405–423.

Sayres, Sohnya, et al., eds. *The 60's without Apology.* Minneapolis: University of Minnesota Press, 1984.

Scanlan, Charles M. *Indian Creek Massacre and Captivity of Hall Girls . . . ,* 2d ed. Milwaukee: Reic Publishing Co., 1913.

Schoolcraft, Henry Rowe. *Algic Researches.* [1839].

————. *Historical and Statistical Information Respecting the History, Condition, and Prospects of the Indian Tribes of the United States.* Philadelphia: Paledin, 1969 [1851–1857].

Schubnell, Matthias. *N. Scott Momaday: The Cultural and Literary Background.* Norman: University of Oklahoma Press, 1985.

Schwitters, Kurt. "abloesung." *Transition* 22 (1933): 38–39.

Shweder, Richard. "Preview: A Colloquy of Culture Theorists." Shweder and LeVine, 1–24.

Shweder, Richard, and Robert LeVine, eds. *Culture Theory: Essays on Mind, Self and Emotion.* Cambridge: Cambridge University Press, 1984.

Silko, Leslie Marmon. "An Old-Time Indian Attack Conducted in Two Parts." *Shantih* 4 (1979): 3–5.

————. *Ceremony.* New York: Viking, 1977.

————. "Landscape, History, and the Pueblo Imagination." *Antaeus* 51 (1986): 83–94.

————. *Storyteller.* New York: Seaver Books, 1981.

Simpson, Louis, *North of Jamaica.* New York: Harper, 1972.

Slotkin, Richard. *Regeneration through Violence: The Mythology of the American Frontier, 1600–1860.* Middletown, Conn.: Wesleyan University Press, 1973.

Smith, Barbara Herrnstein. "Contingencies of Value." von Hallberg, 5–40.

Smith, Henry Nash. "Book Review." *The Graduate School Record* (Ohio State University), June 1953: 7–8.

————. *Virgin Land.* Cambridge: Harvard University Press, 1950.

Smith, Lawrence A. "A Conversation with Louis Simpson." *Chicago Review* 27 (1975).

Snyder, Gary. *He Who Hunted Birds in His Father's Village: The Dimensions of a Haida Myth.* San Francisco: Grey Fox, 1979.

————. *Myths and Texts*. New York: New Directions, 1978 [1960].

Soper, Kate. *Humanism and Anti-Humanism*. London: Hutchinson, 1986.

Spitzer, Leo. "*Geistesgeschicte* vs. History of Ideas as Applied to Hitlerism." *Journal of the History of Ideas* 5 (1944): 191–203.

————. "History of Ideas versus Reading of Poetry." *The Southern Review* 6 (1941): 584–609.

Stephanson, Anders. "Regarding Postmodernism—A Conversation with Fredric Jameson." *Social Text* 17 (1987): 29–54.

Swann, Brian. "Introduction." Niatum, 1988, xiii–xxxii.

————, ed. *Smoothing the Ground: Essays on Native American Oral Literature*. Berkeley, Los Angeles, London: University of California Press, 1983.

————. *Song of the Sky: Versions of Native American Songs and Poems*. N.p.: Four Zoas Night House, 1985.

Swann, Brian, and Arnold Krupat, eds. *I Tell You Now: Autobiographical Essays by Native American Writers*. Lincoln: University of Nebraska Press, 1987.

————, and Arnold Krupat, eds. *Recovering the Word: Essays on Native American Literature*. Berkeley, Los Angeles, London: University of California Press, 1987a.

Tanner, Stephen. *Paul Elmer More: Literary Criticism as the History of Ideas*. Provo: Brigham Young University Press, 1987.

Tarn, Nathaniel. "Preface." Snyder, 1979, xiii–xix.

Tate, James. "One Dreams of Indians." *The Lost Pilot*. New York: 1982.

Tedlock, Dennis. *Finding the Center: Narrative Poetry of the Zuni Indians*. University of Nebraska Press, 1978 [1972].

————. *The Spoken Word and the Work of Interpretation*. Philadelphia: University of Pennsylvania Press, 1983.

————. "Toward an Oral Poetics." *New Literary History* 8 (1977):

Thatcher, B. B. *Indian Biography*. Glorieta, N.M.: Rio Grande, 1973 [1832].

Timberlake, Lt. Henry. *Memoirs: 1756–1765*. Salem, N.H.: Ayer, 1971.

Toelken, Barre, and Tacheeni Scott. "Poetic Retranslation and the 'Pretty Languages' of Yellowman." Kroeber, 65–116.

Tomkins, Jane. " 'Indians': Textualism, Morality, and the Problem of History." *Critical Inquiry* 13 (1986): 101–119.

————. "Sentimental Power: *Uncle Tom's Cabin* and the Politics of Literary History." Bercovitch and Jehlen, 267–292.

Tyler, Stephen. "Post-modern Ethnography: From Document of the Occult to Occult Document." Clifford and Marcus, 122–140.

————. "The Vision Quest in the West or What the Mind's Eye Sees." *Journal of Anthropological Research* 40 (1984): 23–40.

United Nations Economic and Social Council. *Study of the Problem of Discrimination against Indigenous Populations*. A Report of the Working Group on Indigenous Populations on its Fifth Session, 1987.

Untermeyer, Louis, ed. *American Poetry: From the Beginning to Whitman*. New York: Harcourt, 1931.

———. "The Indian as Poet." *Dial,* 8 March, 1919.

———. "Native Ballads and Folk Songs: American Indian Poetry." Untermeyer, 1931, 687–689.

Veeser, Cyrus. Letter to the editor of the *New York Times.* June 23, 1988.

Velie, Alan R. *Four American Indian Literary Masters: N. Scott Momaday, James Welch, Leslie Marmon Silko, and Gerald Vizenor.* Norman: University of Oklahoma Press, 1982.

von Hallberg, Robert, ed. *Canons.* Chicago: University of Chicago Press, 1984.

Wakefield, J. A. *A History of the War between the United States and the Sac and Fox Nations of Indians.* Jacksonville, Ill., 1834.

Washburn, Wilcomb E. "Distinguishing History from Moral Philosophy and Public Advocacy." Martin, 91–97.

———. *The Indian in America.* New York: Harper and Row, 1975.

Welch, James. "Snow Country Weavers." Sanders and Peek, 470.

———. *Winter in the Blood.* New York: Penguin, 1986 [1974].

Wellek, René. *History of Modern Criticism,* vol. 1. New Haven: Yale University Press, 1955.

White, Allon. "The Struggle for Bakhtin: Fraternal Reply to Robert Young." *Cultural Critique* 8 (1987–1988): 217–241.

White, Hayden. *Metahistory.* Baltimore: Johns Hopkins University Press: 1973.

Whitewolf, Jim. *The Life of a Kiowa Apache Indian,* ed. Charles S. Brant. New York: Dover, 1969.

Wiget, Andrew. *Native American Literature.* Boston: Twayne, 1985.

———. "Telling the Tale: A Performance Analysis of a Hopi Coyote Story." Swann and Krupat, 297–338.

Williams, Raymond. "Base and Superstructure in Marxist Cultural Theory." *Problems in Materialism and Culture.* London: Verso, 1980, 31–49.

———. *Keywords.* New York: Oxford University Press, 1976.

———. *Marxism and Literature.* Oxford: Oxford University Press, 1977.

Williams, William Carlos. *In the American Grain.* New York: New Directions, 1956 [1925].

Winters, Yvor. *The Collected Poems of Yvor Winters.* Manchester 1978.

———. "The Indian in English." *Uncollected Essays and Reviews,* ed. Francis Murphy. University of Chicago Press, 1975.

Wooden Leg. *Wooden Leg: A Warrior Who Fought Custer.* Interpreted by Thomas B. Marquis. Lincoln: University of Nebraska Press, 1931.

Yellow Wolf. *Yellow Wolf: His Own Story.* Ed. Lucullus Virgil McWhorter. Caldwell, ID: the Caxton Printers, 1940.

Index

Compositor: Huron Valley Graphics
Text: 10.5/15 Bembo
Display: Bembo
Printer: Edwards Bros., Inc.
Binder: Edwards Bros., Inc.